Selected
Prayers of Prophet Muhammad
ﷺ
and Great Muslim Saints

Selected
Prayers of
Prophet Muhammad

and Great Muslim Saints

Compiled by

M. Fethullah Gülen

Translated by Ali Keeler

TUGHRA
BOOKS

New Jersey

Copyright © 2009 by Tughra Books
Originally published in Turkish as *Mealli Dua Mecmuası* 2002

12 11 10 09   2 3 4 5

*All rights reserved. No part of this book may be reproduced or transmitted in any
form or by any means, electronic or mechanical, including photocopying, recording
or by any information storage and retrieval system without permission in writing from
the Publisher.*

Published by Tughra Books
345 Clifton Ave., Clifton, NJ, 07011, USA

www.tughrabooks.com

ISBN 978-1-59784-226-6

Printed by
Çağlayan A.Ş., Izmir - Turkey

Table of Contents

In the name of Allah the Merciful the Compassionate

Preface

All praise is due to Allah the One and Only, the Clear Truth, Who has no partner. I have rejected all other than Him. And I bear witness that Muhammad is His servant, His Messenger, His elected and His beloved, the best of His creation and the noblest of all who preceded him and all who come after him. May the blessings of Allah and peace descend upon him, upon his brothers from amongst the prophets and messengers, upon the angels God made nearest to Him, and upon His righteous servants from the company of the heavens and the earth.

Supplication is worship, for through supplication the servant approaches Allah Almighty and turns away from all other than Him. Supplication is the believer's sword, for with it he can ward off misfortune. Can this be otherwise, when Allah Most High has said: "Call on me and I will answer you"? And He has said: "And if My servant asks about Me, know for certain that I am near; I answer the supplication of every supplicant when he calls on Me." And He has said: "So who [else] answers the one in need when he calls on Him, and who else lifts away harm?"

In addition, the Prophet, peace and blessings be upon him, said on the same matter: "Supplication (to Allah) is worship," and: "Supplication is the essence of worship." He also said: "Supplicate, for truly supplication wards off misfortune," and lastly: "No caution avails you in the face of destiny, but supplication is beneficial with regard to whatever has happened and whatever has not yet happened, so supplication is incumbent on you, O servants of Allah!"

Therefore know that man is in no better state than when he is supplicating His Lord and confiding in Him, and when he is practicing the invocations transmitted by the master of the messengers, may the most perfect greetings be upon him.

Indeed, for centuries our scholars have gone to great pains in the compilation of numerous books of supplications and invocations for daily practice—may Allah recompense them with the best reward and benefit the whole Muslim community by their works! My aim was to make their work more accessible to aspirants by selecting [from those compilations] that which can be practiced on a daily basis by all those who petition and invoke (their Lord).

Allah is the Compassionate, the Beneficent, the Loving, and the Responsive, and from Him I ask for success, guidance, piety, and His unceasing bestowal of every kind of favor and splendor. In addition, I ask to be united with Muhammad, peace and blessings be upon him and his companions.

Allah is my sufficiency, there is no god but Him, in Him have I put my trust and He is the Lord of the Supreme Throne (Tawba 9:129). Glory be to Allah! There is no strength except in Him. Whatever He wills comes to be and what He wills not does not come to pass. I know that Allah has power over all things and His knowledge encompasses everything. I place in Allah's safekeeping my religion, my worldly affairs, my parents, my teacher, my brothers and sisters, for what better protector is there than He?

Note 1: In Arabic, the direction of writing is from right to the left; therefore pages start and flow from the right. This book also follows the same system, as the prayers are originally Arabic.

Note 2: Numbers in brackets found next to some of the prayers refer to the number of times that the invocation should be repeated.

1. O Hearer of voices in all the different languages! I ask You for protection, safety, well-being, benevolence, grace, and satisfaction.

2. Enrich me through Your bounty such that I depend on none other than You!

3. O Most Merciful of the merciful! (3)

4. "Peace is the word from a Merciful Lord." (Ya Sin 36:58) (19)

5. Blessings from Allah, the Benefactor, the Merciful, upon our master Muhammad, the perfect master, the opener, the seal, and upon his family, his companions, his wives, his progeny, commensurate with the number of souls, moments, drops, plants, and all of creation, at each time he is remembered by the people of remembrance and each time the heedless neglect his remembrance.

6. And all praise is due to Allah, the Lord of the worlds.

يَا سَامِعَ الْأَصْوَاتِ عَلَى اخْتِلَافِ اللُّغَاتِ أَسْأَلُكَ الْعِصْمَةَ وَالْأَمْنَ وَالسَّلَامَةَ وَاللُّطْفَ وَالْبَرَكَةَ وَالْقَنَاعَةَ ﴿١﴾ وَأَغْنِنَا بِفَضْلِكَ عَمَّنْ سِوَاكَ ﴿٢﴾

يَا أَرْحَمَ الرَّاحِمِينَ (٣) ﴿٣﴾

﴿سَلَامٌ قَوْلًا مِنْ رَبٍّ رَحِيمٍ﴾ (١٩) ﴿٤﴾

وَصَلَوَاتُ اللهِ الْبَرِّ الرَّحِيمِ عَلَى سَيِّدِنَا مُحَمَّدٍ السَّيِّدِ الْكَامِلِ الْفَاتِحِ الْخَاتِمِ وَعَلَى آلِهِ وَأَصْحَابِهِ وَأَزْوَاجِهِ وَذُرِّيَّاتِهِ عَدَدَ الْأَنْفَاسِ وَاللَّحَظَاتِ وَالْقَطْرِ وَالنَّبَاتَاتِ وَجَمِيعِ مَا فِي الْكَائِنَاتِ كُلَّمَا ذَكَرَهُ الذَّاكِرُونَ وَغَفَلَ عَنْ ذِكْرِهِ الْغَافِلُونَ ﴿٥﴾

وَالْحَمْدُ للهِ رَبِّ الْعَالَمِينَ ﴿٦﴾

1. Let me drink a quenching cup of the draught of Your love, and leave me not among the despairing, *Ya Hu, Ya Hu, Ya Hu, Ya Ahiyyan, Sharahiyyan,*[12] O Possessor of the far-reaching proof! O Lord of Greatness and Power! O All-Living, Self-Subsistent [Lord]! O Possessor of Majesty and Bounty!

2. My Lord, how sublime is Your affair! How mighty Your authority!

3. By You, O Allah, I have alighted and You are the best at bringing [us] to our station.

4. On You do I rely for You are the best of helpers.

5. And by You I was guided to the straight path.

6. Avert from me the ill of everything reprehensible.

7. Let my prayer be accompanied by a response from You with benevolence, nurturing care, great favors, generous bestowals, and elevations which bring me into Your Presence, and make me worthy of hearing the Speech!

8. O the Quick (Answerer of prayers), O the Originator, O Raiser of ranks!

---

[12] *Ahiyyan* and *Sharahiyan* are Syriac names used for God.

وَاسْقِنِي كَأْساً رَوِيّاً مِنْ شَرَابِ مَحَبَّتِكَ وَلَا

تَجْعَلْنِي مِنَ الْقَانِطِينَ يَا هُوَ يَا هُوَ يَا هُوَ يَا هُوَ يَا اهِيّاً

شَرَاهِيّاً يَا ذَا الْحُجَّةِ الْبَالِغَةِ يَا ذَا الْعَظَمَةِ وَالْقُدْرَةِ

يَا حَيُّ يَا قَيُّومُ يَا ذَا الْجَلَالِ وَالْإِكْرَامِ ﴿١﴾ إِلهِي مَا

أَعْظَمَ شَأْنَكَ وَأَعَزَّ سُلْطَانَكَ ﴿٢﴾ بِكَ اللّهُمَّ نَزَلْتُ

وَأَنْتَ خَيْرُ الْمُنْزِلِينَ ﴿٣﴾ وَبِكَ اعْتَصَمْتُ وَأَنْتَ خَيْرُ

النَّاصِرِينَ ﴿٤﴾ وَبِكَ اهْتَدَيْتُ إِلَى صِرَاطِكَ الْمُسْتَقِيمِ

﴿٥﴾ فَاكْفِنِي اللّهُمَّ شَرَّ كُلِّ مَكْرُوهٍ ﴿٦﴾ وَاجْعَلْ دُعَائِي

مَقْرُوناً بِإِجَابَتِكَ مَعَ اللُّطْفِ وَالرِّعَايَةِ وَالْمِنَحِ الْجِسَامِ

وَالتَّلَقِّيَاتِ الْكِرَامِ وَتَرَقِّيَاتِ الْوُصُولِ إِلَى حَضْرَتِكَ

وَأَهِّلْنِي لِسَمَاعِ الْخِطَابِ ﴿٧﴾ يَا سَرِيعُ يَا بَدِيعُ يَا

رَفِيعَ الدَّرَجَاتِ ﴿٨﴾

1. And bring me thereby close to Your noble presence! Make me one who holds fast to the divine law (*al-sharia*), most pure, receptive to the knowledge and wisdom that You cast through Your favor into my heart from the effusion of Your lights.

2. Protect me, O Allah, from conceit, pride, ostentation, hypocrisy, and hidden association (*shirk*), and purge me of filth, misdeeds and faults, both the hidden and apparent!

3. Make me safe from the punishment of the grave and its trials and let my life be led in obedience to You!

4. Grant me understanding of the knowledge from Your presence (*al-dunni*)!

5. Grant me the companionship of Your righteous servants, the highest saints (*abdal*) and Your truthful servants (*siddiqin*),

6. And include me among them through Your mercy, Most Merciful of the merciful!

7. Allah! Deliver me from every tribulation, and save me from everything that leads to ruin!

8. And don't make me among the depraved!

وَاجْعَلْنِي فِي ذَلِكَ قَرِيباً مِنْ حَضْرَتِكَ الشَّرِيفَةِ مُتَمَسِّكاً بِالشَّرِيعَةِ الْمُطَهَّرَةِ مُتَلَقِّياً لِلْعُلُومِ وَالْحِكْمَةِ الَّتِي تَقْذِفُهَا بِفَضْلِكَ فِي قَلْبِي مِنْ فَيْضِ أَنْوَارِكَ ﴿١﴾

وَاحْفَظْنِيَ اللَّهُمَّ مِنَ الْعُجْبِ وَالْكِبْرِ وَالرِّيَاءِ وَالنِّفَاقِ وَالشِّرْكِ الْخَفِيِّ وَطَهِّرْنِي مِنَ الدَّنَسِ وَالزَّلَّاتِ وَالْعُيُوبِ الْبَاطِنَةِ وَالظَّاهِرَةِ ﴿٢﴾

وَاجْعَلْنِي آمِناً مِنْ عَذَابِ الْقَبْرِ وَفِتْنَتِهِ وَاجْعَلْ حَيَاتِي فِي طَاعَتِكَ ﴿٣﴾ وَفَهِّمْنِي فِي عِلْمِكَ اللَّدُنِّيِّ ﴿٤﴾ وَأَصْحِبْنِي فِي عِبَادِكَ الصَّالِحِينَ وَالْأَبْدَالِ وَالصِّدِّيقِينَ ﴿٥﴾ وَاجْعَلْنِي مِنْهُمْ بِرَحْمَتِكَ يَا أَرْحَمَ الرَّاحِمِينَ ﴿٦﴾ اَللَّهُمَّ عَافِنِي مِنْ كُلِّ بَلِيَّةٍ وَنَجِّنِي مِنْ كُلِّ هَلَكَةٍ ﴿٧﴾ وَلَا تَجْعَلْنِي مِنَ السَّافِلِينَ ﴿٨﴾

1. I ask You, O my Lord, with that with which Your Prophets called upon You, and with which the bearers of Your Throne and those of Your angels (You made nearest to You) glorify and magnify You, to make me fully protected and preserved from every enemy among jinn, men and all other worlds, from those about which I know and those of which I am unaware.

   Grant me the secret of the support of lights from the reserves of Your Mighty and Impregnable Care, which is screened from all evil, immersed in the sea of the light of Your Grandeur, supported from You by the Holy Spirit (the Archangel Gabriel).

2. And be for me, O Allah, a Protector, Helper, Guarantor, Guardian, Reckoner, and Preserver for the sake of Your Mercy, Bounty, Favor, and Might. And place all Your creatures at my beck and call, and the keys to their hearts in my hand. Make me loved, honored, respected and revered by them, so they don't disobey my command, and so that I never experience that which is disagreeable from them and am protected from their harm, due to the intensity of their love, friendship and affection [for me].[11]

---

[11] When a person gives himself or herself to God's service, God in turn places all creatures at his or her service.

وَاسْأَلُكَ يَارَبِّ بِمَا دَعَاكَ بِهِ أَنْبِيَاؤُكَ وَبِمَا يُسَبِّحُكَ

وَيُمَجِّدُكَ حَمَلَةُ عَرْشِكَ وَالْمُقَرَّبُونَ مِنْ مَلَئِكَتِكَ أَنْ

تَجْعَلَنِي مُحَصَّناً مَحْفُوظاً مِنْ كُلِّ عَدُوٍّ مِنَ الْجِنِّ وَالْأَنْسِ

وَسَائِرِ الْعَوَالِمِ مَا عَلِمْتُ مِنْهَا وَمَا لَمْ أَعْلَمْ وَأَدْخِلْنِي فِي

سِرِّ إِمْدَادِ أَنْوَارِ خَزَائِنِ حِرْزِكَ الْعَزِيزِ الْمَنِيعِ مَحْجُوباً

عَنْ كُلِّ سُوءٍ مَغْمُوساً فِي بَحْرٍ مِنْ نُورِ هَيْبَتِكَ مُؤَيَّداً

مِنْكَ بِرُوحِ الْقُدُسِ ۞ وَكُنِ اللَّهُمَّ لِي وَلِيّاً وَنَاصِراً

وَكَفِيلاً وَوَكِيلاً وَحَسِيباً وَحَفِيظاً بِرَحْمَتِكَ وَفَضْلِكَ

وَمَنِّكَ وَطَوْلِكَ وَاجْعَلْ جَمِيعَ مَخْلُوقَاتِكَ طَوْعَ يَدِي

مَالِكاً أَزِمَّةَ قُلُوبِهِمْ مَحْبُوباً عِنْدَهُمْ مُعَزَّزاً مُكَرَّماً مُهَاباً

لَا يَعْصُونَ أَمْرِي وَلَا أَنَالُ مِنْهُمْ مَكْرُوهاً أَبَداً مَعْصُوماً

مِنْ أَذَاهُمْ بِشِدَّةِ الْمَحَبَّةِ وَالْأُلْفَةِ وَالْمَوَدَّةِ ۞

1. I clad myself in the armor of the majesty of the magnificent radiance of His Greatest Name, [and His names]: the All-Living, Self-Subsistent, and Possessor of Majesty and Bounty.

2. I hold fast to and take shelter in the blazes of light [emanating] from the secrets of His sublime speech.

3. I cling to His innermost benevolence, in all its excellence and beauty.

4. It is to His mighty pillar that I flee for refuge and support; glorified be He and to Him be praise!

5. "There is nothing like unto Him, and He is the All-Hearing, the All-Seeing." (Shura 42:11)

6. [He is] Opening, All-Knowing, Expanding, Honoring, Munificent, Generous, Most-High, and All-Tremendous.

7. O Allah! Verily I ask You by Your perfect words, the magnified names, radiant letters, revealed scriptures, and clear signs.

8. [I ask You] by the awesomeness, majesty, power, and greatness which emanates from the canopies of Your tremendous Throne. I ask You by the special merits and secrets with which You have charged the letters and names, by the noble presence before You, by the divine law most purified, by the five prescribed prayers, and by the connection of the elite of Your servants to Your secrets and Your mercy.

وَبِجَلَالِ بَهَاءِ سَنَاءِ اسْمِهِ الْأَعْظَمِ الْأَكْبَرِ الْحَيِّ الْقَيُّومِ ذِي الْجَلَالِ وَالْإِكْرَامِ تَدَرَّعْتُ ﴿١﴾ وَبِبَوَارِقِ أَنْوَارِ أَسْرَارِ كَلَامِهِ الْعَظِيمِ احْتَجَبْتُ وَتَمَسَّكْتُ ﴿٢﴾ وَبِخَفِيِّ لُطْفِهِ الْحَسَنِ الْجَمِيلِ تَعَلَّقْتُ ﴿٣﴾ وَبِرُكْنِهِ الْقَوِيِّ الْتَجَأْتُ وَاسْتَنَدْتُ سُبْحَانَهُ وَبِحَمْدِهِ ﴿٤﴾ ﴿لَيْسَ كَمِثْلِهِ شَيْءٌ وَهُوَ السَّمِيعُ الْبَصِيرُ﴾ ﴿٥﴾ فَتَّاحٌ عَلِيمٌ بَاسِطٌ مُعِزٌّ جَوَادٌ كَرِيمٌ عَلِيٌّ عَظِيمٌ ﴿٦﴾ اللَّهُمَّ إِنِّي أَسْأَلُكَ بِالْكَلِمَاتِ التَّامَّاتِ وَالْأَسْمَاءِ الْمُعَظَّمَاتِ وَالْأَحْرُفِ النُّورَانِيَّاتِ وَالْكُتُبِ الْمُنْزَلَاتِ وَالْآيَاتِ الْبَيِّنَاتِ ﴿٧﴾ بِمَا وَارَدَتْهُ سُرَادِقَاتُ عَرْشِكَ الْعَظِيمِ مِنَ الْهَيْبَةِ وَالْجَلَالِ وَالْقُدْرَةِ وَالْعَظَمَةِ وَبِمَا أَوْدَعْتَ فِي الْحُرُوفِ وَالْأَسْمَاءِ مِنَ الْخَوَاصِّ وَالْأَسْرَارِ بِالْحَضْرَةِ الشَّرِيفَةِ وَالشَّرِيعَةِ الْمُطَهَّرَةِ وَالصَّلَوَاتِ الْخَمْسِ وَاتِّصَالِ الْأَسْرَارِ وَالرَّحْمَةِ لِلْخَوَاصِّ مِنْ عِبَادِكَ ﴿٨﴾

In the name of Allah, the All-Merciful, the Beneficent.

1. In the name of Allah, on my right.
2. In the name of Allah, on my left.
3. In the name of Allah behind me.
4. In the name of Allah in front of me.
5. In the name of Allah above me.
6. In the name of Allah I seek protection.
7. I have entered into His guarded care.
8. And I have taken cover in His impregnable fortress.
9. I clothe myself with the [apparel of] His beautiful names,
10. and enrobe myself with the secret of the lights of His name, the Sublime (*Al-Jalil*).
11. With the power of the influence of the secrets of His names the Most Strong, the Subduer (*Al-Qawiyy, Al-Qahhar*), I rise and conquer my enemies among jinn, humankind, and all other creatures, shield myself, prevail [over them] and gain victory.

بِسْمِ اللهِ الرَّحْمٰنِ الرَّحِيمِ

بِسْمِ اللهِ عَلَى يَمِينِي ﴿١﴾ بِسْمِ اللهِ عَلَى شِمَالِي

﴿٢﴾ بِسْمِ اللهِ عَلَى خَلْفِي ﴿٣﴾ بِسْمِ اللهِ عَلَى أَمَامِي

﴿٤﴾ بِسْمِ اللهِ عَلَى فَوْقِي ﴿٥﴾ بِسْمِ اللهِ اكْتَنَفْتُ ﴿٦﴾

وَفِي حِرْزِهِ الْحَصِينِ دَخَلْتُ ﴿٧﴾ وَبِحِصْنِهِ الْمَنِيعِ

احْتَجَبْتُ ﴿٨﴾ وَبِأَسْمَائِهِ الْحُسْنَى تَسَرْبَلْتُ ﴿٩﴾ وَبِسِرِّ

أَنْوَارِ اسْمِهِ الْجَلِيلِ تَرَدَّيْتُ ﴿١٠﴾ وَبِقُوَّةِ إِمْدَادِ أَسْرَارِ اسْمِهِ

الْقَوِيِّ الْقَاهِرِ عَلَوْتُ وَغَلَبْتُ أَعْدَائِي مِنَ الْجِنِّ وَالْإِنْسِ

وَسَائِرِ الْمَخْلُوقِينَ وَاحْتَجَبْتُ وَقَهَرْتُ وَانْتَصَرْتُ ﴿١١١﴾

١٨٨

حِزْبُ الْحَصِينِ

THE LITANY OF
THE PROTECTED

1. "He is Allah besides Whom there is no other god; Knower of the Unseen and the visible. He is the All-Merciful, the All-Compassionate. ◉ He is Allah, there is no god but He; the Sovereign, the All-Holy, the Source of Peace, the Source of Security; the Guardian, the All-Mighty; the Compeller, the Majestic. Transcendent is He above all that they ascribe as partner (to Him)! ◉ He is Allah; the Creator, the Producer, the Fashioner (Who has brought His creatures to existence and fashioned them in the best form and perfect harmony, making them undergo different phases). His are the most beautiful names. All that is in the heavens and the earth glorifies Him. He is the All-Mighty, the All-Wise." (Hashr 59:22-4)

2. There is no god but Allah, Alone without associate. His is the dominion and to Him belongs all praise, and He has power over all things.

3. "There is no god but You; Glory be to You! Truly I have been among the wrongdoers." (Anbiya 21:87)

4. O Allah! Send blessings upon our master Muhammad, from pre-eternity up to eternity, commensurate with what is encompassed by Allah's knowledge, and upon his family and companions, with peace.

(This should be recited 19 times)

هُوَ اللهُ الَّذِي لَا إِلٰهَ إِلَّا هُوَ عَالِمُ الْغَيْبِ وَالشَّهَادَةِ

هُوَ الرَّحْمٰنُ الرَّحِيمُ ۞ هُوَ اللهُ الَّذِي لَا إِلٰهَ إِلَّا هُوَ

اَلْمَلِكُ الْقُدُّوسُ السَّلَامُ الْمُؤْمِنُ الْمُهَيْمِنُ الْعَزِيزُ

الْجَبَّارُ الْمُتَكَبِّرُ سُبْحَانَ اللهِ عَمَّا يُشْرِكُونَ ۞ هُوَ اللهُ

الْخَالِقُ الْبَارِئُ الْمُصَوِّرُ لَهُ الْأَسْمَاءُ الْحُسْنٰى يُسَبِّحُ لَهُ مَا

فِي السَّمٰوَاتِ وَالْأَرْضِ وَهُوَ الْعَزِيزُ الْحَكِيمُ ﴿١﴾

لَا إِلٰهَ إِلَّا اللهُ وَحْدَهُ لَا شَرِيكَ لَهُ، لَهُ الْمُلْكُ وَلَهُ

الْحَمْدُ وَهُوَ عَلٰى كُلِّ شَيْءٍ قَدِيرٌ ﴿٢﴾

لَا إِلٰهَ إِلَّا أَنْتَ سُبْحَانَكَ إِنِّي كُنْتُ مِنَ الظَّالِمِينَ ﴿٣﴾

اَللّٰهُمَّ صَلِّ عَلٰى سَيِّدِنَا مُحَمَّدٍ مِنَ الْأَزَلِ إِلَى الْأَبَدِ

عَدَدَ مَا فِي عِلْمِ اللهِ وَعَلٰى اٰلِهِ وَصَحْبِهِ وَسَلِّمْ ﴿٤﴾

(ألا كل شخص يقرأها ١٩ مرة)

١٨٦

1. O Allah! I ask You, for to You is due all praise. There is no god but You, the Favorer, Originator of the heavens and the earth, Possessor of Majesty and Bounty. O All-Living, Self-Subsistent [Lord]!

2. "And Your God is one God; there is no god but He, the All-Merciful, the All-Compassionate." (Baqara 2:163)

3. "Allah! There is no god but He, the All-Living, Self-Subsistent. Neither does slumber overtake Him nor sleep and to Him belongs whatever is in the heavens and the earth. Who can intercede with Him except by His leave? He knows what is before them and what is behind them and they comprehend of His knowledge only that which He wills. His Throne encompasses the heavens and the earth, and maintaining them both tires Him not. He is the Exalted, the Sublime." (Ayat al-Kursi / Baqara 2:255)

4. "(O Muhammad) Say! O Allah, Owner of sovereignty, You bestow sovereignty on whom You will and take away sovereignty from whom You will; You exalt whom You will and You abase whom You will. All goodness is in Your hand; indeed You have power over all things." (Al Imran 3:26)

5. "You cause the night to pass into the day and the day to pass into the night. You bring forth the living from the dead and the dead from the living; and You give sustenance to whom You will without stint." (Al Imran 3:27)

اَللّٰهُمَّ إِنِّي أَسْأَلُكَ بِأَنَّ لَكَ الْحَمْدَ لَا إِلٰهَ إِلَّا أَنْتَ الْمَنَّانُ بَدِيعُ السَّمٰوَاتِ وَالْأَرْضِ ذُو الْجَلَالِ وَالْإِكْرَامِ يَا حَيُّ يَا قَيُّومُ ۝١ وَالٰهُكُمْ إِلٰهٌ وَاحِدٌ لَا إِلٰهَ إِلَّا هُوَ الرَّحْمٰنُ الرَّحِيمُ ۝٢ اَللّٰهُ لَا إِلٰهَ إِلَّا هُوَ الْحَيُّ الْقَيُّومُ لَا تَأْخُذُهُ سِنَةٌ وَلَا نَوْمٌ لَهُ مَا فِي السَّمٰوَاتِ وَمَا فِي الْأَرْضِ مَنْ ذَا الَّذِي يَشْفَعُ عِنْدَهُ إِلَّا بِإِذْنِهِ يَعْلَمُ مَا بَيْنَ أَيْدِيهِمْ وَمَا خَلْفَهُمْ وَلَا يُحِيطُونَ بِشَيْءٍ مِنْ عِلْمِهِ إِلَّا بِمَا شَاءَ وَسِعَ كُرْسِيُّهُ السَّمٰوَاتِ وَالْأَرْضَ وَلَا يَؤُودُهُ حِفْظُهُمَا وَهُوَ الْعَلِيُّ الْعَظِيمُ ۝٣ قُلِ اللّٰهُمَّ مَالِكَ الْمُلْكِ تُؤْتِي الْمُلْكَ مَنْ تَشَاءُ وَتَنْزِعُ الْمُلْكَ مِمَّنْ تَشَاءُ وَتُعِزُّ مَنْ تَشَاءُ وَتُذِلُّ مَنْ تَشَاءُ بِيَدِكَ الْخَيْرُ إِنَّكَ عَلَى كُلِّ شَيْءٍ قَدِيرٌ ۝٤ تُولِجُ الَّيْلَ فِي النَّهَارِ وَتُولِجُ النَّهَارَ فِي الَّيْلِ وَتُخْرِجُ الْحَيَّ مِنَ الْمَيِّتِ وَتُخْرِجُ الْمَيِّتَ مِنَ الْحَيِّ وَتَرْزُقُ مَنْ تَشَاءُ بِغَيْرِ حِسَابٍ ۝٥

1. "We shall show them our signs in the world around them and within themselves until it becomes apparent that it (this Qur'an) is the Truth. Is it not enough that your Lord is witness over all things?" (Fussilat 41:53)

2. "When you said to the believers: Is it not sufficient for you that your Lord should support you with three thousand angels sent down?" (Al Imran 3:124)

3. "Is not Allah enough for His servant?" (Zumar 39:36)

4. "Is not Allah the wisest of judges?" (Hud 11:45)

Allah, Almighty has spoken the truth.

5. I ask You, O Allah! O He (*Ya Huwa*)! O All-Merciful (*Ya Rahman*)! O All-Compassionate (*Ya Rahim*)! O All-Living (*Ya Hayy*)! O Self-Subsistent (*Ya Qayyum*)! O Possessor of Majesty and Bounty (*Ya Dhal Jalali wal Ikram*)!

6. O Allah! Verily I ask You, for truly You are Allah; there is no god but You; the Affectionate, the Favorer; the Originator of the heavens and the earth; the Possessor of Majesty and Bounty.

7. O Allah, truly I ask You, for I bear witness that truly You are Allah; there is no god but You; the One and Only, the Absolute, who begets not, nor is He begotten, and there is no one like unto Him.

سَنُرِيهِمْ اٰيَاتِنَا فِي الْاٰفَاقِ وَفِي أَنْفُسِهِمْ حَتّٰى يَتَبَيَّنَ لَهُمْ أَنَّهُ الْحَقُّ أَوَلَمْ يَكْفِ بِرَبِّكَ أَنَّهُ عَلٰى كُلِّ شَيْءٍ شَهِيدٌ ۝١ إِذْ تَقُولُ لِلْمُؤْمِنِينَ أَلَنْ يَكْفِيَكُمْ أَنْ يُمِدَّكُمْ رَبُّكُمْ بِثَلٰثَةِ اٰلَافٍ مِنَ الْمَلٰئِكَةِ مُنْزَلِينَ ۝٢ أَلَيْسَ اللهُ بِكَافٍ عَبْدَهُ ۝٣ أَلَيْسَ اللهُ بِأَحْكَمِ الْحَاكِمِينَ ۝٤ صَدَقَ اللهُ الْعَظِيمُ

أَسْأَلُكَ يَا اَللهُ يَا هُوَ يَا رَحْمٰنُ يَا رَحِيمُ يَا حَيُّ يَا قَيُّومُ يَا ذَا الْجَلَالِ وَالْإِكْرَامِ ۝٥ اَللّٰهُمَّ إِنِّيٓ أَسْأَلُكَ بِأَنَّكَ أَنْتَ اللهُ لَآ إِلٰهَ إِلَّآ أَنْتَ الْحَنَّانُ الْمَنَّانُ بَدِيعُ السَّمٰوَاتِ وَالْأَرْضِ ذُو الْجَلَالِ وَالْإِكْرَامِ ۝٦ اَللّٰهُمَّ إِنِّيٓ أَسْأَلُكَ بِأَنِّيٓ أَشْهَدُ أَنَّكَ أَنْتَ اللهُ الَّذِي لَآ إِلٰهَ إِلَّآ أَنْتَ الْأَحَدُ الصَّمَدُ الَّذِي لَمْ يَلِدْ وَلَمْ يُولَدْ وَلَمْ يَكُنْ لَهُ كُفُوًا أَحَدٌ ۝٧

١٨٤

1. "Say: Sufficient is Allah as witness between me and you, and he who has knowledge of the scripture." (Ra'd 13:43)

2. "Read your book, for sufficient is your soul as reckoner over you this day." (Isra 17:14)

3. "Sufficient is your Lord as guide and helper." (Furqan 25:31)

4. "Say: Sufficient is Allah as witness between me and you; He knows what is in the heavens and the earth." (Ankabut 29:52)

5. "And Allah repulsed the unbelievers in their fury; they gained no good. Allah averted their attack from the believers for truly He is ever Strong, Triumphant." (Ahzab 33:25)

6. "Those who deliver the messages of Allah and fear Him, and they do not fear anyone except Allah. Sufficient is Allah as Reckoner." (Ahzab 33:39)

7. "He is sufficient as a witness between me and you, and He is the All-Forgiving, the All-Compassionate." (Ahqaf 46:8)

8. "He it is who sent His Messenger with guidance and the religion of truth, to make it prevail over all religions and sufficient is Allah as witness." (Fath 48:28)

9. "Verily, we have averted from you the mockers." (Hijr 15:95)

قُلْ كَفَى بِاللَّهِ شَهِيداً بَيْنِي وَبَيْنَكُمْ وَمَنْ عِنْدَهُ عِلْمُ الْكِتَابِ ﴿١﴾ اقْرَأْ كِتَابَكَ كَفَى بِنَفْسِكَ الْيَوْمَ عَلَيْكَ حَسِيباً ﴿٢﴾ وَكَفَى بِرَبِّكَ هَادِياً وَنَصِيراً ﴿٣﴾

قُلْ كَفَى بِاللَّهِ بَيْنِي وَبَيْنَكُمْ شَهِيداً يَعْلَمُ مَا فِي السَّمَوَاتِ وَالْأَرْضِ ﴿٤﴾

وَرَدَّ اللَّهُ الَّذِينَ كَفَرُوا بِغَيْظِهِمْ لَمْ يَنَالُوا خَيْراً وَكَفَى اللَّهُ الْمُؤْمِنِينَ الْقِتَالَ وَكَانَ اللَّهُ قَوِيًّا عَزِيزاً ﴿٥﴾

الَّذِينَ يُبَلِّغُونَ رِسَالَاتِ اللَّهِ وَيَخْشَوْنَهُ وَلَا يَخْشَوْنَ أَحَداً إِلَّا اللَّهَ وَكَفَى بِاللَّهِ حَسِيباً ﴿٦﴾

كَفَى بِهِ شَهِيداً بَيْنِي وَبَيْنَكُمْ وَهُوَ الْغَفُورُ الرَّحِيمُ ﴿٧﴾ هُوَ الَّذِي أَرْسَلَ رَسُولَهُ بِالْهُدَى وَدِينِ الْحَقِّ لِيُظْهِرَهُ عَلَى الدِّينِ كُلِّهِ وَكَفَى بِاللَّهِ شَهِيداً ﴿٨﴾

إِنَّا كَفَيْنَاكَ الْمُسْتَهْزِئِينَ ﴿٩﴾

1. "Those who remained steadfast and in their Lord put their trust." (Nahl 16:42)

2. "And whoever puts his trust in His Lord, truly Allah is All-Honored, All-Wise." (Anfal 8:49)

3. "And if they incline to peace, incline to it also, and trust in Allah. Assuredly, He is the All-Hearing, the All-Knowing." (Anfal 8:61)

4. "And their messengers said to them, we are only mortals like you, but Allah shows His favor on whomever He wills of His servants. And it is not for us to bring for you a warrant except by the permission of Allah, so in Allah let the believers put their trust!" (Ibrahim 14:11)

5. "Allah, there is no god but Him, and in Him let the believers put their trust." (Taghabun 64:13)

6. "We are your protecting friends in this life and in the Hereafter and you will have there whatever your souls desire, and you will have there whatever you call for." (Fussilat 41:31)

7. "And Allah is sufficient as Reckoner." (Nisa 4:6)

8. "Whatever good reaches you it is from Allah, and whatever ill afflicts you it is from yourself. We sent you as a Messenger for people, and sufficient is Allah as witness." (Nisa 4:79)

اَلَّذِينَ صَبَرُوا وَعَلَى رَبِّهِمْ يَتَوَكَّلُونَ ﴿١﴾ وَمَنْ يَتَوَكَّلْ عَلَى اللهِ فَإِنَّ اللهَ عَزِيزٌ حَكِيمٌ ﴿٢﴾

وَإِنْ جَنَحُوا لِلسَّلْمِ فَاجْنَحْ لَهَا وَتَوَكَّلْ عَلَى اللهِ إِنَّهُ هُوَ السَّمِيعُ الْعَلِيمُ ﴿٣﴾ قَالَتْ لَهُمْ رُسُلُهُمْ إِنْ نَحْنُ إِلَّا بَشَرٌ مِثْلُكُمْ وَلَكِنَّ اللهَ يَمُنُّ عَلَى مَنْ يَشَاءُ مِنْ عِبَادِهِ وَمَا كَانَ لَنَا أَنْ نَأْتِيَكُمْ بِسُلْطَانٍ إِلَّا بِإِذْنِ اللهِ وَعَلَى اللهِ فَلْيَتَوَكَّلِ الْمُؤْمِنُونَ ﴿٤﴾

اللهُ لَا إِلَهَ إِلَّا هُوَ وَعَلَى اللهِ فَلْيَتَوَكَّلِ الْمُؤْمِنُونَ ﴿٥﴾ نَحْنُ أَوْلِيَاؤُكُمْ فِي الْحَيَوةِ الدُّنْيَا وَفِي الْآخِرَةِ وَلَكُمْ فِيهَا مَا تَشْتَهِي أَنْفُسُكُمْ وَلَكُمْ فِيهَا مَا تَدَّعُونَ ﴿٦﴾ وَكَفَى بِاللهِ حَسِيبًا ﴿٧﴾ مَآ أَصَابَكَ مِنْ حَسَنَةٍ فَمِنَ اللهِ وَمَآ أَصَابَكَ مِنْ سَيِّئَةٍ فَمِنْ نَفْسِكَ وَأَرْسَلْنَاكَ لِلنَّاسِ رَسُولًا وَكَفَى بِاللهِ شَهِيدًا ﴿٨﴾

1. "Verily those of humankind who have the best claim to Abraham are those who followed him, and this Prophet and those who believe, and Allah is the Protector of the believers." (Al Imran 3:68)

2. "When two parties from among you nearly gave in and Allah was their Protector; so in Allah let the believers put their trust." (Al Imran 3:122)

3. "Verily, to Allah belongs the kingdom of the heavens and the earth; He gives life and brings death, and without Allah you have no protector, nor helper." (Tawba 9:116)

4. "Allah is He Who created the heavens and the earth and what is between them in six days, then He established Himself on the Throne. Without Him you have no protector, nor intercessor. Do you not then take heed?" (Sajda 32:4)

5. "Or have they taken [for themselves] protectors other than Him, while Allah is the Protector; He revives the dead and has power over all things." (Shura 42:9)

6. "And He it is who sends down the rain after they had fallen into despair and spreads His mercy, and He is the Protector, the Owner of Praise." (Shura 42:28)

7. "Verily, he (Satan) has no authority over those who believe and put their trust in their Lord." (Nahl 16:99)

إِنَّ أَوْلَى النَّاسِ بِإِبْرْهِيمَ لَلَّذِينَ اتَّبَعُوهُ وَهٰذَا النَّبِيُّ وَالَّذِينَ اٰمَنُوا وَاللهُ وَلِيُّ الْمُؤْمِنِينَ ۝ إِذْ هَمَّتْ طَائِفَتَانِ مِنْكُمْ أَنْ تَفْشَلَا وَاللهُ وَلِيُّهُمَا وَعَلَى اللهِ فَلْيَتَوَكَّلِ الْمُؤْمِنُونَ ۝ إِنَّ اللهَ لَهُ مُلْكُ السَّمٰوَاتِ وَالْأَرْضِ يُحْيِي وَيُمِيتُ وَمَا لَكُمْ مِنْ دُونِ اللهِ مِنْ وَلِيٍّ وَلَا نَصِيرٍ ۝

اَللهُ الَّذِي خَلَقَ السَّمٰوَاتِ وَالْأَرْضَ وَمَا بَيْنَهُمَا فِي سِتَّةِ أَيَّامٍ ثُمَّ اسْتَوٰى عَلَى الْعَرْشِ مَا لَكُمْ مِنْ دُونِهِ مِنْ وَلِيٍّ وَلَا شَفِيعٍ أَفَلَا تَتَذَكَّرُونَ ۝

أَمِ اتَّخَذُوا مِنْ دُونِهِ أَوْلِيَاءَ فَاللهُ هُوَ الْوَلِيُّ وَهُوَ يُحْيِي الْمَوْتٰى وَهُوَ عَلٰى كُلِّ شَيْءٍ قَدِيرٌ ۝

وَهُوَ الَّذِي يُنَزِّلُ الْغَيْثَ مِنْ بَعْدِ مَا قَنَطُوا وَيَنْشُرُ رَحْمَتَهُ وَهُوَ الْوَلِيُّ الْحَمِيدُ ۝ إِنَّهُ لَيْسَ لَهُ سُلْطَانٌ عَلَى الَّذِينَ اٰمَنُوا وَعَلٰى رَبِّهِمْ يَتَوَكَّلُونَ ۝

1. "And to Allah belongs whatever is in the heavens and whatever is in the earth, and He is sufficient as Guardian." (Nisa 4:132)

2. "And to Allah belongs that which is unseen in the heavens and the earth and to Him returns every matter. So worship Him and rely on Him for Allah is not unaware of what you do." (Hud 11:123)

3. "And put your trust in the All-Living who dies not and glorify Him with His praise. It is enough that He is fully aware of the sins of His servants." (Furqan 25:58)

4. "And put your trust in the All-Honored, the All-Compassionate." (Shuara 26:217)

5. "So [Muhammad] put your trust in Allah, for you stand upon the plain truth." (Naml 27:79)

6. "And Moses said: O my people if you believe in Allah, then in Him put your trust if you are Muslims." (Yunus 10:85)

7. "Truly, over My servants you have no authority, and sufficient is Allah as Guardian." (Isra 17:65)

8. "Do you not know that to Allah belongs the kingdom of the heavens and the earth, and besides Allah you have no protector nor helper?" (Baqara 2:107)

9. "Allah is the Protector of those who believe; He takes them out of the darkness into the light." (Baqara 2:257)

وَلِلّٰهِ مَا فِي السَّمٰوَاتِ وَمَا فِي الْأَرْضِ وَكَفٰى بِاللّٰهِ وَكِيلاً ﴿١﴾ وَلِلّٰهِ غَيْبُ السَّمٰوَاتِ وَالْأَرْضِ وَإِلَيْهِ يُرْجَعُ الْأَمْرُ كُلُّهُ فَاعْبُدْهُ وَتَوَكَّلْ عَلَيْهِ وَمَا رَبُّكَ بِغَافِلٍ عَمَّا تَعْمَلُونَ ﴿٢﴾ وَتَوَكَّلْ عَلَى الْحَيِّ الَّذِي لَا يَمُوتُ وَسَبِّحْ بِحَمْدِهِ وَكَفٰى بِهِ بِذُنُوبِ عِبَادِهِ خَبِيراً ﴿٣﴾ وَتَوَكَّلْ عَلَى الْعَزِيزِ الرَّحِيمِ ﴿٤﴾ فَتَوَكَّلْ عَلَى اللّٰهِ إِنَّكَ عَلَى الْحَقِّ الْمُبِينِ ﴿٥﴾

وَقَالَ مُوسٰى يَا قَوْمِ إِنْ كُنْتُمْ اٰمَنْتُمْ بِاللّٰهِ فَعَلَيْهِ تَوَكَّلُوا إِنْ كُنْتُمْ مُسْلِمِينَ ﴿٦﴾ إِنَّ عِبَادِي لَيْسَ لَكَ عَلَيْهِمْ سُلْطَانٌ وَكَفٰى بِرَبِّكَ وَكِيلاً ﴿٧﴾

أَلَمْ تَعْلَمْ أَنَّ اللّٰهَ لَهُ مُلْكُ السَّمٰوَاتِ وَالْأَرْضِ وَمَا لَكُمْ مِنْ دُونِ اللّٰهِ مِنْ وَلِيٍّ وَلَا نَصِيرٍ ﴿٨﴾ اَللّٰهُ وَلِيُّ الَّذِينَ اٰمَنُوا يُخْرِجُهُمْ مِنَ الظُّلُمَاتِ إِلَى النُّورِ ﴿٩﴾

1. "You are our Protector, so forgive us and have mercy on us, for You are the best of those who forgive." (Maida 5:155)

2. "Verily, my Protector is Allah, who revealed the Book, and he takes care of the righteous." (A'raf 7:196)

3. "O you who believe! Remember Allah's favor to you when a people designed to lay their hands upon you and He kept their hands from [harming] you, so fear Allah, and in Allah let the believers place their trust." (Maida 5:11)

4. "For them is the abode of peace in the presence of their Lord and He is their Protector because of what they used to do." (An'am 6:128)

5. "As for what you have been given, it is for the enjoyment of the life of this world, but what is with Allah is better and more lasting for those who believe and put their trust in their Lord." (Shura 42:36)

6. "It was by the mercy of Allah that you were gentle with them for had you been stern and harsh of heart, they would have dispersed from around you, so pardon them, seek forgiveness for them and consult them on the course of affairs. And when you are resolved, put your trust in Allah. Verily Allah loves those who put their trust [in Him]." (Al Imran 3:159)

   "And put your trust in Allah, for Allah is sufficient as Guardian." (Nisa 4:81)

أَنْتَ وَلِيُّنَا فَاغْفِرْ لَنَا وَارْحَمْنَا وَأَنْتَ خَيْرُ الْغَافِرِينَ ۞ إِنَّ وَلِيِّيَ اللهُ الَّذِي نَزَّلَ الْكِتَابَ وَهُوَ يَتَوَلَّى الصَّالِحِينَ ۞ يَا أَيُّهَا الَّذِينَ اٰمَنُوا اذْكُرُوا نِعْمَتَ اللهِ عَلَيْكُمْ إِذْ هَمَّ قَوْمٌ أَنْ يَبْسُطُوا إِلَيْكُمْ أَيْدِيَهُمْ فَكَفَّ أَيْدِيَهُمْ عَنْكُمْ وَاتَّقُوا اللهَ وَعَلَى اللهِ فَلْيَتَوَكَّلِ الْمُؤْمِنُونَ ۞ لَهُمْ دَارُ السَّلَامِ عِنْدَ رَبِّهِمْ وَهُوَ وَلِيُّهُمْ بِمَا كَانُوا يَعْمَلُونَ ۞ فَمَا أُوتِيتُمْ مِنْ شَيْءٍ فَمَتَاعُ الْحَيَوةِ الدُّنْيَا وَمَا عِنْدَ اللهِ خَيْرٌ وَأَبْقَى لِلَّذِينَ اٰمَنُوا وَعَلَى رَبِّهِمْ يَتَوَكَّلُونَ ۞ فَبِمَا رَحْمَةٍ مِنَ اللهِ لِنْتَ لَهُمْ وَلَوْ كُنْتَ فَظًّا غَلِيظَ الْقَلْبِ لَا نْفَضُّوا مِنْ حَوْلِكَ فَاعْفُ عَنْهُمْ وَاسْتَغْفِرْ لَهُمْ وَشَاوِرْهُمْ فِى الْأَمْرِ فَإِذَا عَزَمْتَ فَتَوَكَّلْ عَلَى اللهِ إِنَّ اللهَ يُحِبُّ الْمُتَوَكِّلِينَ وَتَوَكَّلْ عَلَى اللهِ وَكَفَى بِاللهِ وَكِيلًا ۞

1. "Indeed there is an excellent example for you in Abraham and those who were with him when they said to their people: Truly we are immune from you and that which you worship besides Allah and we reject you. Hostility and hatred have arisen between us forever, unless you believe in Allah alone—except for the saying of Abraham to his father: I will implore forgiveness for you, although I have not the power to do anything for you before Allah. Our Lord! In You have we put our trust, to You do we turn in repentance, and unto You is the journeying." (Mumtahana 60:4)

2. "Say: He is the All-Merciful. We believe in Him, and in Him have we put our trust. Thereafter you will know who is in clear error." (Mulk 67:29)

3. "Why should we not put our trust in Allah and He has guided us on our paths. We will definitely remain steadfast in the face of that with which you have caused us harm. So in Allah let the trusting put their trust. (Ibrahim 14:12)

4. "It is only Allah who is your Protecting Friend, and His Messenger, and those who believe, who establish the prayer, pay the *zakat* and bow down [in prayer]." (Maida 5:55)

قَدْ كَانَتْ لَكُمْ أُسْوَةٌ حَسَنَةٌ فِي إِبْرَهِيمَ وَالَّذِينَ مَعَهُ إِذْ قَالُوا لِقَوْمِهِمْ إِنَّا بُرَءَآؤُا مِنكُمْ وَمِمَّا تَعْبُدُونَ مِن دُونِ اللهِ كَفَرْنَا بِكُمْ وَبَدَا بَيْنَنَا وَبَيْنَكُمُ الْعَدَاوَةُ وَالْبَغْضَاءُ أَبَداً حَتَّى تُؤْمِنُوا بِاللهِ وَحْدَهُ إِلَّا قَوْلَ إِبْرَهِيمَ لِأَبِيهِ لَأَسْتَغْفِرَنَّ لَكَ وَمَا أَمْلِكُ لَكَ مِنَ اللهِ مِن شَيْءٍ رَبَّنَا عَلَيْكَ تَوَكَّلْنَا وَإِلَيْكَ أَنَبْنَا وَإِلَيْكَ الْمَصِيرُ ﴿١﴾ قُلْ هُوَ الرَّحْمَنُ ءَامَنَّا بِهِ وَعَلَيْهِ تَوَكَّلْنَا فَسَتَعْلَمُونَ مَنْ هُوَ فِي ضَلَالٍ مُبِينٍ ﴿٢﴾ وَمَا لَنَا أَلَّا نَتَوَكَّلَ عَلَى اللهِ وَقَدْ هَدَينَا سُبُلَنَا وَلَنَصْبِرَنَّ عَلَى مَا ءَاذَيْتُمُونَا وَعَلَى اللهِ فَلْيَتَوَكَّلِ الْمُتَوَكِّلُونَ ﴿٣﴾ إِنَّمَا وَلِيُّكُمُ اللهُ وَرَسُولُهُ وَالَّذِينَ ءَامَنُوا الَّذِينَ يُقِيمُونَ الصَّلَوةَ وَيُؤْتُونَ الزَّكَوةَ وَهُمْ رَاكِعُونَ ﴿٤﴾

1. "He (Jacob) said, O my sons! Don't enter by one gate, but enter by different gates. I cannot avail you aught against Allah. The judgment is His alone. In Him have I put my trust, and in Him let the trusting place their trust." (Yusuf 12:67)

2. "Say: He is my Lord, there is no god but Him, in Him have I put my trust and to Him is my return." (Ra'd 13:30)

3. "And whatever you differ about, its judgment returns to Allah, that is Allah, my Lord. In Him have I put my trust and unto Him I turn in repentance." (Shura 42:10)

4. "We will not be able to return to it unless Allah, our Lord wills it. Our Lord encompasses everything in His knowledge. In Allah have we put our trust. Our Lord! Decide with truth between us and our people, for You are the best of those who decide." (A'raf 7:89)

5. "So they said: In Allah have we put our trust. Our Lord! Don't make us a lure for the oppressing people." (Yunus 10:86)

وَقَالَ يَا بَنِيَّ لَا تَدْخُلُوا مِنْ بَابٍ وَاحِدٍ وَادْخُلُوا مِنْ أَبْوَابٍ مُتَفَرِّقَةٍ وَمَا أُغْنِي عَنْكُمْ مِنَ اللهِ مِنْ شَيْءٍ إِنِ الْحُكْمُ إِلَّا لِلّٰهِ عَلَيْهِ تَوَكَّلْتُ وَعَلَيْهِ فَلْيَتَوَكَّلِ الْمُتَوَكِّلُونَ ﴿١﴾

قُلْ هُوَ رَبِّي لَا إِلٰهَ إِلَّا هُوَ عَلَيْهِ تَوَكَّلْتُ وَإِلَيْهِ مَتَابِ ﴿٢﴾ وَمَا اخْتَلَفْتُمْ فِيهِ مِنْ شَيْءٍ فَحُكْمُهُ إِلَى اللهِ ذٰلِكُمُ اللهُ رَبِّي عَلَيْهِ تَوَكَّلْتُ وَإِلَيْهِ أُنِيبُ ﴿٣﴾

وَمَا يَكُونُ لَنَا أَنْ نَعُودَ فِيهَا إِلَّا أَنْ يَشَاءَ اللهُ رَبُّنَا وَسِعَ رَبُّنَا كُلَّ شَيْءٍ عِلْماً عَلَى اللهِ تَوَكَّلْنَا رَبَّنَا افْتَحْ بَيْنَنَا وَبَيْنَ قَوْمِنَا بِالْحَقِّ وَأَنْتَ خَيْرُ الْفَاتِحِينَ ﴿٤﴾

فَقَالُوا عَلَى اللهِ تَوَكَّلْنَا رَبَّنَا لَا تَجْعَلْنَا فِتْنَةً لِلْقَوْمِ الظَّالِمِينَ ﴿٥﴾

1. "Say: Have you considered [concerning] those you are calling on besides Allah: if Allah wills harm for me, is there anyone who can lift away His harm, or if He wills mercy for me, is there anyone who can withhold His mercy? Say: Allah suffices me, in Him do the trusting place their trust." (Zumar 39:38)

2. "Recite to them the story of Noah when he said to his people: O my people, if my dwelling [amongst you] and my reminder [to you] of Allah's signs, is offensive to you, in Allah have I put my trust, so put together your course of action with your partners and afterwards let it not be a cause of grievance to you. Then exact your sentence on me and don't give me respite." (Yunus 10:72)

3. "Truly, I have put my trust in my Lord and your Lord, there's not a beast that He does not grasp by the forelock. Verily my Lord is upon the straight path." (Hud 11:56)

4. "He said: O my people, do you not see that if I am acting on a clear proof from my Lord and he has provided me with a good provision? I do not wish to be contrary and do that which I have forbidden you to do; I only want to reform as much as I can. My success is only from Allah. In Him have I put my trust and to Him do I turn." (Hud 11:88)

قُلْ أَفَرَأَيْتُمْ مَا تَدْعُونَ مِنْ دُونِ اللهِ إِنْ أَرَادَنِيَ اللهُ بِضُرٍّ

هَلْ هُنَّ كَاشِفَاتُ ضُرِّهِ أَوْ أَرَادَنِي بِرَحْمَةٍ هَلْ هُنَّ مُمْسِكَاتُ

رَحْمَتِهِ قُلْ حَسْبِيَ اللهُ عَلَيْهِ يَتَوَكَّلُ الْمُتَوَكِّلُونَ ﴿١﴾

وَاتْلُ عَلَيْهِمْ نَبَأَ نُوحٍ إِذْ قَالَ لِقَوْمِهِ يَا قَوْمِ إِنْ

كَانَ كَبُرَ عَلَيْكُمْ مَقَامِي وَتَذْكِيرِي بِآيَاتِ اللهِ فَعَلَى اللهِ

تَوَكَّلْتُ فَأَجْمِعُوا أَمْرَكُمْ وَشُرَكَاءَكُمْ ثُمَّ لَا يَكُنْ أَمْرُكُمْ

عَلَيْكُمْ غُمَّةً ثُمَّ اقْضُوا إِلَيَّ وَلَا تُنْظِرُونِ ﴿٢﴾

إِنِّي تَوَكَّلْتُ عَلَى اللهِ رَبِّي وَرَبِّكُمْ مَا مِنْ دَابَّةٍ إِلَّا هُوَ

اخِذٌ بِنَاصِيَتِهَا إِنَّ رَبِّي عَلَى صِرَاطٍ مُسْتَقِيمٍ ﴿٣﴾

قَالَ يَا قَوْمِ أَرَأَيْتُمْ إِنْ كُنْتُ عَلَى بَيِّنَةٍ مِنْ رَبِّي

وَرَزَقَنِي مِنْهُ رِزْقاً حَسَناً وَمَا أُرِيدُ أَنْ أُخَالِفَكُمْ إِلَى

مَا أَنْهَاكُمْ عَنْهُ إِنْ أُرِيدُ إِلَّا الْإِصْلَاحَ مَا اسْتَطَعْتُ وَمَا

تَوْفِيقِي إِلَّا بِاللهِ عَلَيْهِ تَوَكَّلْتُ وَإِلَيْهِ أُنِيبُ ﴿٤﴾

1. "He it is who sends down the rain after they had despaired, and spreads His mercy, and He is the Protector, Owner of Praise." (Shura 42:28)

2. "And whoever fears Allah, He makes for him a way out. ⚙ And He provides for him from whence he doesn't expect it. And whoever puts his trust in Allah, He suffices him. Allah will surely bring about what He decrees. He has set a measure for all things." (Talaq 65:2-3)

3. "And if they wish to deceive you, truly Allah suffices you. He it is who aided you with His support and with the believers." (Anfal 8:62)

4. "O Prophet! Allah suffices you and those who follow you among the believers." (Anfal 8:64)

5. "Those to whom men said: Indeed the people have gathered against you, so fear them. But their faith was increased and they replied: Allah suffices us and what an excellent Guardian [He is]!" (Al Imran 3:173)

6. "If only they were content with what Allah and His Messenger had brought them and said: Allah suffices us. Allah will grant us from His bounty and so will His Messenger. Truly it is to Allah that we turn our hopes." (Tawba 9:59)

وَهُوَ الَّذِي يُنَزِّلُ الْغَيْثَ مِنْ بَعْدِ مَا قَنَطُوا وَيَنْشُرُ

رَحْمَتَهُ وَهُوَ الْوَلِيُّ الْحَمِيدُ ﴿١﴾

وَمَنْ يَتَّقِ اللَّهَ يَجْعَلْ لَهُ مَخْرَجاً ۞ وَيَرْزُقْهُ مِنْ حَيْثُ

لَا يَحْتَسِبُ وَمَنْ يَتَوَكَّلْ عَلَى اللَّهِ فَهُوَ حَسْبُهُ إِنَّ اللَّهَ بَالِغُ

أَمْرِهِ قَدْ جَعَلَ اللَّهُ لِكُلِّ شَيْءٍ قَدْراً ﴿٢﴾

وَإِنْ يُرِيدُوا أَنْ يَخْدَعُوكَ فَإِنَّ حَسْبَكَ اللَّهُ هُوَ الَّذِي

أَيَّدَكَ بِنَصْرِهِ وَبِالْمُؤْمِنِينَ ﴿٣﴾

يَا أَيُّهَا النَّبِيُّ حَسْبُكَ اللَّهُ وَمَنِ اتَّبَعَكَ مِنَ الْمُؤْمِنِينَ ﴿٤﴾

الَّذِينَ قَالَ لَهُمُ النَّاسُ إِنَّ النَّاسَ قَدْ جَمَعُوا لَكُمْ فَاخْشَوْهُمْ

فَزَادَهُمْ إِيمَاناً وَقَالُوا حَسْبُنَا اللَّهُ وَنِعْمَ الْوَكِيلُ ﴿٥﴾

وَلَوْ أَنَّهُمْ رَضُوا مَا آتَيْهُمُ اللَّهُ وَرَسُولُهُ وَقَالُوا حَسْبُنَا اللَّهُ

سَيُؤْتِينَا اللَّهُ مِنْ فَضْلِهِ وَرَسُولُهُ إِنَّا إِلَى اللَّهِ رَاغِبُونَ ﴿٦﴾

1. "Two men who feared [their Lord] and whom Allah had favored, said: Enter upon them by the gate, for if you enter by it you will surely be victorious. So put your trust in Allah if you are believers." (Maida 5:23)

2. "You alone do we worship and from You alone do we seek help." (Fatiha 1:3)

3. "O you who believe seek help in patience and prayer. Verily Allah is with the patient." (Baqara 2:153)

4. "Moses said to his people: seek help from Allah and show patience. Truly the earth belongs to Allah; He bequeaths it to whomsoever He wills among His servants. And the final outcome is for the pious." (A'raf 128)

5. "And Allah is He whose help is to be sought with regard to what you describe." (Yusuf 12:18)

6. "He said: My Lord! Judge by what is right. Our Lord is He whose help is to be sought against what you attribute [to Him]." (Anbiya 21:112)

7. "And seek help through patience and prayer, and indeed it is heavy [upon all] save the humble." (Baqara 2:45)

8. "When you sought the help of your Lord, and He answered: I am supporting you with a thousand angels rank upon rank." (Anfal 8:9)

قَالَ رَجُلَانِ مِنَ الَّذِينَ يَخَافُونَ أَنْعَمَ اللهُ عَلَيْهِمَا

ادْخُلُوا عَلَيْهِمُ الْبَابَ فَإِذَا دَخَلْتُمُوهُ فَإِنَّكُمْ غَالِبُونَ وَعَلَى

اللهِ فَتَوَكَّلُوا إِنْ كُنْتُمْ مُؤْمِنِينَ ﴿١﴾

إِيَّاكَ نَعْبُدُ وَإِيَّاكَ نَسْتَعِينُ ﴿٢﴾

يَا أَيُّهَا الَّذِينَ آمَنُوا اسْتَعِينُوا بِالصَّبْرِ وَالصَّلٰوةِ إِنَّ اللهَ مَعَ

الصَّابِرِينَ ﴿٣﴾

قَالَ مُوسٰى لِقَوْمِهِ اسْتَعِينُوا بِاللهِ وَاصْبِرُوا إِنَّ الْأَرْضَ للهِ

يُورِثُهَا مَنْ يَشَاءُ مِنْ عِبَادِهِ وَالْعَاقِبَةُ لِلْمُتَّقِينَ ﴿٤﴾

وَاللهُ الْمُسْتَعَانُ عَلٰى مَا تَصِفُونَ ﴿٥﴾ قَالَ رَبِّ احْكُمْ

بِالْحَقِّ وَرَبُّنَا الرَّحْمٰنُ الْمُسْتَعَانُ عَلٰى مَا تَصِفُون ﴿٦﴾

وَاسْتَعِينُوا بِالصَّبْرِ وَالصَّلٰوةِ وَإِنَّهَا لَكَبِيرَةٌ إِلَّا عَلَى

الْخَاشِعِينَ ﴿٧﴾ إِذْ تَسْتَغِيثُونَ رَبَّكُمْ فَاسْتَجَابَ لَكُمْ أَنِّي

مُمِدُّكُمْ بِأَلْفٍ مِنَ الْمَلَئِكَةِ مُرْدِفِينَ ﴿٨﴾

1. "And those who knew that they will meet with Allah said: How many a little company has overcome a mighty host by Allah's leave, and Allah is with the patient." (Baqara 2:249)

2. "Allah has written: Surely I will be victorious, I and my messengers. Indeed, Allah is the Strong, the Triumphant." (Mujadila 58:21)

3. "O Prophet! Exhort the believers to fight, and if there are among you twenty steadfast, they shall overcome two hundred, and if there are among you a hundred steadfast, they shall overcome a thousand of the unbelievers because they are a people who do not comprehend. ✪ Now Allah has lightened [your burden] for He knows that there is a weakness in you, so if there are among you a hundred steadfast they shall overcome two hundred and if there are among you one thousand steadfast they shall overcome two thousand by the permission of Allah. Allah is with the steadfast." (Anfal 8:65-6)

4. "*Alif, Lam, Mim.* ✪ The Romans have been defeated. ✪ In the nearest land, and after their defeat they will be victorious." (Rum 30:1-3)

5. "And Allah is controlling his affairs, but most people know not." (Yusuf 12:21)

قَالَ الَّذِينَ يَظُنُّونَ أَنَّهُمْ مُلَاقُوا اللهِ كَمْ مِنْ فِئَةٍ قَلِيلَةٍ غَلَبَتْ فِئَةً كَثِيرَةً بِإِذْنِ اللهِ وَاللهُ مَعَ الصَّابِرِينَ ﴿١﴾

كَتَبَ اللهُ لَأَغْلِبَنَّ أَنَا وَرُسُلِي إِنَّ اللهَ قَوِيٌّ عَزِيزٌ ﴿٢﴾

يَا أَيُّهَا النَّبِيُّ حَرِّضِ الْمُؤْمِنِينَ عَلَى الْقِتَالِ إِنْ يَكُنْ مِنْكُمْ عِشْرُونَ صَابِرُونَ يَغْلِبُوا مِائَتَيْنِ وَإِنْ يَكُنْ مِنْكُمْ مِائَةٌ يَغْلِبُوا أَلْفًا مِنَ الَّذِينَ كَفَرُوا بِأَنَّهُمْ قَوْمٌ لَا يَفْقَهُونَ ۞ الْآنَ خَفَّفَ اللهُ عَنْكُمْ وَعَلِمَ أَنَّ فِيكُمْ ضَعْفًا فَإِنْ يَكُنْ مِنْكُمْ مِائَةٌ صَابِرَةٌ يَغْلِبُوا مِائَتَيْنِ وَإِنْ يَكُنْ مِنْكُمْ أَلْفٌ يَغْلِبُوا أَلْفَيْنِ بِإِذْنِ اللهِ وَاللهُ مَعَ الصَّابِرِينَ ﴿٣﴾

الٓمٓ ۞ غُلِبَتِ الرُّومُ ۞ فِي أَدْنَى الْأَرْضِ وَهُمْ مِنْ بَعْدِ غَلَبِهِمْ سَيَغْلِبُونَ ﴿٤﴾ وَاللهُ غَالِبٌ عَلَى أَمْرِهِ وَلَٰكِنَّ أَكْثَرَ النَّاسِ لَا يَعْلَمُونَ ﴿٥﴾

1. "And if they turn away, know that Allah is your Protector, a blessed Protector, and a blessed Helper." (Anfal 8:40)

2. "And strive for Allah with the endeavor that He has a right to. He chose you and did not encumber you with hardship in religion. [It is] the faith of your forefather Abraham; He named you Muslims from before and in this [scripture], so that the Messenger can be a witness for you and you can be witnesses for humankind. Therefore, establish the prayer, pay the *zakat* (alms), and hold fast to Allah for He is your Protector; an excellent Protector and an excellent Helper." (Hajj 22:78)

3. "And Allah is more knowledgeable about your enemies. And Allah suffices as Protector and suffices as Helper." (Nisa 4:45)

4. "What is it with you that you don't fight for Allah's cause and for the weak among men, women and children who are crying: Our Lord! Take us away from this town whose inhabitants are oppressors and send us from Your Presence a protector, and send from Your Presence a helper!" (Nisa 4:75)

5. "And your Lord is sufficient as Guide and Helper." (Furqan 25:31)

6. "And that verily they would be helped. ❂ And that Our host would verily be the victors." (Saffat 37:172-3)

وَإِنْ تَوَلَّوْا فَاعْلَمُوا أَنَّ اللهَ مَوْلٰيكُمْ نِعْمَ الْمَوْلٰى وَنِعْمَ النَّصِيرُ ﴿١﴾ وَجَاهِدُوا فِي اللهِ حَقَّ جِهَادِهِ هُوَ اجْتَبٰيكُمْ وَمَا جَعَلَ عَلَيْكُمْ فِي الدِّينِ مِنْ حَرَجٍ مِلَّةَ أَبِيكُمْ إِبْرٰهِيمَ هُوَ سَمّٰيكُمُ الْمُسْلِمِينَ مِنْ قَبْلُ وَفِي هٰذَا لِيَكُونَ الرَّسُولُ شَهِيداً عَلَيْكُمْ وَتَكُونُوا شُهَدَاءَ عَلَى النَّاسِ فَأَقِيمُوا الصَّلٰوةَ وَاٰتُوا الزَّكٰوةَ وَاعْتَصِمُوا بِاللهِ هُوَ مَوْلٰيكُمْ فَنِعْمَ الْمَوْلٰى وَنِعْمَ النَّصِيرُ ﴿٢﴾ وَاللهُ أَعْلَمُ بِأَعْدَائِكُمْ وَكَفٰى بِاللهِ وَلِيًّا وَكَفٰى بِاللهِ نَصِيراً ﴿٣﴾ وَمَا لَكُمْ لَا تُقَاتِلُونَ فِي سَبِيلِ اللهِ وَالْمُسْتَضْعَفِينَ مِنَ الرِّجَالِ وَالنِّسَاءِ وَالْوِلْدَانِ الَّذِينَ يَقُولُونَ رَبَّنَا أَخْرِجْنَا مِنْ هٰذِهِ الْقَرْيَةِ الظَّالِمِ أَهْلُهَا وَاجْعَلْ لَنَا مِنْ لَدُنْكَ وَلِيًّا وَاجْعَلْ لَنَا مِنْ لَدُنْكَ نَصِيراً ﴿٤﴾ وَكَفٰى بِرَبِّكَ هَادِياً وَنَصِيراً ﴿٥﴾ إِنَّهُمْ لَهُمُ الْمَنْصُورُونَ ۞ وَإِنَّ جُنْدَنَا لَهُمُ الْغَالِبُونَ ﴿٤﴾

1. "And [He will give you] something else that you will love: help from Allah, and approaching victory. So give good tidings to the believers." (Saff 61:13)

2. "When Allah's help arrives and victory ❀ And you see people entering the religion of Allah in droves." (Nasr 110:1-2)

3. "Verily prophets have been denied before you [Muhammad] and they showed patience in the face of denial and persecution, till Our help reached them. And no one can change the words of Allah. And already have some tidings of the messengers reached you." (An'am 6:34)

4. "Thus does Allah strengthen with His support whom He wills. Verily in this there is a lesson for those who can see." (Al Imran 3:13)

5. "And if they wish to deceive you, truly Allah is your sufficiency. He it is Who strengthened you with His support and with the believers." (Anfal 8:62)

6. "Those who are being fought have been given permission as they have been oppressed, and assuredly Allah has the power to support them." (Hajj 22:39)

7. "O you who believe, be the helpers of Allah, even as Jesus son of Mary said unto the disciples: Who are my helpers for Allah. They said: We are the helpers of Allah, so a party of the Children of Israel believed while a party disbelieved, and We aided those who believed over their foe, so they became the uppermost." (Saff 61:14)

وَأُخْرَىٰ تُحِبُّونَهَا نَصْرٌ مِنَ اللهِ وَفَتْحٌ قَرِيبٌ وَبَشِّرِ الْمُؤْمِنِينَ ۞ إِذَا جَاءَ نَصْرُ اللهِ وَالْفَتْحُ ۞ وَرَأَيْتَ النَّاسَ يَدْخُلُونَ فِي دِينِ اللهِ أَفْوَاجاً ۞ وَلَقَدْ كُذِّبَتْ رُسُلٌ مِنْ قَبْلِكَ فَصَبَرُوا عَلَىٰ مَا كُذِّبُوا وَأُوذُوا حَتَّىٰ أَتَيْهُمْ نَصْرُنَا وَلَا مُبَدِّلَ لِكَلِمَاتِ اللهِ وَلَقَدْ جَاءَكَ مِنْ نَبَإِ الْمُرْسَلِينَ ۞ وَاللهُ يُؤَيِّدُ بِنَصْرِهِ مَنْ يَشَاءُ إِنَّ فِي ذَٰلِكَ لَعِبْرَةً لِأُولِي الْأَبْصَارِ ۞ وَإِنْ يُرِيدُوا أَنْ يَخْدَعُوكَ فَإِنَّ حَسْبَكَ اللهُ هُوَ الَّذِي أَيَّدَكَ بِنَصْرِهِ وَبِالْمُؤْمِنِينَ ۞ أُذِنَ لِلَّذِينَ يُقَاتَلُونَ بِأَنَّهُمْ ظُلِمُوا وَإِنَّ اللهَ عَلَىٰ نَصْرِهِمْ لَقَدِيرٌ ۞ يَا أَيُّهَا الَّذِينَ آمَنُوا كُونُوا أَنْصَارَ اللهِ كَمَا قَالَ عِيسَى ابْنُ مَرْيَمَ لِلْحَوَارِيِّينَ مَنْ أَنْصَارِي إِلَى اللهِ قَالَ الْحَوَارِيُّونَ نَحْنُ أَنْصَارُ اللهِ فَآمَنَتْ طَائِفَةٌ مِنْ بَنِي إِسْرَائِيلَ وَكَفَرَتْ طَائِفَةٌ فَأَيَّدْنَا الَّذِينَ آمَنُوا عَلَىٰ عَدُوِّهِمْ فَأَصْبَحُوا ظَاهِرِينَ ۞

1. "He said: My Lord! Help me for they deny me." (Mu'minun 23:26)

2. "He said: My Lord! Help me against the corrupt people." (Ankabut 29:30)

3. "Save those who believe and do righteous deeds, and remember Allah much, and who vindicated themselves after being oppressed; and the oppressors will know to what overturning they will be overturned." (Shuara 26:227)

4. "So he cried unto his Lord [saying] I am overwhelmed, so vanquish [them]!" (Qamar 54:10)

5. "Or do you think that you will enter Paradise when you haven't yet received the like of those who passed away before you; they were afflicted by hardship and suffering and shaken as if by an earthquake till the Messenger and those who believed with him said: When will Allah's help arrive? Assuredly, Allah's help is near." (Baqara 2:214)

6. "And Allah only made it as good tidings for you, and so that your hearts would become serene by it. Victory is only from Allah, All-Honorable, All-Wise." (Anfal 8:10)

7. "Verily we sent before you [Muhammad] messengers to their own peoples and they brought them clear proofs, and we took vengeance on the wrong doers, and it is incumbent upon Us to help the believers." (Rum 30:47)

قَالَ رَبِّ انْصُرْنِي بِمَا كَذَّبُونِ ﴿١﴾ قَالَ رَبِّ انْصُرْنِي عَلَى الْقَوْمِ الْمُفْسِدِينَ ﴿٢﴾ إِلَّا الَّذِينَ آمَنُوا وَعَمِلُوا الصَّالِحَاتِ وَذَكَرُوا اللَّهَ كَثِيرًا وَانْتَصَرُوا مِنْ بَعْدِ مَا ظُلِمُوا وَسَيَعْلَمُ الَّذِينَ ظَلَمُوا أَيَّ مُنْقَلَبٍ يَنْقَلِبُونَ ﴿٣﴾ فَدَعَا رَبَّهُ أَنِّي مَغْلُوبٌ فَانْتَصِرْ ﴿٤﴾ أَمْ حَسِبْتُمْ أَنْ تَدْخُلُوا الْجَنَّةَ وَلَمَّا يَأْتِكُمْ مَثَلُ الَّذِينَ خَلَوْا مِنْ قَبْلِكُمْ مَسَّتْهُمُ الْبَأْسَاءُ وَالضَّرَّاءُ وَزُلْزِلُوا حَتَّى يَقُولَ الرَّسُولُ وَالَّذِينَ آمَنُوا مَعَهُ مَتَى نَصْرُ اللَّهِ أَلَا إِنَّ نَصْرَ اللَّهِ قَرِيبٌ ﴿٥﴾

وَمَا جَعَلَهُ اللَّهُ إِلَّا بُشْرَى لَكُمْ وَلِتَطْمَئِنَّ قُلُوبُكُمْ بِهِ وَمَا النَّصْرُ إِلَّا مِنْ عِنْدِ اللَّهِ الْعَزِيزِ الْحَكِيمِ ﴿٦﴾ وَلَقَدْ أَرْسَلْنَا مِنْ قَبْلِكَ رُسُلًا إِلَى قَوْمِهِمْ فَجَاءُوهُمْ بِالْبَيِّنَاتِ فَانْتَقَمْنَا مِنَ الَّذِينَ أَجْرَمُوا وَكَانَ حَقًّا عَلَيْنَا نَصْرُ الْمُؤْمِنِينَ ﴿٧﴾

1. "Indeed we have sent our messengers with clear proofs, and we sent with them the Scriptures and the standard by which people may establish justice. And we revealed iron a [source of] great strength with benefits for people, and so that Allah may know who helps Him and His messengers in the unseen. Verily Allah is the Strong, All-Honorable." (Hadid 57:25)

2. "And [the spoils] are for the poor immigrants who were driven from their homes and wealth while seeking Allah's favor and good pleasure, and supporting Allah and His Messenger; these are the truthful." (Hashr 59:8)

3. "Indeed Allah is your Protector and He is the best of helpers." (Al Imran 3:150)

4. "And their saying was naught except to say: Our Lord, forgive us our sins and any excess in our affairs, make us steadfast, and support us against the unbelieving people." (Al Imran 3:147)

5. "Allah does not charge a soul beyond its capacity. It shall be requited only for the good it earned and the evil it committed. Our Lord! Do not take us to task when we forget or make mistakes! Our Lord! Do not lay on us a burden like that you laid on those who came before us! Our Lord! Do not charge us with more than we can bear! Pardon us, forgive us, and have mercy on us! You are our Master, grant us victory over the unbelievers." (Baqara 2: 286)

لَقَدْ أَرْسَلْنَا رُسُلَنَا بِالْبَيِّنَاتِ وَأَنزَلْنَا مَعَهُمُ الْكِتَابَ

وَالْمِيزَانَ لِيَقُومَ النَّاسُ بِالْقِسْطِ وَأَنزَلْنَا الْحَدِيدَ فِيهِ بَأْسٌ

شَدِيدٌ وَمَنَافِعُ لِلنَّاسِ وَلِيَعْلَمَ اللّهُ مَن يَنصُرُهُ وَرُسُلَهُ بِالْغَيْبِ

إِنَّ اللّهَ قَوِيٌّ عَزِيزٌ ۞ لِلْفُقَرَاءِ الْمُهَاجِرِينَ الَّذِينَ أُخْرِجُوا مِن

دِيَارِهِمْ وَأَمْوَالِهِمْ يَبْتَغُونَ فَضْلاً مِنَ اللّهِ وَرِضْوَاناً وَيَنصُرُونَ

اللّهَ وَرَسُولَهُ أُوْلَئِكَ هُمُ الصَّادِقُونَ ۞ بَلِ اللّهُ مَوْلِيكُمْ وَهُوَ

خَيْرُ النَّاصِرِينَ ۞ وَمَا كَانَ قَوْلَهُمْ إِلاَّ أَنْ قَالُوا رَبَّنَا اغْفِرْ لَنَا

ذُنُوبَنَا وَإِسْرَافَنَا فِي أَمْرِنَا وَثَبِّتْ أَقْدَامَنَا وَانْصُرْنَا عَلَى الْقَوْمِ

الْكَافِرِينَ ۞ لاَ يُكَلِّفُ اللّهُ نَفْساً إِلاَّ وُسْعَهَا لَهَا مَا كَسَبَتْ

وَعَلَيْهَا مَا اكْتَسَبَتْ رَبَّنَا لاَ تُؤَاخِذْنَا إِن نَسِينَا أَوْ أَخْطَأْنَا رَبَّنَا

وَلاَ تَحْمِلْ عَلَيْنَا إِصْراً كَمَا حَمَلْتَهُ عَلَى الَّذِينَ مِن قَبْلِنَا رَبَّنَا

وَلاَ تُحَمِّلْنَا مَا لاَ طَاقَةَ لَنَا بِهِ وَاعْفُ عَنَّا وَاغْفِرْ لَنَا وَارْحَمْنَا

أَنتَ مَوْلاَنَا فَانصُرْنَا عَلَى الْقَوْمِ الْكَافِرِينَ ۞

1. "If Allah supports you, then no one can overcome you, and if He forsakes you, who is there to come to your aid besides Him? So in Allah let the believers put their trust." (Al Imran 3:160)

2. "Fight them and Allah will punish them at your hands, disgrace them, give you victory over them, and heal the hearts of a believing people." (Tawba 9:14)

3. "Verily Allah helps whoever helps Him (His religion). Indeed, He is the Strong, the Triumphant." (Hajj 22:40)

4. "That [is so]. And whoever retaliated with the like of that which he was made to suffer and then is wronged [again] Allah will surely come to his aid. Indeed He is the Pardoning, the Forgiving." (Hajj 22:60)

5. "And, O my people! Who would deliver me from Allah if I drove them away? Will you not take heed?" (Hud 11:30)

6. "He said: O my people! Don't you see that if I am [acting] on a clear proof from my Lord, and He has granted me a mercy from Himself, who will save me from Allah if I disobey Him? You will do naught for me except increase my perdition." (Hud 11:63)

إِنْ يَنْصُرْكُمُ اللهُ فَلَا غَالِبَ لَكُمْ وَإِنْ يَخْذُلْكُمْ فَمَنْ

ذَا الَّذِي يَنْصُرُكُمْ مِنْ بَعْدِهِ وَعَلَى اللهِ فَلْيَتَوَكَّلِ الْمُؤْمِنُونَ

﴿١﴾ قَاتِلُوهُمْ يُعَذِّبْهُمُ اللهُ بِأَيْدِيكُمْ وَيُخْزِهِمْ وَيَنْصُرْكُمْ

عَلَيْهِمْ وَيَشْفِ صُدُورَ قَوْمٍ مُؤْمِنِينَ ﴿٢﴾

وَلَيَنْصُرَنَّ اللهُ مَنْ يَنْصُرُهُ إِنَّ اللهَ لَقَوِيٌّ عَزِيزٌ ﴿٣﴾

ذَلِكَ وَمَنْ عَاقَبَ بِمِثْلِ مَا عُوقِبَ بِهِ ثُمَّ بُغِيَ عَلَيْهِ

لَيَنْصُرَنَّهُ اللهُ إِنَّ اللهَ لَعَفُوٌّ غَفُورٌ ﴿٤﴾

وَيَا قَوْمِ مَنْ يَنْصُرُنِي مِنَ اللهِ إِنْ طَرَدْتُهُمْ أَفَلَا

تَذَكَّرُونَ ﴿٥﴾

قَالَ يَا قَوْمِ أَرَأَيْتُمْ إِنْ كُنْتُ عَلَى بَيِّنَةٍ مِنْ رَبِّي

وَآتَانِي مِنْهُ رَحْمَةً فَمَنْ يَنْصُرُنِي مِنَ اللهِ إِنْ عَصَيْتُهُ فَمَا

تَزِيدُونَنِي غَيْرَ تَخْسِيرٍ ﴿٦﴾

1. "Those who follow the Messenger, the Unlettered Prophet whom they find described in the Torah and Gospel [which are] with them. He enjoins on them the good and forbids them that which is evil. He makes lawful for them the wholesome things and prohibits for them that which is foul. He will relieve them of their burden and the shackles which [weighed] upon them…

2. (continued) Then those who believe in him, revere him, support him and follow the light which was sent down with him; these are the successful." (A'raf 7:157)

3. "When Allah made [His] covenant with the Prophets, [He said]: Behold that which I have given you of scripture and wisdom. And afterwards [when] there comes unto you a Messenger confirming [the truth of] what is with you, you shall believe in him and support him. He said: Do you agree and thereby take up My burden [upon yourselves] in this [matter]? They said: We agree. He said: Then bear witness and I am with you among the witnesses." (Al Imran 3:81)

4. "O you who believe, if you help (the religion of) Allah He will help you and make you steadfast." (Muhammad 47:7)

5. "[…….. the believers shall rejoice] ❂ At the help of Allah. He helps whomsoever He wills, and He is the All-Mighty, the Merciful." (Rum 30:5)

6. "And that Allah may help you with a mighty help." (Fath 48:3)

اَلَّذِينَ يَتَّبِعُونَ الرَّسُولَ النَّبِيَّ الْأُمِّيَّ الَّذِي يَجِدُونَهُ
مَكْتُوباً عِنْدَهُمْ فِي التَّوْرٰيةِ وَالْإِنْجِيلِ يَأْمُرُهُمْ بِالْمَعْرُوفِ
وَيَنْهٰيهُمْ عَنِ الْمُنْكَرِ وَيُحِلُّ لَهُمُ الطَّيِّبَاتِ وَيُحَرِّمُ عَلَيْهِمُ
الْخَبَائِثَ وَيَضَعُ عَنْهُمْ إِصْرَهُمْ وَالْأَغْلَالَ الَّتِي كَانَتْ
عَلَيْهِمْ ۞ فَالَّذِينَ اٰمَنُوا بِهِ وَعَزَّرُوهُ وَنَصَرُوهُ وَاتَّبَعُوا
النُّورَ الَّذِي أُنْزِلَ مَعَهُ أُولٰئِكَ هُمُ الْمُفْلِحُونَ ۞

وَإِذْ أَخَذَ اللهُ مِيثَاقَ النَّبِيِّينَ لَمَا اٰتَيْتُكُمْ مِنْ كِتَابٍ
وَحِكْمَةٍ ثُمَّ جَاءَكُمْ رَسُولٌ مُصَدِّقٌ لِمَا مَعَكُمْ لَتُؤْمِنُنَّ بِهِ
وَلَتَنْصُرُنَّهُ قَالَ ءَأَقْرَرْتُمْ وَأَخَذْتُمْ عَلٰى ذٰلِكُمْ إِصْرِي قَالُوا
أَقْرَرْنَا قَالَ فَاشْهَدُوا وَأَنَا مَعَكُمْ مِنَ الشَّاهِدِينَ ۞

يَا أَيُّهَا الَّذِينَ اٰمَنُوا إِنْ تَنْصُرُوا اللهَ يَنْصُرْكُمْ وَيُثَبِّتْ
أَقْدَامَكُمْ ۞ بِنَصْرِ اللهِ يَنْصُرُ مَنْ يَشَاءُ وَهُوَ الْعَزِيزُ
الرَّحِيمُ ۞ وَيَنْصُرَكَ اللهُ نَصْراً عَزِيزاً ۞

١٦٧

For Allah's support

In the name of Allah, the All-Merciful, the All-Compassionate.

1. "Verily did Allah support you at Badr when you were feeble, so fear Allah that you may be among the grateful." (Al Imran 3:123)

2. "Verily has Allah supported you in many places and on the day of Hunayn when you were complacent with your large numbers, but that did not avail you one bit, for the earth around you closed in on you after being spacious, and then you turned on your heels." (Tawba 9:25)

3. "We supported him against a people who denied Our signs. Truly they were a wicked people, so We drowned them all." (Anbiya 21:77)

4. "We helped them, so they were victorious." (Saffat 37:116)

5. "Verily those who believed and left their homes and strove with their wealth and their lives for Allah's cause, and those who took them in and helped them; these are protecting friends of one another." (Anfal 8:72)

6. "And those who believed and left their homes and strove for Allah's cause, and those who took them in and helped them; these are believers in truth and for them is forgiveness and a generous provision." (Anfal 8:74)

نُصْرَةُ اللهِ:

بِسْمِ اللهِ الرَّحْمٰنِ الرَّحِيمِ

وَلَقَدْ نَصَرَكُمُ اللهُ بِبَدْرٍ وَأَنْتُمْ أَذِلَّةٌ فَاتَّقُوا اللهَ لَعَلَّكُمْ
تَشْكُرُونَ ۝ لَقَدْ نَصَرَكُمُ اللهُ فِي مَوَاطِنَ كَثِيرَةٍ وَيَوْمَ
حُنَيْنٍ إِذْ أَعْجَبَتْكُمْ كَثْرَتُكُمْ فَلَمْ تُغْنِ عَنْكُمْ شَيْئًا وَضَاقَتْ
عَلَيْكُمُ الْأَرْضُ بِمَا رَحُبَتْ ثُمَّ وَلَّيْتُمْ مُدْبِرِينَ ۝

وَنَصَرْنَاهُ مِنَ الْقَوْمِ الَّذِينَ كَذَّبُوا بِآيَاتِنَا إِنَّهُمْ كَانُوا
قَوْمَ سَوْءٍ فَأَغْرَقْنَاهُمْ أَجْمَعِينَ ۝ وَنَصَرْنَاهُمْ فَكَانُوا
هُمُ الْغَالِبِينَ ۝ إِنَّ الَّذِينَ آمَنُوا وَهَاجَرُوا وَجَاهَدُوا
بِأَمْوَالِهِمْ وَأَنْفُسِهِمْ فِي سَبِيلِ اللهِ وَالَّذِينَ آوَوْا وَنَصَرُوا
أُولَئِكَ بَعْضُهُمْ أَوْلِيَاءُ بَعْضٍ ۝ وَالَّذِينَ آمَنُوا وَهَاجَرُوا
وَجَاهَدُوا فِي سَبِيلِ اللهِ وَالَّذِينَ آوَوْا وَنَصَرُوا أُولَئِكَ هُمُ
الْمُؤْمِنُونَ حَقًّا لَهُمْ مَغْفِرَةٌ وَرِزْقٌ كَرِيمٌ ۝

The prayer for Allah's help and victory

1. In the name of Allah, the All-Merciful, the All-Compassionate.

   Allah is the Greatest! (*Allahu Akbar* 10 times)

2. He is the Absolutely Independent One, All-Living, Self-Subsistent, All-Judging, All-Just, and All-Holy.

3. O Allah! Bless our master Muhammad, commensurate with the total number of all that is encompassed by the knowledge of Allah, with a blessing which lasts for the duration of the dominion of Allah, and upon his family and companions with peace!

دُعَاءُ النَّصْرِ وَالْغَلَبَةِ:

بِسْمِ اللهِ الرَّحْمٰنِ الرَّحِيمِ

اَللهُ أَكْبَرُ، اَللهُ أَكْبَرُ، اَللهُ أَكْبَرُ، اَللهُ أَكْبَرُ،

اَللهُ أَكْبَرُ، اَللهُ أَكْبَرُ، اَللهُ أَكْبَرُ، اَللهُ أَكْبَرُ،

اَللهُ أَكْبَرُ، اَللهُ أَكْبَرُ ﴿١﴾

فَرْدٌ حَيٌّ قَيُّومٌ حَكَمٌ عَدْلٌ قُدُّوسٌ ﴿٢﴾

اَللّٰهُمَّ صَلِّ عَلَى سَيِّدِنَا مُحَمَّدٍ عَدَدَ مَا فِي عِلْمِ
اللهِ صَلَاةً دَائِمَةً بِدَوَامِ مُلْكِ اللهِ وَعَلَى اٰلِهِ وَصَحْبِهِ
وَسَلِّمْ ﴿٣﴾

دُعَاءُ النّصْرِ وَالْغَلَبَةِ

THE PRAYER FOR HELP AND VICTORY

1. "Verily He who enjoined upon You the Qur'an will bring you back to the place of return." (Qasas 28:85)

   "Our Lord grant us mercy from You, and put our affairs in order with rectitude." (Kehf 18:10)

   Grant me relief from my plight and a way out.

   "Verily Allah and His angels bless the Prophet. O you who believe send blessings on him and greetings of peace!" (Ahzab 33:56)[10]

   May the blessings of Allah, His peace, His greetings, His mercy, and His grace, be upon our master Muhammad, Your servant, Your prophet, Your beloved, Your Messenger, the unlettered prophet, and upon his family and his companions with peace, commensurate with the number of the even and the odd (all creatures in pairs and individually), and the number of perfect and blessed words of Allah.

2. O Allah, send a perfect blessing and complete peace upon our master Muhammad by whom all problems are solved, tribulations are lifted, needs are fulfilled, wishes and good ends attained, and for whose noble countenance the clouds pour down rain; and [send perfect blessings and peace] upon his family and companions with each glance [of the eye] and breath and to the number of all things known to You.

---

10 From P.236/2–P.239/4 is the prayer of Ibn Mashish.

﴿إِنَّ الَّذِي فَرَضَ عَلَيْكَ الْقُرْاٰنَ لَرَادُّكَ إِلٰى مَعَادٍ﴾

﴿رَبَّنَا اٰتِنَا مِنْ لَدُنْكَ رَحْمَةً وَهَيِّئْ لَنَا مِنْ أَمْرِنَا رَشَداً﴾

اجْعَلْ لِي مِنْ أَمْرِي فَرَجاً وَمَخْرَجاً ﴿إِنَّ اللهَ وَمَلٰئِكَتَهُ

يُصَلُّونَ عَلَى النَّبِيِّ يَا أَيُّهَا الَّذِينَ اٰمَنُوا صَلُّوا عَلَيْهِ وَسَلِّمُوا

تَسْلِيماً﴾ صَلَوَاتُ اللهِ وَسَلَامُهُ وَتَحِيَّتُهُ وَرَحْمَتُهُ وَبَرَكَاتُهُ

عَلٰى سَيِّدِنَا مُحَمَّدٍ عَبْدِكَ وَنَبِيِّكَ وَحَبِيبِكَ وَرَسُولِكَ النَّبِيِّ

الْأُمِّيِّ وَعَلٰى اٰلِهِ وَصَحْبِهِ وَسَلِّمْ عَدَدَ الشَّفْعِ وَالْوَتْرِ وَعَدَدَ

كَلِمَاتِ اللهِ التَّامَّاتِ الْمُبَارَكَاتِ ﴿١﴾

اَللّٰهُمَّ صَلِّ صَلَاةً كَامِلَةً وَسَلِّمْ سَلَاماً تَامًّا عَلٰى سَيِّدِنَا

مُحَمَّدٍ الَّذِي تَنْحَلُّ بِهِ الْعُقَدُ، وَتَنْفَرِجُ بِهِ الْكُرَبُ، وَتُقْضٰى

بِهِ الْحَوَائِجُ، وَتُنَالُ بِهِ الرَّغَائِبُ وَحُسْنُ الْخَوَاتِمِ، وَيُسْتَسْقٰى

الْغَمَامُ بِوَجْهِهِ الْكَرِيمِ، وَعَلٰى اٰلِهِ وَصَحْبِهِ فِي كُلِّ لَمْحَةٍ

وَنَفَسٍ بِعَدَدِ كُلِّ مَعْلُومٍ لَكَ ﴿٢﴾

O Allah! Verily he is the most comprehensive secret, leading to You, and he is the greatest aide-de-camp, standing before You.

1. O Allah! Join me to his lineage, and make me worthy of his high esteem! Grant me an acquaintance with him through which I will be saved from the sources of ignorance, and drink from the streams of [Your] bounty. Carry me along his path to Your presence, bearing me with Your all-encompassing support! Hurl me against falsehood so that I stamp it out, plunge me into the seas of oneness, and put me into the very ocean of Divine Unity, such that I do not see, or hear, or find, or sense except through [that Unity]!

2. O Allah! Make the greatest aide-de-camp (Muhammad) the life of my soul, his spirit the secret of my reality, his reality that which assembles my being, with the realization of the First Truth. O [You Who are] the First, Last, Manifest, and Hidden! Listen to my cry, as You listened to the cry of Zechariah, peace be upon him! Grant me aid in the way (leading to Your good pleasure), support me in Your way with Your power, make me close to you and come between me and all other than You! Allah, Allah, Allah!

هُوَ أَهْلُهُ، اَللّٰهُمَّ إِنَّهُ سِرُّكَ الْجَامِعُ الدَّالُّ عَلَيْكَ وَحِجَابُكَ الْأَعْظَمُ الْقَائِمُ لَكَ بَيْنَ يَدَيْكَ ﴿٣﴾ اَللّٰهُمَّ أَلْحِقْنِي بِنَسَبِهِ وَحَقِّقْنِي بِحَسَبِهِ وَعَرِّفْنِي إِيَّاهُ مَعْرِفَةً أَسْلَمُ بِهَا مِنْ مَوَارِدِ الْجَهْلِ وَأَكْرَعُ بِهَا مِنْ مَوَارِدِ الْفَضْلِ واحْمِلْنِي عَلٰى سَبِيلِهِ إِلٰى حَضْرَتِكَ حَمْلاً مَحْفُوفًا بِنُصْرَتِكَ واقْذِفْ بِي عَلَى الْبَاطِلِ فَأَدْمَغَهُ وَزُجَّ بِي فِي بِحَارِ الْأَحَدِيَّةِ وَأَغْرِقْنِي فِي عَيْنِ بَحْرِ الْوَحْدَةِ حَتّٰى لَا أَرٰى وَلَا أَسْمَعَ وَلَا أَجِدَ وَلَا أُحِسَّ إِلَّا بِهَا ﴿١﴾ واجْعَلِ اللّٰهُمَّ الْحِجَابَ الْأَعْظَمَ حَيَاةَ رُوحِي، وَرُوحَهُ سِرَّ حَقِيقَتِي، وَحَقِيقَتَهُ جَامِعَ عَوَالِمِي بِتَحْقِيقِ الْحَقِّ الْأَوَّلِ يَا أَوَّلُ يَا آخِرُ يَا ظَاهِرُ يَا بَاطِنُ اسْمَعْ نِدَائِي بِمَا سَمِعْتَ بِهِ نِدَاءَ عَبْدِكَ زَكَرِيَّا عَلَيْهِ السَّلَامُ وانْصُرْنِي بِكَ لَكَ وَأَيِّدْنِي بِكَ لَكَ واجْمَعْ بَيْنِي وَبَيْنَكَ وَحُلْ بَيْنِي وَبَيْنَ غَيْرِكَ، اللهُ، اللهُ، اللهُ ﴿٢﴾

1. O Allah! Bless the essence of Muhammad, subtle and unique, the sun of the firmament of secrets, the medium for the manifestation of lights, the axis of majesty, and the pole of the celestial sphere of beauty!

2. O Allah! For the sake of his secret with You, and his journey to You, calm my fears, reduce my mistakes, and remove my grief and my greed! Be [there] for me, take me unto You, away from my self, and grant me the state of extinction (*fana*)![8] of my self. Let me not be tempted by my self, or veiled by my senses, and reveal to me every unspoken secret, O All-Living, Self-Subsistent [Lord]! (*Ya Hayy, Ya Qayyum*) O All-Living, Self-Subsistent [Lord]! O All-Living, Self-Subsistent [Lord]! (3)

3. O Allah! Bless him through whom secrets were disclosed, lights burst forth, and in whom realities arose (and find their real values). To whom the knowledge of Adam descended, showing the inadequacy of creatures. Before him intellects are confounded, and not one of us can reach [his level], neither those who preceded us nor those who will come after. The gardens of the celestial kingdom are made fair by the flowers of his beauty, and the pools of His world of Names and Attributes (*jabarut*, or the intermediary world) effuse with the overflowing of his lights. Nothing is there that is not conditioned by him and if it was not for the intermediary that which is mediated for would perish.[9] [Bless him] with a blessing which truly befits You, from You to him as is meet for him.

---

8 *Fana* literally means "annihilation," a spiritual state in which the self is erased through absorption in the presence of the One.

9 If Allah were to communicate to His servants in this life without the intermediary of the Messenger, they could not bear it and would perish.

اَللّٰهُمَّ صَلِّ عَلٰى ذَاتِ الْمُحَمَّدِيَّةِ اللَّطِيفَةِ الْأَحَدِيَّةِ
شَمْسِ سَمَاءِ الْأَسْرَارِ وَمَظْهَرِ الْأَنْوَارِ وَمَرْكَزِ مَدَارِ الْجَلَالِ
وَقُطْبِ فَلَكِ الْجَمَالِ ۞ اَللّٰهُمَّ بِسِرِّهِ لَدَيْكَ وَبِسَيْرِهِ إِلَيْكَ
اٰمِنْ خَوْفِي وَأَقِلْ عَثْرَتِي وَأَذْهِبْ حُزْنِي وَحِرْصِي وَكُنْ لِي
وَخُذْنِي إِلَيْكَ مِنِّي وَارْزُقْنِي الْفَنَاءَ عَنِّي وَلَا تَجْعَلْنِي مَفْتُوناً
بِنَفْسِي مَحْجُوباً بِحِسِّي وَاكْشِفْ لِي عَنْ كُلِّ سِرٍّ مَكْتُومٍ يَا
حَيُّ يَا قَيُّومُ يَا حَيُّ يَا قَيُّومُ يَا حَيُّ يَا قَيُّومُ (ثلاثاً) ۞ اَللّٰهُمَّ
صَلِّ عَلٰى مَنْ مِنْهُ انْشَقَّتِ الْأَسْرَارُ وَانْفَلَقَتِ الْأَنْوَارُ وَفِيهِ
ارْتَقَتِ الْحَقَائِقُ وَتَنَزَّلَتْ عُلُومُ اٰدَمَ فَأَعْجَزَ الْخَلَائِقَ وَلَهُ
تَضَاءَلَتِ الْفُهُومُ فَلَمْ يُدْرِكْهُ مِنَّا سَابِقٌ وَلَا لَاحِقٌ فَرِيَاضُ
الْمَلَكُوتِ بِأَزْهَارِ جَمَالِهِ مُونِقَةٌ وَحِيَاضُ الْجَبَرُوتِ بِفَيْضِ
أَنْوَارِهِ مُتَدَفِّقَةٌ وَلَا شَيْءَ إِلَّا وَهُوَ بِهِ مَنُوطٌ، إِذْ لَوْلَا الْوَاسِطَةُ
لَذَهَبَ كَمَا قِيلَ الْمَوْسُوطُ صَلَاةً تَلِيقُ بِكَ مِنْكَ إِلَيْهِ كَمَا

1. O Allah, bless our master Muhammad and his family with each succession of day and night, with each return of the late afternoon, with each repetition of night and day, and at each rising of the two bright stars of Ursa Minor!

2. Send greetings and peace to his soul and the souls of his household on our behalf!

3. And send mercy, grace and peace upon him and them, in abundance up to the Day of the Gathering and Settlement!

    And forgive us and have mercy on us, and treat us with kindness, O our Lord, with every blessing [You send]!

    O Allah bless our master Muhammad, ocean of Your lights, substance of Your secrets, spring of your providence, sun of Your guidance, the most distinguished one among those nearest to God, and the foremost in Your presence!

    And the best of Your creation, the most beloved creature to You, Your servant, Your beloved, Your Messenger, the unlettered prophet whom You made the seal of the prophets and the messengers. And bless all the prophets and the messengers, their families and companions, the angels you made nearest to You, and Your righteous servants among the company of the heavens and earth! May the good pleasure of Allah, Most High, be upon us and upon all of them! Amin. And all praise is due to Allah.

اَللّٰهُمَّ صَلِّ عَلَى سَيِّدِنَا مُحَمَّدٍ وَعَلَى اٰلِهِ كُلَّمَا اخْتَلَفَ
الْمَلَوَانِ وَتَعَاقَبَ الْعَصْرَانِ وَكَرَّرَ الْجَدِيدَانِ وَاسْتَقْبَلَ الْفَرْقَدَانِ
وَبَلِّغْ رُوحَهُ وَأَرْوَاحَ أَهْلِ بَيْتِهِ مِنَّا التَّحِيَّةَ وَالسَّلَامَ وَارْحَمْ
وَبَارِكْ وَسَلِّمْ عَلَيْهِ وَعَلَيْهِمْ كَثِيراً كَثِيراً إِلَى يَوْمِ الْحَشْرِ وَالْقَرَارِ
﴿١﴾ وَاغْفِرْ لَنَا وَارْحَمْنَا وَالْطُفْ بِنَا يَا إِلٰهَنَا بِكُلِّ صَلَاةٍ مِنْهَا
﴿٢﴾ اَللّٰهُمَّ صَلِّ عَلَى سَيِّدِنَا مُحَمَّدٍ بَحْرِ أَنْوَارِكَ وَمَعْدِنِ
أَسْرَارِكَ وَعَيْنِ عِنَايَتِكَ وَشَمْسِ هِدَايَتِكَ وَعَرُوسِ مَمْلَكَتِكَ
وَإِمَامِ حَضْرَتِكَ وَخَيْرِ خَلْقِكَ وَأَحَبِّ الْخَلْقِ إِلَيْكَ عَبْدِكَ
وَحَبِيبِكَ وَرَسُولِكَ النَّبِيِّ الْأُمِّيِّ الَّذِي خَتَمْتَ بِهِ الْأَنْبِيَاءَ
وَالْمُرْسَلِينَ وَعَلَى سَائِرِ الْأَنْبِيَاءِ وَالْمُرْسَلِينَ وَعَلَى اٰلِهِ وَصَحْبِهِ
أَجْمَعِينَ وَعَلَى الْمَلَئِكَةِ الْمُقَرَّبِينَ وَعَلَى عِبَادِكَ الصَّالِحِينَ
مِنْ أَهْلِ السَّمٰوَاتِ وَأَهْلِ الْأَرَضِينَ رِضْوَانُ اللهِ تَعَالَى عَلَيْنَا
وَعَلَيْهِمْ أَجْمَعِينَ اٰمِينَ وَالْحَمْدُ لِلّٰهِ رَبِّ الْعَالَمِينَ ﴿٣﴾

1. "Verily Allah and His angels bless the Prophet. Oh you who believe, send blessings upon him and greetings of peace." (Ahzab 33:56)

   At Your command.

2. O Allah! Bless our master Muhammad and the family of our master Muhammad with a blessing whereby You save us from all terror and disasters, fulfill for us all our needs, cleanse us of all our misdeeds, raise us to the highest ranks in Your presence, and whereby You might cause us to attain our highest aspirations in all that is good, in this life and after death. Amin, O Answerer of prayers! And all praise is due to Allah, the Lord of the worlds.

﴿إِنَّ اللهَ وَمَلَئِكَتَهُ يُصَلُّونَ عَلَى النَّبِيِّ يَا أَيُّهَا الَّذِينَ آمَنُوا صَلُّوا عَلَيْهِ وَسَلِّمُوا تَسْلِيماً﴾ لَبَّيْكَ ﴿١﴾

اَللَّهُمَّ صَلِّ عَلَى سَيِّدِنَا مُحَمَّدٍ وَعَلَى آلِ سَيِّدِنَا مُحَمَّدٍ صَلَاةً تُنْجِينَا بِهَا مِنْ جَمِيعِ الْأَهْوَالِ وَالْآفَاتِ، وَتَقْضِي لَنَا بِهَا جَمِيعَ الْحَاجَاتِ، وَتُطَهِّرُنَا بِهَا مِنْ جَمِيعِ السَّيِّئَاتِ، وَتَرْفَعُنَا بِهَا عِنْدَكَ أَعْلَى الدَّرَجَاتِ، وَتُبَلِّغُنَا بِهَا أَقْصَى الْغَايَاتِ مِنْ جَمِيعِ الْخَيْرَاتِ فِي الْحَيَاةِ وَبَعْدَ الْمَمَاتِ، أَمِينَ يَا مُجِيبَ الدَّعَوَاتِ وَالْحَمْدُ لِلهِ رَبِّ الْعَالَمِينَ ﴿٢﴾

اَلصَّلَوَاتُ عَلَى سَيِّدِ السَّادَاتِ

INVOKING BLESSINGS ON
PROPHET MUHAMMAD
THE MASTER OF PRINCES

1. O Allah! I ask You, bearing witness that You are Allah; there is no god but You; the One and Only, the Absolute, Who begets not, nor is He begotten and there is none like unto Him.

2. O Allah! Truly I ask You, as all praise belongs to You, and there is no god but You, the Bounteous, the Originator of the heavens and the earth, the Lord of Majesty and Bounty, O All-Living, Self-Subsistent [Lord]!

3. O Allah! Truly I ask You, as all praise belongs to You; there is no god but You, Alone without associate. You are the Bounteous, the Originator of the heavens and the earth, the Lord of Majesty and Bounty.

4. O Affectionate [One]! O Bounteous [One]! O Originator of the heavens and the earth! O Lord of Majesty and Bounty! I ask of You Paradise, and I seek refuge in You from the Hellfire.

5. O Allah, make good the outcome of all our affairs and save us from disgrace in this life and the punishment in the Hereafter!

Here ends the Qur'an- and the hadith-sourced supplications.

اَللّٰهُمَّ إِنِّي أَسْأَلُكَ بِأَنِّي أَشْهَدُ أَنَّكَ أَنْتَ اللهُ لَا إِلٰهَ إِلَّا

أَنْتَ الْأَحَدُ الصَّمَدُ الَّذِي لَمْ يَلِدْ وَلَمْ يُولَدْ وَلَمْ يَكُنْ لَهُ

كُفُوًا أَحَدٌ ﴿١﴾ اَللّٰهُمَّ إِنِّي أَسْأَلُكَ بِأَنَّ لَكَ الْحَمْدَ لَا إِلٰهَ

إِلَّا أَنْتَ الْمَنَّانُ بَدِيعُ السَّمٰوَاتِ وَالْأَرْضِ ذُو الْجَلَالِ

وَالْإِكْرَامِ يَا حَيُّ يَا قَيُّومُ ﴿٢﴾

اَللّٰهُمَّ إِنِّي أَسْأَلُكَ بِأَنَّ لَكَ الْحَمْدَ لَا إِلٰهَ إِلَّا أَنْتَ

وَحْدَكَ لَا شَرِيكَ لَكَ، أَنْتَ الْمَنَّانُ بَدِيعُ السَّمٰوَاتِ

وَالْأَرْضِ ذُو الْجَلَالِ وَالْإِكْرَامِ ﴿٣﴾ يَا حَنَّانُ يَا مَنَّانُ يَا بَدِيعَ

السَّمٰوَاتِ وَالْأَرْضِ يَا ذَا الْجَلَالِ وَالْإِكْرَامِ أَسْأَلُكَ الْجَنَّةَ

وَأَعُوذُ بِكَ مِنَ النَّارِ ﴿٤﴾ اَللّٰهُمَّ أَحْسِنْ عَاقِبَتَنَا فِي الْأُمُورِ

كُلِّهَا وَأَجِرْنَا مِنْ خِزْيِ الدُّنْيَا وَعَذَابِ الْاٰخِرَةِ ﴿٥﴾

تمت الأدعية المأثورة

١٥٧

1   "He is Allah besides Whom there is no other god; Knower of the Unseen and the visible. He is the All-Merciful, the All-Compassionate. ❂ He is Allah, there is no god but He; the Sovereign, the All-Holy, the Source of Peace, the Source of Security; the Guardian, the All-Mighty; the Compeller, the Majestic. Transcendent is He above all that they ascribe as partner (to Him)! ❂ He is Allah; the Creator, the Producer, the Fashioner (Who has brought His creatures to existence and fashioned them in the best form and perfect harmony, making them undergo different phases). His are the most beautiful names. All that is in the heavens and the earth glorifies Him. He is the All-Mighty, the All-Wise." (Hashr 59:22-4)

2.   "Alif, Lam, Mim. There is no god but He; the All-Living, the Self-Subsistent." (Al Imran 3:1)

3.   "And Your God is one God, there is no god but He, the All-Merciful, the All-Compassionate." (Baqara 2:163)

4.   Allah; there is no god but "He, the One and Only, the Absolute Eternal, Who begets not, nor is He begotten and there is none like unto Him." (Ikhlas 112: Second part of verse 1-3)

5.   I ask You, O Allah! He!; All-Merciful!; The All-Compassionate! The All-Living! The Self-Subsistent! Lord of Majesty and Bounty! (*Ya Hu, Ya Rahman, Ya Rahim, Ya Hayy, Ya Qayyum, Ya Dhal Jalali wal Ikram*)

﴿هُوَ اللهُ الَّذِي لَا إِلَهَ إِلَّا هُوَ عَالِمُ الْغَيْبِ وَالشَّهَادَةِ هُوَ الرَّحْمَنُ الرَّحِيمُ ۞ هُوَ اللهُ الَّذِي لَا إِلَهَ إِلَّا هُوَ الْمَلِكُ الْقُدُّوسُ السَّلَامُ الْمُؤْمِنُ الْمُهَيْمِنُ الْعَزِيزُ الْجَبَّارُ الْمُتَكَبِّرُ سُبْحَانَ اللهِ عَمَّا يُشْرِكُونَ ۞ هُوَ اللهُ الْخَالِقُ الْبَارِئُ الْمُصَوِّرُ لَهُ الْأَسْمَاءُ الْحُسْنَى يُسَبِّحُ لَهُ مَا فِي السَّمَوَاتِ وَالْأَرْضِ وَهُوَ الْعَزِيزُ الْحَكِيمُ ﴿١﴾﴾

﴿الٓمٓ ۞ اللهُ لَا إِلَهَ إِلَّا هُوَ الْحَيُّ الْقَيُّومُ ﴿٢﴾﴾

﴿وَإِلَهُكُمْ إِلَهٌ وَاحِدٌ لَا إِلَهَ إِلَّا هُوَ الرَّحْمَنُ الرَّحِيمُ ﴿٣﴾﴾

اللهُ لَا إِلَهَ إِلَّا هُوَ الْأَحَدُ الصَّمَدُ الَّذِي لَمْ يَلِدْ وَلَمْ يُولَدْ وَلَمْ يَكُنْ لَهُ كُفُوًا أَحَدٌ ﴿٤﴾

أَسْأَلُكَ يَا اللهُ يَا هُوَ يَا رَحْمَنُ يَا رَحِيمُ يَا حَيُّ يَا قَيُّومُ يَا ذَا الْجَلَالِ وَالْإِكْرَامِ ﴿٥﴾

1. "There is no god but You, Glory be to You! Truly I have been among the wrongdoers." (Anbiya 21:87)

2. "Allah! There is no god but He, the All-Living, the Self-Subsistent. Neither does slumber overtake Him nor sleep and to Him belongs whatever is in the heavens and the earth. Who can intercede with Him except by His leave? He knows what is before them and what is behind them and they comprehend of His knowledge only that which He wills. His Throne encompasses the heavens and the earth, and maintaining them both tires Him not. He is the Exalted, the Sublime." (Ayat al-Kursi / Baqara 2:255)

3. "Say! O Allah, Owner of sovereignty, You bestow sovereignty on whom You will and take away sovereignty from whom You will; You exalt whom You will and You abase whom You will. All goodness is in Your hand; indeed You have power over all things." (Al Imran 3:26)

﴿لَا إِلَهَ إِلَّا أَنْتَ سُبْحَانَكَ إِنِّي كُنْتُ مِنَ الظَّالِمِينَ﴾ ①

﴿اَللهُ لَا إِلَهَ إِلَّا هُوَ اَلْحَيُّ الْقَيُّومُ لَا تَأْخُذُهُ سِنَةٌ وَلَا نَوْمٌ لَهُ مَا فِي السَّمَوَاتِ وَمَا فِي الْأَرْضِ مَنْ ذَا الَّذِي يَشْفَعُ عِنْدَهُ إِلَّا بِإِذْنِهِ يَعْلَمُ مَا بَيْنَ أَيْدِيهِمْ وَمَا خَلْفَهُمْ وَلَا يُحِيطُونَ بِشَيْءٍ مِنْ عِلْمِهِ إِلَّا بِمَا شَاءَ وَسِعَ كُرْسِيُّهُ السَّمَوَاتِ وَالْأَرْضَ وَلَا يَؤُودُهُ حِفْظُهُمَا وَهُوَ الْعَلِيُّ الْعَظِيمُ﴾ ②

﴿قُلِ اللَّهُمَّ مَالِكَ الْمُلْكِ تُؤْتِي الْمُلْكَ مَنْ تَشَاءُ وَتَنْزِعُ الْمُلْكَ مِمَّنْ تَشَاءُ وَتُعِزُّ مَنْ تَشَاءُ وَتُذِلُّ مَنْ تَشَاءُ بِيَدِكَ الْخَيْرُ إِنَّكَ عَلَى كُلِّ شَيْءٍ قَدِيرٌ﴾ ③

دُعَاءُ اسْمِ اللهِ الْأَعْظَمِ

THE PRAYER OF
THE GREATEST NAME

The Equitable (*Al-Muqsit*);
The All-Assembler (*Al-Jami‘*);
The All-Rich (*Al-Ghani*);
The Enricher (*Al-Mughni*);
The Impeder (*Al-Mani‘*);
The Sender of Harm (*Al-Darr*);
The Granter of Benefit (*Al-Nafi‘*);
The Light (*Al-Nur*); The Guide (*Al-Hadi*);
The All-Originator (*Al-Badi‘*);
The Everlasting (*Al-Baqi*);
The All-Inheritor (*Al-Warith*);
The All-Discerning (*Al-Rashid*);
The All-Patient (*Al-Sabur*).

اَلْغَنِيُّ	اَلْجَامِعُ	اَلْمُقْسِطُ
اَلضَّارُّ	اَلْمَانِعُ	اَلْمُغْنِي
اَلْهَادِي	اَلنُّورُ	اَلنَّافِعُ
اَلْوَارِثُ	اَلْبَاقِي	اَلْبَدِيعُ
	اَلصَّبُورُ	اَلرَّشِيدُ

The Self-Sufficient (*Al-Samad*);

The All-Powerful (*Al-Qadir*);

The All-Determiner (*Al-Muqtadir*);

The Hastener (*Al-Muqaddim*);

The Postponer (*Al-Mu'akhkhir*);

The First (*Al-Awwal*);

The Last (*Al-Akhir*);

The Manifest (*Al-Zahir*);

The Hidden (*Al-Batin*);

The All-Ruler (Al-Wali);

The Most Exalted (*Al-Mut'ali*);

The Benefactor (*Al-Barr*);

The Ever-Relenting (*Al-Tawwab*);

The Avenger (*Al-Muntaqim*);

The All-Pardoner (*Al-'Afu*);

The All-Pitying (*Al-Ra'uf*);

The Master of the Kingdom (*Malik al-Mulk*);

The Lord of Majesty and Bounty (*Dhul Jalal wal Ikram*);

اَلْمُقْتَدِرُ	اَلْقَادِرُ	اَلصَّمَدُ
اَلْأَوَّلُ	اَلْمُؤَخِّرُ	اَلْمُقَدِّمُ
اَلْبَاطِنُ	اَلظَّاهِرُ	اَلْاٰخِرُ
اَلْبَرُّ	اَلْمُتَعَالِي	اَلْوَالِي
اَلْعَفُوُّ	اَلْمُنْتَقِمُ	اَلتَّوَّابُ
	مَالِكُ الْمُلْكِ	اَلرَّؤُوفُ
	ذُو الْجَلَالِ وَالْإِكْرَامِ	

The All-Wise (*Al-Hakim*);
The All-Loving (*Al-Wadud*);
The Glorious (*Al-Majeed*);
The Raiser of the dead (*Al-Ba'ith*);
The All-Witnessing (*Al-Shahid*);
The Truth (*Al-Haqq*);
The Most-Reliable (*Al-Wakil*);
The All-Strong (*Al-Qawi*);
The All-Firm (*Al-Matin*);
The Patron (*Al-Wali*);
The Owner of Praise (*Al-Hamid*);
The All-Calculating (*Al-Muhsi*);
The Initiator (*Al-Mubdi'*);
The Restorer (*Mu'id*);
The Giver of Life (*Al-Muhyi*);
The Giver of Death (*Al-Mumit*);
The All-Living (*Al-Hayy*);
The Self-Subsistent (*Al-Qayyum*);
The Founder (*Al-Wajid*);
The Noble (*Al-Maajid*);
The One (*Al-Wahid*);

اَلْمَجِيدُ	۞	اَلْوَدُودُ	۞	اَلْحَكِيمُ
اَلْحَقُّ	۞	اَلشَّهِيدُ	۞	اَلْبَاعِثُ
اَلْمَتِينُ	۞	اَلْقَوِيُّ	۞	اَلْوَكِيلُ
اَلْمُحْصِي	۞	اَلْحَمِيدُ	۞	اَلْوَلِيُّ
اَلْمُحْيِي	۞	اَلْمُعِيدُ	۞	اَلْمُبْدِئُ
اَلْقَيُّومُ	۞	اَلْحَيُّ	۞	اَلْمُمِيتُ
اَلْوَاحِدُ	۞	اَلْمَاجِدُ	۞	اَلْوَاجِدُ

The Debaser (*Al-Khafid*);

The Exalter (*Al-Rafi'*);

The Honorer (*Al-Mu'izz*);

The Abaser (*Al-Mudhill*);

The All-Hearing (*Al-Sami'*);

The All-Seeing (*Al-Basir*);

The Judge (*Al-Hakam*);

The All-Just (*Al-'Adl*);

The Benevolent and Subtle (*Al-Latif*);

The All-Cognizant (*Al-Khabir*);

The All-Clement (*Al-Halim*);

The All-Mighty (*Al-'Azim*);

The All-Forgiving (*Al-Ghafur*);

The Rewarder of Thankfulness (*Al-Shakur*);

The All-High (*Al-'Ali*); The Great (*Al-Kabir*);

The All-Protecting (*Al-Hafiz*);

The All-Nourisher (*Al-Muqit*);

The All-Reckoner (*Al-Hasib*);

The Sublime (*Al-Jalil*);

The All-Generous (*Al-Karim*);

The All-Vigilant (*Al-Raqib*);

The Responding (*Al-Mujib*);

The Vast (*Al-Wasi'*);

اَلْمُعِزُّ	❀	اَلرَّافِعُ	❀	اَلْخَافِضُ
اَلْبَصِيرُ	❀	اَلسَّمِيعُ	❀	اَلْمُذِلُّ
اَللَّطِيفُ	❀	اَلْعَدْلُ	❀	اَلْحَكَمُ
اَلْعَظِيمُ	❀	اَلْحَلِيمُ	❀	اَلْخَبِيرُ
اَلْعَلِيُّ	❀	اَلشَّكُورُ	❀	اَلْغَفُورُ
اَلْمُقِيتُ	❀	اَلْحَفِيظُ	❀	اَلْكَبِيرُ
اَلْكَرِيمُ	❀	اَلْجَلِيلُ	❀	اَلْحَسِيبُ
اَلْوَاسِعُ	❀	اَلْمُجِيبُ	❀	اَلرَّقِيبُ

He is Allah besides Whom there is no other god;

The All-Merciful (*Al-Rahman: Who is essentially merciful*);

The All-Compassionate (*Al-Rahim: Who shows compassion to His creatures*);

The Sovereign (*Al-Malik: The Absolute owner of everything*);

The All-Holy (*Al-Quddus: Who purifies everything and Who is exempt from any impurity*);

The Flawless (*Al-Salam: Who is without any flaws, imperfections, and grants well-being to His creatures*);

The Source of Security (*Al-Mu'min*);

The Guardian (*Al-Muhaymin*);

The All-Honored and Triumphant with irresistible Might (*Al-'Aziz*);

The Compeller (*Al-Jabbar: Who regulates His servants' affairs, and directs them as He wills*);

The Majestic (*Al-Mutakabbir: Who is the sole possessor of Greatness*);

The Creator (*Al-Khaliq*);

The Producer (*Al-Bari'*); The Fashioner (*Al-Musawwir*);

The Most Forgiving (*Al-Ghaffar*);

The Subduer (*Al-Qahhar*);

The Bestower (*Al-Wahhab*);

The All-Providing (*Al-Razzaq*);

The All-Opener (*Al-Fattah*);

The All-Knowing (*Al-'Alim*);

The Constricting (*Al-Qabid*);

The Expander (*Al-Basit*);

هُوَ اللهُ الَّذِي لَا إِلٰهَ إِلَّا هُوَ

اَلْمَلِكُ	۞	اَلرَّحِيمُ	۞	اَلرَّحْمٰنُ
اَلْمُؤْمِنُ	۞	اَلسَّلَامُ	۞	اَلْقُدُّوسُ
اَلْجَبَّارُ	۞	اَلْعَزِيزُ	۞	اَلْمُهَيْمِنُ
اَلْبَارِئُ	۞	اَلْخَالِقُ	۞	اَلْمُتَكَبِّرُ
اَلْقَهَّارُ	۞	اَلْغَفَّارُ	۞	اَلْمُصَوِّرُ
اَلْفَتَّاحُ	۞	اَلرَّزَّاقُ	۞	اَلْوَهَّابُ
اَلْبَاسِطُ	۞	اَلْقَابِضُ	۞	اَلْعَلِيمُ

اَلْأَسْمَاءُ الْحُسْنَى

THE MOST BEAUTIFUL
NAMES

1. O Allah! Grant me goodness in this life, goodness in the Hereafter, and deliver me from the Hellfire.

2. O Allah! Verily we ask of You the good for which Your Prophet Muhammad—may Allah bless him and grant him peace—asked You; and we seek refuge in You from the evil from which Your Prophet Muhammad—may Allah bless him and grant him peace—sought refuge in You. You are the One whose help is sought, the realization [of all desires] is in Your hands, and there is no strength or power except in Allah.

3. O Allah! Truly I take refuge in You from associating anything with You, that I am aware of, and I seek Your forgiveness from that which I am not aware of.

4. O Allah! Lord of Prophet Muhammad, forgive me my sins, root out the rancor of my heart, and save me from all trials that cause people to go astray.

اَللّٰهُمَّ اٰتِنَا فِي الدُّنْيَا حَسَنَةً وَفِي الْاٰخِرَةِ حَسَنَةً وَقِنَا

عَذَابَ النَّارِ ﴿١﴾ اَللّٰهُمَّ إِنَّا نَسْأَلُكَ مِنْ خَيْرِ مَا سَأَلَكَ

مِنْهُ نَبِيُّكَ مُحَمَّدٌ ﷺ وَنَعُوذُ بِكَ مِنْ شَرِّ مَا اسْتَعَاذَكَ

مِنْهُ نَبِيُّكَ مُحَمَّدٌ ﷺ وَأَنْتَ الْمُسْتَعَانُ وَعَلَيْكَ الْبَلَاغُ

وَلَاحَوْلَ وَلَا قُوَّةَ إِلَّا بِاللهِ ﴿٢﴾

اَللّٰهُمَّ إِنِّيٓ أَعُوذُ بِكَ مِنْ أَنْ أُشْرِكَ بِكَ شَيْئًا وَأَنَا

أَعْلَمُ وَأَسْتَغْفِرُكَ لِمَا لَآ أَعْلَمُ ﴿٣﴾

اَللّٰهُمَّ رَبَّ النَّبِيِّ مُحَمَّدٍ اغْفِرْ لِي ذَنْبِي وَأَذْهِبْ

غَيْظَ قَلْبِي وَأَجِرْنِي مِنْ مُضِلَّاتِ الْفِتَنِ ﴿٤﴾

1. O Allah! Apportion to us fear of You which obstructs us from Your disobedience, obedience to You by which we gain Your Paradise, and certainty that makes it easy for us to endure the afflictions of this life. Let us enjoy our hearing, sight, and strength as long as You keep us alive.

   Keep those faculties intact and healthy. Let our vengeance be on those who have oppressed us, and support us against those who have committed aggression against us. Let not our calamity be in our religion, nor let this life be our major concern or the full extent of our knowledge, and place not someone in authority over us who does not treat us with mercy.

2. O Allah! Truly we ask You for the means of deserving Your mercy, the means of being certain of Your forgiveness, protection from every sin, the benefit of every virtue, the triumph of Paradise, and deliverance from the Hellfire.

3. O Allah! Leave us not with a sin without forgiving it, or a worry without relieving it, or a debt without settling it, or a need in this life and the Hereafter, which You approve of, without fulfilling it, O Most Merciful of those who show mercy!

اَللّٰهُمَّ اقْسِمْ لَنَا مِنْ خَشْيَتِكَ مَا تَحُولُ بِهِ بَيْنَنَا وَبَيْنَ مَعَاصِيكَ وَمِنْ طَاعَتِكَ مَا تُبَلِّغُنَا بِهِ جَنَّتَكَ وَمِنَ الْيَقِينِ مَا تُهَوِّنُ بِهِ عَلَيْنَا مَصَائِبَ الدُّنْيَا وَمَتِّعْنَا بِأَسْمَاعِنَا وَأَبْصَارِنَا وَقُوَّتِنَا مَا أَحْيَيْتَنَا وَاجْعَلْهُ الْوَارِثَ مِنَّا وَاجْعَلْ ثَأْرَنَا عَلٰى مَنْ ظَلَمَنَا وَانْصُرْنَا عَلٰى مَنْ عَادَانَا وَلَا تَجْعَلْ مُصِيبَتَنَا فِي دِينِنَا وَلَا تَجْعَلِ الدُّنْيَا أَكْبَرَ هَمِّنَا وَلَا مَبْلَغَ عِلْمِنَا وَلَا تُسَلِّطْ عَلَيْنَا مَنْ لَا يَرْحَمُنَا ﴿١﴾

اَللّٰهُمَّ إِنَّا نَسْأَلُكَ مُوجِبَاتِ رَحْمَتِكَ وَعَزَائِمَ مَغْفِرَتِكَ وَالسَّلَامَةَ مِنْ كُلِّ إِثْمٍ وَالْغَنِيمَةَ مِنْ كُلِّ بِرٍّ وَالْفَوْزَ بِالْجَنَّةِ وَالنَّجَاةَ مِنَ النَّارِ ﴿٢﴾

اَللّٰهُمَّ لَا تَدَعْ لَنَا ذَنْبًا إِلَّا غَفَرْتَهُ وَلَا هَمًّا إِلَّا فَرَّجْتَهُ وَلَا دَيْنًا إِلَّا قَضَيْتَهُ وَلَا حَاجَةً مِنْ حَوَائِجِ الدُّنْيَا وَالْآخِرَةِ هِيَ لَكَ رِضًا إِلَّا قَضَيْتَهَا يَا أَرْحَمَ الرَّاحِمِينَ ﴿٣﴾

1. We seek refuge in Allah from the punishment of the Hellfire. We seek refuge in Allah from the temptation which is apparent and that which is hidden. We seek refuge in Allah from the trial of the Antichrist (*Al Dajjal*).

2. O Allah! Truly do we take refuge in You from the pain of tribulation the baseness of damnation, an unfortunate decree, and the malicious delight of the enemy [at our misfortune].

3. O Allah, Disposer of hearts! Direct our hearts to Your obedience!

4. O Allah, Turner of hearts! Bind my heart to Your religion!

5. O Allah! Forgive us, show mercy on us, and be content with us! Accept from us [our deeds], enter us into Paradise, save us from the Hellfire and put right all our affairs!

6. O Allah! Give us increase (in Your blessings), and don't take from us; honor us and don't humiliate us, bestow on us and don't deprive us, favor us and don't favor others instead of us; make us contented and be content with us, O Most Merciful of the merciful!

7. O Allah! Assist us in remembering You, showing gratitude toward You, and worshipping You properly!

8. O Allah! Grant us a good outcome in all of our affairs, and save us from disgrace in this life and punishment in the Hereafter!

نَعُوذُ بِاللهِ مِنْ عَذَابِ النَّارِ، نَعُوذُ بِاللهِ مِنَ الْفِتَنِ مَا

ظَهَرَ مِنْهَا وَمَا بَطَنَ، نَعُوذُ بِاللهِ مِنْ فِتْنَةِ الدَّجَّالِ ﴿١﴾

اَللّٰهُمَّ إِنَّا نَعُوذُ بِكَ مِنْ جَهْدِ الْبَلَاءِ وَدَرْكِ الشَّقَاءِ

وَسُوءِ الْقَضَاءِ وَشَمَاتَةِ الْأَعْدَاءِ ﴿٢﴾ اَللّٰهُمَّ يَا مُصَرِّفَ

الْقُلُوبِ صَرِّفْ قُلُوبَنَا إِلَى طَاعَتِكَ ﴿٣﴾

اَللّٰهُمَّ يَا مُقَلِّبَ الْقُلُوبِ ثَبِّتْ قَلْبِي عَلَى دِينِكَ ﴿٤﴾

اَللّٰهُمَّ اغْفِرْ لَنَا وَارْحَمْنَا وَارْضَ عَنَّا وَتَقَبَّلْ مِنَّا وَأَدْخِلْنَا

الْجَنَّةَ وَنَجِّنَا مِنَ النَّارِ وَأَصْلِحْ لَنَا شَأْنَنَا كُلَّهُ ﴿٥﴾

اَللّٰهُمَّ زِدْنَا وَلَا تَنْقُصْنَا وَأَكْرِمْنَا وَلَا تُهِنَّا وَأَعْطِنَا

وَلَا تَحْرُمْنَا وَآثِرْنَا وَلَا تُؤْثِرْ عَلَيْنَا وَأَرْضِنَا وَارْضَ عَنَّا

يَا أَرْحَمَ الرَّاحِمِينَ ﴿٦﴾ اَللّٰهُمَّ أَعِنَّا عَلَى ذِكْرِكَ وَشُكْرِكَ

وَحُسْنِ عِبَادَتِكَ ﴿٧﴾ اَللّٰهُمَّ أَحْسِنْ عَاقِبَتَنَا فِي الْأُمُورِ

كُلِّهَا وَأَجِرْنَا مِنْ خِزْيِ الدُّنْيَا وَعَذَابِ الْآخِرَةِ ﴿٨﴾

1. O Allah! Purify me of my sins just as a white garment is cleansed of filth!

2. O Allah! Distance me from my misdeeds as You have distanced the East from the West! This is what Muhammad (peace and blessings be upon him) asked of His Lord.

3. O Allah! Save me from the Hellfire! I ask You for Your forgiveness during the night and the day, and a righteous station. Amin.

4. O Allah! Truly I ask You for deliverance in a sound state from the Hellfire, and to enter me into Paradise in safety. Amin.

5. O You, the One Who has revealed what is beautiful and concealed what is ugly; the One Who does not take [someone] to account for (immediately after) an offence,[7] and Who does not break the veil between Him and any of His servants! O You, the One Who is most lenient! O You, the One Whose forgiveness is all-embracing, the One Who gives out His mercy with open hands, the One Who is party to every secret discourse; the One Whom every complaint reaches, the One Who pardons generously, the One Whose favors are immense, and the One Who brings blessings into existence before they can be claimed by anyone.

6. Our Lord! Our Master! Our heart's desire! I ask You, O Allah, not to roast my body in the Hellfire.

---

[7] Allah does not punish people immediately after their offence but gives them respite allowing them time to repent for their crime.

144

اَللّٰهُمَّ نَقِّنِي مِنْ خَطَايَايَ كَمَا يُنَقّى الثَّوْبُ الْأَبْيَضُ مِنَ الدَّنَسِ ﴿١﴾ اَللّٰهُمَّ بَاعِدْ بَيْنِي وَبَيْنَ خَطَايَايَ كَمَا بَاعَدْتَ بَيْنَ الْمَشْرِقِ وَالْمَغْرِبِ هٰذَا مَا سَأَلَهُ مُحَمَّدٌ رَبَّهُ ﴿٢﴾ اَللّٰهُمَّ نَجِّنِي مِنَ النَّارِ وَأَسْأَلُكَ مَغْفِرَةً بِاللَّيْلِ وَالنَّهَارِ وَالْمَنْزِلَ الصَّالِحَ اٰمِينَ ﴿٣﴾

اَللّٰهُمَّ إِنِّي أَسْأَلُكَ خَلَاصاً مِنَ النَّارِ سَالِماً وَأَدْخِلْنِي الْجَنَّةَ اٰمِناً ﴿٤﴾ يَا مَنْ أَظْهَرَ الْجَمِيلَ وَسَتَرَ الْقَبِيحَ، يَا مَنْ لَا يُؤَاخِذُ بِالْجَرِيمَةِ وَلَا يَهْتِكُ السِّتْرَ، يَا حَسَنَ التَّجَاوُزِ، يَا وَاسِعَ الْمَغْفِرَةِ، يَا بَاسِطَ الْيَدَيْنِ بِالرَّحْمَةِ، يَا صَاحِبَ كُلِّ نَجْوٰى، يَا مُنْتَهٰى كُلِّ شَكْوٰى، يَا كَرِيمَ الصَّفْحِ، يَا عَظِيمَ الْمَنِّ، يَا مُبْتَدِئَ النِّعَمِ قَبْلَ اسْتِحْقَاقِهَا ﴿٥﴾

يَا رَبَّنَا وَيَا سَيِّدَنَا وَيَا غَايَةَ رَغْبَتِنَا أَسْأَلُكَ يَا اَللهُ أَنْ لَا تَشْوِيَ خَلْقِي بِالنَّارِ ﴿٦﴾

1. O Allah! Truly I ask You of the best that I [can] produce, the best that I [can] do, and the best of my acts; the best of that which I hide, the best of that which I show. [I ask You] to accord me the highest degrees in Paradise. Amin.

2. O Allah! Truly I ask You to make my memory honored, lift my burden (of sin) from me, put right my affairs, purify my heart, safeguard my private parts, illuminate my heart and forgive me my sins. And I ask You to accord me the highest degrees in Paradise. Amin.

3. O Allah! Truly I ask You to bless me in my hearing, in my sight, in my spirit, in my constitution, in my character, in my family, in my life, in my death, and in my works. Accept my good deeds and grant me the highest rank in Paradise. Amin.

4. O Allah! You are the First; there was nothing before You, and You are the Last; there is nothing after You. I seek refuge in You from every beast in Your charge, and I take refuge from the [burden] of sin, and the [yoke] of heavy debt.

اَللّٰهُمَّ إِنِّيٓ أَسْأَلُكَ خَيْرَ مَآ اٰتِي وَخَيْرَ مَآ أَفْعَلُ وَخَيْرَ
مَآ أَعْمَلُ وَخَيْرَ مَآ أُبْطِنُ وَخَيْرَ مَآ أُظْهِرُ وَالدَّرَجَاتِ
الْعُلٰى مِنَ الْجَنَّةِ اٰمِينَ ۝ اَللّٰهُمَّ إِنِّيٓ أَسْأَلُكَ أَنْ تَرْفَعَ
ذِكْرِي وَتَضَعَ وِزْرِي وَتُصْلِحَ أَمْرِي وَتُطَهِّرَ قَلْبِي
وَتُحَصِّنَ فَرْجِي وَتُنَوِّرَ قَلْبِي وَتَغْفِرَ لِي ذَنْبِي وَأَسْأَلُكَ
الدَّرَجَاتِ الْعُلٰى مِنَ الْجَنَّةِ اٰمِينَ ۝

اَللّٰهُمَّ إِنِّيٓ أَسْأَلُكَ أَنْ تُبَارِكَ لِي فِي سَمْعِي وَفِي
بَصَرِي وَفِي رُوحِي وَفِي خَلْقِي وَفِي خُلُقِي وَفِيٓ أَهْلِي
وَفِي مَحْيَايَ وَفِي مَمَاتِي وَفِي عَمَلِي وَتَقَبَّلَ حَسَنَاتِي
وَأَسْأَلُكَ الدَّرَجَاتِ الْعُلٰى مِنَ الْجَنَّةِ اٰمِينَ ۝

اَللّٰهُمَّ أَنْتَ الْأَوَّلُ فَلَا شَيْءَ قَبْلَكَ وَأَنْتَ الْاٰخِرُ فَلَا
شَيْءَ بَعْدَكَ أَعُوذُ بِكَ مِنْ شَرِّ كُلِّ دَآبَّةٍ نَاصِيَتُهَا بِيَدِكَ
وَأَعُوذُ بِكَ مِنَ الْمَأْثَمِ وَالْمَغْرَمِ ۝

You respond to those in desperate need, and You remove harm. You cure the sick, forgive sins, and accept repentance. No one can repay [You] for Your blessings, and no one who possesses a tongue can praise You as You deserve [to be praised].

1. O Allah! Truly I ask You for knowledge which is beneficial, take refuge in You from knowledge which yields no benefit, and ask You for deeds which are accepted.

2. O Allah! Make Your most abundant provision for me when I have grown old and at my departure from this life.

3. O Allah! Truly I ask You [that I should make] the best request, the best supplication, [and I ask You to grant me] the best success, the best deed, the best reward, the best life and the best death!

4. Make me steadfast (in religion), make my scales heavy [with good deeds], and realize my faith for me! Raise my rank, accept my prayers, and forgive me for my misdeeds! I ask You to accord me the highest degrees in paradise. Amin.

5. O Allah! Truly I ask of You the openings to goodness, and the outcome which goodness brings—its entirety: its beginning, its end, its outward, and its inward. [I ask You] to accord me the highest degrees in Paradise. Amin.

وَتُجِيبُ الْمُضْطَرَّ وَتَكْشِفُ الضُّرَّ وَتَشْفِي السَّقِيمَ وَتَغْفِرُ الذَّنْبَ وَتَقْبَلُ التَّوْبَةَ وَلَا يَجْزِي بِآلَائِكَ أَحَدٌ وَلَا يَبْلُغُ مِدْحَتَكَ قَوْلُ قَائِلٍ ﴿٥﴾ اَللّٰهُمَّ إِنِّي أَسْأَلُكَ عِلْماً نَافِعاً وَأَعُوذُ بِكَ مِنْ عِلْمٍ لَا يَنْفَعُ وَأَسْأَلُكَ عَمَلاً مُتَقَبَّلاً ﴿١﴾ اَللّٰهُمَّ اجْعَلْ أَوْسَعَ رِزْقِكَ عَلَيَّ عِنْدَ كِبَرِ سِنِّي وَانْقِطَاعِ عُمُرِي ﴿٢﴾ اَللّٰهُمَّ إِنِّي أَسْأَلُكَ خَيْرَ الْمَسْأَلَةِ وَخَيْرَ الدُّعَاءِ وَخَيْرَ النَّجَاحِ وَخَيْرَ الْعَمَلِ وَخَيْرَ الثَّوَابِ وَخَيْرَ الْحَيَاةِ وَخَيْرَ الْمَمَاتِ ﴿٣﴾ وَثَبِّتْنِي وَثَقِّلْ مَوَازِينِي وَحَقِّقْ إِيمَانِي وَارْفَعْ دَرَجَتِي وَتَقَبَّلْ صَلَاتِي وَاغْفِرْ خَطِيئَتِي وَأَسْأَلُكَ الدَّرَجَاتِ الْعُلَى مِنَ الْجَنَّةِ اٰمِينَ ﴿٤﴾ اَللّٰهُمَّ إِنِّي أَسْأَلُكَ فَوَاتِحَ الْخَيْرِ وَخَوَاتِمَهُ وَجَوَامِعَهُ وَأَوَّلَهُ وَاٰخِرَهُ وَظَاهِرَهُ وَبَاطِنَهُ وَالدَّرَجَاتِ الْعُلَى مِنَ الْجَنَّةِ اٰمِينَ ﴿٥﴾

1. O Allah! Bless me in my religion through which is the safeguarding of my affairs. Bless me in my Hereafter which is my journey's end, and in my worldly life in which is my means of attainment. Make my life [a means of] increase in every good, and let my death be a [means of finding] repose from every evil.

2. O Allah! I ask You to grant me a pure life, a good end and a return in the Hereafter free from dishonor or scandal.

3. O Allah! Make me [constantly] patient, and make me ever grateful! Make me insignificant in my own eyes, but great in the eyes of people!

4. My Lord, forgive me, show mercy on me, and guide me to the way which is most upright.

(One prays four *rak'as*, then makes the following supplication):

5. Your Light was perfected, and You guided [by it] so to You is due all praise. Your forbearance is immense, and You forgave, so to You belongs all praise. You bestowed open-handedly, so to You belongs all praise. Our Lord, Your Countenance is the noblest of all countenances, Your station is the most sublime of stations, and Your bestowal is the greatest of bestowals and the most delightful. When You are obeyed, our Lord, You show gratitude, and when You are disobeyed You forgive.

اَللّٰهُمَّ بَارِكْ لِي فِي دِينِيَ الَّذِي هُوَ عِصْمَةُ أَمْرِي وَفِي
أُخِرَتِيَ الَّتِي إِلَيْهَا مَصِيرِي وَفِي دُنْيَايَ الَّتِي فِيهَا بَلَاغِي
وَاجْعَلِ الْحَيَاةَ زِيَادَةً لِي فِي كُلِّ خَيْرٍ وَاجْعَلِ الْمَوْتَ
رَاحَةً لِي مِنْ كُلِّ شَرٍّ ﴿١﴾ اَللّٰهُمَّ إِنِّي أَسْأَلُكَ عِيشَةً نَقِيَّةً
وَمِيتَةً سَوِيَّةً وَمَرَدًّا غَيْرَ مَخْزًى وَلَا فَاضِحٍ ﴿٢﴾
اَللّٰهُمَّ اجْعَلْنِي صَبُورًا وَاجْعَلْنِي شَكُورًا وَاجْعَلْنِي
فِي عَيْنِي صَغِيرًا وَفِي أَعْيُنِ النَّاسِ كَبِيرًا ﴿٣﴾
رَبِّ اغْفِرْ وَارْحَمْ وَاهْدِنِي السَّبِيلَ الْأَقْوَمَ ﴿٤﴾

(ويصلي أربع ركعات ثم يدعو:)

تَمَّ نُورُكَ فَهَدَيْتَ فَلَكَ الْحَمْدُ، عَظُمَ حِلْمُكَ فَغَفَرْتَ
فَلَكَ الْحَمْدُ، بَسَطْتَ يَدَكَ فَأَعْطَيْتَ فَلَكَ الْحَمْدُ، رَبَّنَا
وَجْهُكَ أَكْرَمُ الْوُجُوهِ وَجَاهُكَ أَعْظَمُ الْجَاهِ وَعَطِيَّتُكَ
أَعْظَمُ الْعَطِيَّةِ وَأَهْنَاهَا، تُطَاعُ رَبَّنَا فَتَشْكُرُ وَتُعْصَى فَتَغْفِرُ

١٤١

1. O Allah! Truly I ask You to grant me the ability to do good deeds and leave all objectionable acts and the love of the poor. [I ask You] to forgive me, have mercy on me, and if You intend to put people to trial, take my soul without trial.

2. I ask You for Your Love, and the love of those who love You, and the love of an action which brings me closer to Your love.

3. O Allah! Let me enjoy my hearing and my sight and keep these faculties intact and healthy and help me against those who have wronged me and take vengeance upon them on my behalf.

O He Who is not seen by eyes, nor conceived of by the imagination! No one can describe Him, He is not changed by events, nor does He fear calamities. He knows the weight of the mountains, the volume of the oceans, and the number of raindrops. [He knows] the number of leaves on the trees, and the number of all things that the darkness of night has covered and the light of day has shone upon. No heaven conceals [from Him] another heaven, nor does any earth conceal [from Him] another earth. No sea can conceal [from Him] what is on its bed, nor any mountain conceal what is within its rock.

4. Make the best part of my life its end, the best of my deeds my final deed, and the best of my days the day I meet with You.

اَللّٰهُمَّ إِنِّي أَسْأَلُكَ فِعْلَ الْخَيْرَاتِ وَتَرْكَ الْمُنْكَرَاتِ
وَحُبَّ الْمَسَاكِينِ وَأَنْ تَغْفِرَ لِي وَتَرْحَمَنِي وَإِذَا أَرَدْتَ
فِتْنَةَ النَّاسِ فَتَوَفَّنِي غَيْرَ مَفْتُونٍ ﴿١﴾ وَأَسْأَلُكَ حُبَّكَ
وَحُبَّ مَنْ يُحِبُّكَ وَحُبَّ عَمَلٍ يُقَرِّبُنِي إِلٰى حُبِّكَ ﴿٢﴾
اَللّٰهُمَّ مَتِّعْنِي بِسَمْعِي وَبَصَرِي وَاجْعَلْهُمَا الْوَارِثَ مِنِّي
وَانْصُرْنِي عَلٰى مَنْ ظَلَمَنِي وَخُذْ مِنْهُ بِثَأْرِي يَا مَنْ لَا
تَرَاهُ الْعُيُونُ وَلَا تُخَالِطُهُ الظُّنُونُ وَلَا يَصِفُهُ الْوَاصِفُونَ
وَلَا تُغَيِّرُهُ الْحَوَادِثُ وَلَا يَخْشَى الدَّوَائِرَ وَيَعْلَمُ مَثَاقِيلَ
الْجِبَالِ وَمَكَايِيلَ الْبِحَارِ وَعَدَدَ قَطْرِ الْأَمْطَارِ وَعَدَدَ وَرَقِ
الْأَشْجَارِ وَعَدَدَ مَا أَظْلَمَ عَلَيْهِ اللَّيْلُ وَأَشْرَقَ عَلَيْهِ النَّهَارُ
وَلَا تُوَارِي سَمَاءٌ سَمَاءً وَلَآ أَرْضٌ أَرْضًا وَلَا بَحْرٌ مَا
فِي قَعْرِهِ وَلَا جَبَلٌ مَا فِي وَعْرِهِ ﴿٣﴾
اِجْعَلْ خَيْرَ عُمُرِي اٰخِرَهُ وَخَيْرَ عَمَلِي خَوَاتِمَهُ وَخَيْرَ
أَيَّامِي يَوْمَ أَلْقَاكَ فِيهِ ﴿٤﴾

1. O Allah! Keep me alive as long as life is better for me, and take my soul when death would be better for me!

2. My Lord! Help me, but don't help [another] against me! Support me but don't support [another] against me! Plot for me but don't plot against me! Guide me and facilitate guidance for me and support me against whoever has wronged me!

3. My Lord! Make me perpetually remember You, continuously show gratitude toward You, be ever in awe of You, constantly obedient to You, always humble before You, and one who sighs before You, turning to You in repentance!

4. My Lord! Accept my repentance, wash away my faults, answer my prayer, secure my proof, guide my heart, make my tongue say what is apposite, and root out the resentment from my breast!

5. O Allah! Truly I ask You for steadfastness in my affairs, and I ask You for resolve in [pursuing] right guidance. I ask You for gratitude for Your blessings, and the ability to worship You properly. I ask You for a truthful tongue and a sound heart. I seek refuge in You from the evil that You know about, I ask You for the goodness You know about and I seek Your forgiveness for what You know [best] about, for verily You are the Knower of all that is in the Unseen.

6. O Allah! Inspire in me right guidance, and protect me from the evil of my self.

اَللّٰهُمَّ أَحْيِنِي مَا كَانَتِ الْحَيَاةُ خَيْراً لِي وَتَوَفَّنِي إِذَا كَانَتِ الْوَفَاةُ خَيْراً لِي ﴿١﴾ رَبِّ أَعِنِّي وَلَا تُعِنْ عَلَيَّ وَانْصُرْنِي وَلَا تَنْصُرْ عَلَيَّ وَامْكُرْ لِي وَلَا تَمْكُرْ عَلَيَّ وَاهْدِنِي وَيَسِّرِ الْهُدٰى لِي وَانْصُرْنِي عَلَى مَنْ بَغٰى عَلَيَّ ﴿٢﴾ رَبِّ اجْعَلْنِي لَكَ ذَكَّاراً، لَكَ شَكَّاراً، لَكَ رَهَّاباً، لَكَ مِطْوَاعاً، لَكَ مُخْبِتاً، إِلَيْكَ أَوَّاهاً مُنِيباً ﴿٣﴾ رَبِّ تَقَبَّلْ تَوْبَتِي وَاغْسِلْ حَوْبَتِي وَأَجِبْ دَعْوَتِي وَثَبِّتْ حُجَّتِي وَاهْدِ قَلْبِي وَسَدِّدْ لِسَانِي وَاسْلُلْ سَخِيمَةَ صَدْرِي ﴿٤﴾ اَللّٰهُمَّ إِنِّي أَسْأَلُكَ الثَّبَاتَ فِي الْأَمْرِ وَأَسْأَلُكَ الْعَزِيمَةَ فِي الرُّشْدِ وَأَسْأَلُكَ شُكْرَ نِعْمَتِكَ وَحُسْنَ عِبَادَتِكَ وَأَسْأَلُكَ لِسَاناً صَادِقاً وَقَلْباً سَلِيماً وَأَعُوذُ بِكَ مِنْ شَرِّ مَا تَعْلَمُ وَأَسْأَلُكَ مِنْ خَيْرِ مَا تَعْلَمُ وَأَسْتَغْفِرُكَ بِمَا تَعْلَمُ إِنَّكَ أَنْتَ عَلَّامُ الْغُيُوبِ ﴿٥﴾

اَللّٰهُمَّ أَلْهِمْنِي رُشْدِي وَأَعِذْنِي مِنْ شَرِّ نَفْسِي ﴿٦﴾

1. O Allah! Forgive me my sins, the unintentional and the deliberate!

2. O Allah! Truly I seek Your guidance to put right my affairs, and I take refuge in You from the evil of my self.

3. O Allah! Replenish me, restore me, provide for me and guide me to righteous deeds and morals, for no one provides guidance to these except You, and no one gets rid of their reprehensible opposites except You.

4. O Allah! Truly I seek refuge in You from leprosy, vitiligo,[6] and every malignant illness.

5. O Allah! Forgive me that which [I have done] in earnest, jokingly, unintentionally, and deliberately, for all of these are to my name. Do not deprive me of blessings in that which You have provided for me, and do not try me in that which You have kept from me!

6. O Allah, forgive us our sins, our injustice, that which is in jest, that which is in earnest, that which is deliberate, and that which is unintentional, for we are responsible for all of these.

7. O Allah, rectify for me my religion by which is the safeguarding of my affairs; rectify for me my worldly life in which is my livelihood, and rectify for me my Hereafter to which is my [final] return. Make my life [a means of] increase in every good, and let my death be [a means of finding] repose from every evil!

---

[6] A disease which causes the skin to lose its color and go white.

اَللّٰهُمَّ اغْفِرْ لِي ذُنُوبِي وَخَطَئِي وَعَمْدِي ﴿١﴾

اَللّٰهُمَّ إِنِّيٓ أَسْتَهْدِيكَ لِأُرْشَدَ أَمْرِي وَأَعُوذُ بِكَ مِنْ

شَرِّ نَفْسِي ﴿٢﴾ اَللّٰهُمَّ انْعِشْنِي وَاجْبُرْنِي وَارْزُقْنِي

وَاهْدِنِي لِصَالِحِ الْأَعْمَالِ وَالْأَخْلَاقِ لَا يَهْدِي لِصَالِحِهَا

وَلَا يَصْرِفُ سَيِّئَهَا إِلَّا أَنْتَ ﴿٣﴾ اَللّٰهُمَّ إِنِّيٓ أَعُوذُ بِكَ مِنَ

الْجُذَامِ وَالْبَرَصِ وَسَيِّئِ الْأَسْقَامِ ﴿٤﴾

اَللّٰهُمَّ اغْفِرْ لِي جِدِّي وَهَزْلِي وَخَطَئِي وَعَمْدِي وَكُلُّ

ذٰلِكَ عِنْدِي وَلَا تَحْرِمْنِي بَرَكَةَ مَآ أَعْطَيْتَنِي وَلَا تَفْتِنِّي فِيمَآ

أَحْرَمْتَنِي ﴿٥﴾ اَللّٰهُمَّ اغْفِرْ لَنَا ذُنُوبَنَا وَظُلْمَنَا وَهَزْلَنَا وَجِدَّنَا

وَعَمْدَنَا وَخَطَأَنَا وَكُلُّ ذٰلِكَ عِنْدَنَا ﴿٦﴾ اَللّٰهُمَّ أَصْلِحْ لِي دِينِي

الَّذِي هُوَ عِصْمَةُ أَمْرِي وَأَصْلِحْ لِي دُنْيَايَ الَّتِي فِيهَا مَعَاشِي

وَأَصْلِحْ لِي اٰخِرَتِي الَّتِي فِيهَا مَعَادِي وَاجْعَلِ الْحَيَاةَ زِيَادَةً لِي

فِي كُلِّ خَيْرٍ وَاجْعَلِ الْمَوْتَ رَاحَةً لِي مِنْ كُلِّ شَرٍّ ﴿٧﴾

1. O Allah! Truly I take refuge in You from objectionable characteristics, deeds, desires, and pursuits.

2. O Allah! Truly I take refuge in You from overwhelming debt, subjugation by an enemy, and the malicious gloating of (Your other) servants (people).

3. O Allah! I take refuge in You from worry, grief, incapacity, sloth, cowardice, miserliness, the burden of debt, and subjugation by men.

4. O Allah! Truly I seek refuge in You from knowledge that is not beneficial, a heart devoid of reverence, a prayer which is not listened to, a self which is never satisfied, and from hunger, for verily it is a wretched companion. I seek Your refuge from betrayal, for certainly it is a despicable comrade, and from sloth, cowardice, and miserliness. I seek Your refuge from decrepitude, from declining to the age of senility, from the trial of the Antichrist (*Al Dajjal*), the punishment of the grave, and the trial of life and death.

5. O Allah, truly we ask You [to grant us] sighing, humble, repentant hearts [guided] on Your path.

6. O Allah! Truly we ask You for the means of deserving Your mercy, the means of being certain of Your forgiveness, protection from every sin, the benefit of every virtue, the triumph of Paradise, and deliverance from the Hellfire.

اَللّٰهُمَّ إِنِّي أَعُوذُ بِكَ مِنْ مُنْكَرَاتِ الْأَخْلَاقِ وَالْأَعْمَالِ وَالْأَهْوَاءِ وَالْأَدْوَاءِ ﴿١﴾ اَللّٰهُمَّ إِنِّي أَعُوذُ بِكَ مِنْ غَلَبَةِ الدَّيْنِ وَغَلَبَةِ الْعَدُوِّ وَشَمَاتَةِ الْعِبَادِ ﴿٢﴾ اَللّٰهُمَّ إِنِّي أَعُوذُ بِكَ مِنَ الْهَمِّ وَالْحَزَنِ وَالْعَجْزِ وَالْكَسَلِ وَالْجُبْنِ وَالْبُخْلِ وَضَلَعِ الدَّيْنِ وَغَلَبَةِ الرِّجَالِ ﴿٣﴾ اَللّٰهُمَّ إِنِّي أَعُوذُ بِكَ مِنْ عِلْمٍ لَا يَنْفَعُ وَمِنْ قَلْبٍ لَا يَخْشَعُ وَمِنْ دُعَاءٍ لَا يُسْمَعُ وَمِنْ نَفْسٍ لَا تَشْبَعُ وَمِنَ الْجُوعِ فَإِنَّهُ بِئْسَ الضَّجِيعُ، وَمِنَ الْخِيَانَةِ فَلَبِئْسَ الْبِطَانَةُ، وَمِنَ الْكَسَلِ وَالْجُبْنِ وَالْبُخْلِ وَمِنَ الْهَرَمِ وَمِنْ أَنْ أُرَدَّ إِلَى أَرْذَلِ الْعُمُرِ وَمِنْ فِتْنَةِ الدَّجَّالِ وَعَذَابِ الْقَبْرِ وَفِتْنَةِ الْمَحْيَا وَالْمَمَاتِ ﴿٤﴾ اَللّٰهُمَّ إِنَّا نَسْأَلُكَ قُلُوباً أَوَّاهَةً مُخْبِتَةً مُنِيبَةً فِي سَبِيلِكَ ﴿٥﴾ اَللّٰهُمَّ إِنَّا نَسْأَلُكَ مُوجِبَاتِ رَحْمَتِكَ وَعَزَائِمَ مَغْفِرَتِكَ وَالسَّلَامَةَ مِنْ كُلِّ إِثْمٍ وَالْغَنِيمَةَ مِنْ كُلِّ بِرٍّ وَالْفَوْزَ بِالْجَنَّةِ وَالنَّجَاةَ مِنَ النَّارِ ﴿٦﴾

1. O Allah! Bring out the piety within my soul and purify it, for You are the best one to purify it; You are its Protector and Master.

2. O Allah! Truly I seek refuge in You from knowledge that is not beneficial, a heart devoid of reverence, a self which is never satisfied, and from a prayer which is not answered.

3. O Allah! Truly I seek refuge in You from the evil in that which I have done and from the evil of what I haven't done.

4. O Allah! Truly I seek refuge in You from the evil of what I know and from the evil of what I know not.

5. O Allah! I seek Your refuge from a cessation of Your grace, the removal of Your protection, a sudden disaster, or any of Your wrath. O All-Merciful One! O All-Compassionate One! O Possessor of Majesty and Bounty! O All-Living One! O Self-Subsistent One!

6. O Allah! I take refuge in You from destruction, and I take refuge in You from degeneration. I take refuge in You from drowning, burning or falling into decrepitude. I take refuge in You from Satan causing me to falter at the time of my death, and I take refuge in You from dying from a poisonous bite.

اَللّٰهُمَّ اٰتِ نَفْسِي تَقْوَاهَا وَزَكِّهَا أَنْتَ خَيْرُ مَنْ زَكَّاهَا أَنْتَ وَلِيُّهَا وَمَوْلٰيهَا ﴿١﴾

اَللّٰهُمَّ إِنِّي أَعُوذُ بِكَ مِنْ عِلْمٍ لَا يَنْفَعُ وَمِنْ قَلْبٍ لَا يَخْشَعُ وَمِنْ نَفْسٍ لَا تَشْبَعُ وَمِنْ دَعْوَةٍ لَا يُسْتَجَابُ لَهَا ﴿٢﴾

اَللّٰهُمَّ إِنِّي أَعُوذُ بِكَ مِنْ شَرِّ مَا عَمِلْتُ وَمِنْ شَرِّ مَا لَمْ أَعْمَلْ ﴿٣﴾ اَللّٰهُمَّ إِنِّي أَعُوذُ بِكَ مِنْ شَرِّ مَا عَلِمْتُ وَمِنْ شَرِّ مَا لَمْ أَعْلَمْ ﴿٤﴾ اَللّٰهُمَّ إِنِّي أَعُوذُ بِكَ مِنْ زَوَالِ نِعْمَتِكَ وَتَحَوُّلِ عَافِيَتِكَ وَفَجْأَةِ نِقْمَتِكَ وَجَمِيعِ سَخَطِكَ يَا رَحْمٰنُ يَا رَحِيمُ يَا ذَا الْجَلَالِ وَالْإِكْرَامِ يَا حَيُّ يَا قَيُّومُ ﴿٥﴾ اَللّٰهُمَّ إِنِّي أَعُوذُ بِكَ مِنَ الْهَدْمِ وَأَعُوذُ بِكَ مِنَ التَّرَدِّي وَأَعُوذُ بِكَ مِنَ الْغَرَقِ وَالْحَرَقِ وَالْهَرَمِ وَأَعُوذُ بِكَ مِنْ أَنْ يَتَخَبَّطَنِي الشَّيْطَانُ عِنْدَ الْمَوْتِ وَأَعُوذُ بِكَ مِنْ أَنْ أَمُوتَ لَدِيغًا ﴿٦﴾

1. O Allah! Wash away my sins with the water of snow and hail, purge my heart from sins as a white garment is cleansed of filth, and distance my misdeeds from me as You have distanced the East from the West.

2. O Allah! Truly I take refuge in You from incapacity, sloth, cowardice, and decrepitude. I take refuge in You from the punishment of the grave and I take refuge in You from the trial of life and death.

3. O Allah! I take refuge in You from a hard heart, heedlessness, poverty, humiliation, and deprivation. I take refuge in You from want, unbelief, immorality, divisiveness, esteem seeking, and ostentation. I take refuge in You from deafness, dumbness, insanity, leprosy, and all malignant illnesses.

4. O Allah! Truly do I complain to You of my lack of strength and ability, and my ineffectualness with people.

اَللّٰهُمَّ اغْسِلْ خَطَايَايَ بِمَاءِ الثَّلْجِ وَالْبَرَدِ وَنَقِّ قَلْبِي مِنَ الْخَطَايَا كَمَا يُنَقَّى الثَّوْبُ الْأَبْيَضُ مِنَ الدَّنَسِ وَبَاعِدْ بَيْنِي وَبَيْنَ خَطَايَايَ كَمَا بَاعَدْتَ بَيْنَ الْمَشْرِقِ وَالْمَغْرِبِ ﴿١﴾

اَللّٰهُمَّ إِنِّي أَعُوذُ بِكَ مِنَ الْعَجْزِ وَالْكَسَلِ وَالْجُبْنِ وَالْهَرَمِ وَأَعُوذُ بِكَ مِنْ عَذَابِ الْقَبْرِ وَأَعُوذُ بِكَ مِنْ فِتْنَةِ الْمَحْيَا وَالْمَمَاتِ ﴿٢﴾

اَللّٰهُمَّ إِنِّي أَعُوذُ بِكَ مِنَ الْقَسْوَةِ وَالْغَفْلَةِ وَالْعَيْلَةِ وَالذِّلَّةِ وَالْمَسْكَنَةِ وَأَعُوذُ بِكَ مِنَ الْفَقْرِ وَالْكُفْرِ وَالْفُسُوقِ وَالشِّقَاقِ وَالسُّمْعَةِ وَالرِّيَاءِ وَأَعُوذُ بِكَ مِنَ الصَّمَمِ وَالْبَكَمِ وَالْجُنُونِ وَالْجُذَامِ وَسَيِّئِ الْأَسْقَامِ ﴿٣﴾

اَللّٰهُمَّ إِنِّي أَشْكُو إِلَيْكَ ضَعْفَ قُوَّتِي وَقِلَّةَ حِيلَتِي وَهَوَانِي عَلَى النَّاسِ ﴿٤﴾

1. O Allah! Truly I ask of You pardon and well-being in this life and the Hereafter.

2. O Allah! Truly I ask You for exoneration and well-being in this life and in the Hereafter, Most Merciful of the merciful, Possessor of Majesty and Bounty!

3. "Allah is sufficient for us, and what an excellent Guardian!" (Al Imran 3:173)

4. "What an excellent Protector, and what an excellent Helper!" (Anfal 8:40) There is no power or strength except in Allah, the Exalted, the Sublime.

5. O Allah! Bless our master Muhammad and his brothers from among the prophets and messengers, according to the number of Your creations, corresponding to Your good pleasure, and to the measure of the weight of Your Throne and ink of Your words.

6. O Allah! Bless our master Muhammad and his family to the extent of Allah's perfection, in accordance with what is meet with His perfection, and all praise is due to Allah the Lord of the worlds.

7. O Allah! Truly I take refuge in You from sloth, decrepitude, heavy debt, and the [burden] of sin.

8. O Allah! I take refuge in You from the punishment of the Fire, the tribulation of the Fire and from the punishment of the grave, from the evil of the trial of wealth, from the wretchedness of the trial of poverty, and from the evil of the trial of the Antichrist (*Al Dajjal*).

اَللّٰهُمَّ إِنِّيۤ أَسْأَلُكَ الْعَفْوَ وَالْعَافِيَةَ فِي الدُّنْيَا وَالْاٰخِرَةِ ﴿١﴾ اَللّٰهُمَّ إِنِّيۤ أَسْأَلُكَ الْمُعَافَاةَ وَالْعَافِيَةَ فِي الدُّنْيَا وَالْاٰخِرَةِ يَاۤ أَرْحَمَ الرَّاحِمِينَ يَا ذَا الْجَلَالِ وَالْإِكْرَامِ ﴿٢﴾ ﴿حَسْبُنَا اللهُ وَنِعْمَ الْوَكِيلُ﴾ ﴿٣﴾ ﴿نِعْمَ الْمَوْلٰى وَنِعْمَ النَّصِيرُ﴾ وَلَا حَوْلَ وَلَا قُوَّةَ إِلَّا بِاللهِ الْعَلِيِّ الْعَظِيمِ ﴿٤﴾ اَللّٰهُمَّ صَلِّ عَلٰى سَيِّدِنَا مُحَمَّدٍ وَعَلٰى إِخْوَانِهِ مِنَ النَّبِيِّينَ وَالْمُرْسَلِينَ عَدَدَ خَلْقِكَ وَرِضَا نَفْسِكَ وَزِنَةَ عَرْشِكَ وَمِدَادَ كَلِمَاتِكَ ﴿٥﴾ اَللّٰهُمَّ صَلِّ عَلٰى سَيِّدِنَا مُحَمَّدٍ وَعَلٰى اٰلِهِ عَدَدَ كَمَالِ اللهِ وَكَمَا يَلِيقُ بِكَمَالِهِ وَالْحَمْدُ للهِ رَبِّ الْعَالَمِينَ ﴿٦﴾ اَللّٰهُمَّ إِنِّيۤ أَعُوذُ بِكَ مِنَ الْكَسَلِ وَالْهَرَمِ وَالْمَغْرَمِ وَالْمَأْثَمِ ﴿٧﴾ اَللّٰهُمَّ إِنِّيۤ أَعُوذُ بِكَ مِنْ عَذَابِ النَّارِ وَفِتْنَةِ النَّارِ وَعَذَابِ الْقَبْرِ وَشَرِّ فِتْنَةِ الْغِنَى وَشَرِّ فِتْنَةِ الْفَقْرِ وَمِنْ شَرِّ فِتْنَةِ الْمَسِيحِ الدَّجَّالِ ﴿٨﴾

أَدْعِيَةٌ مُطْلَقَاتٌ غَيْرُ مُقَيَّدَاتٍ

PRAYERS TO BE READ AT ANY TIME

Reading from the Qur'an

One reads a certain portion of the Qur'an each day.

1. Surat al-Fatiha
2. Surat al-Baqara, especially the Ayat al-Kursi and the last verses from "Amana al-Rasul ..." to the end of the sura (Baqara 285-6).
3. The first ten and last ten verses of Surat al-Kahf.
4. Sura Yasin
5. Surat al-Fath
6. Surat al-Zalzala
7. Surat al-Nasr
9. Suras al-Mulk and al-Sajda when he intends to sleep
10. Surat al-Ikhlas and the suras of refuge, al-Falaq and al-Nas (one reads them before going to sleep and then wipes one's hands over one's body).

مَا يُقْرَأُ مِنَ الْقُرْآنِ:

يقرأ من القرآن كل يوم مقداراً معلوماً؛

١. ويقرأ بأُم القرآن

٢. وسورة البقرة لا سيما آية الكرسي وآخر سورة البقرة

﴿آمَنَ الرَّسُولُ... الخ﴾

٣. ومن أول سورة الكهف وآخرها عشر آيات

٤. وسورة يٰس

٥. وسورة الفتح

٦. وسورة الزلزلة

٧. وسورة الكافرون

٨. وسورة النصر

٩. وسورتي الملك والسجدة (حين أراد المنام)

١٠. وسورة الإخلاص والمعوذتين (يقرأها حين ينام ثم
يمسح جسده)

1. Praise be to Allah, to the number of all that He created! Praise be to Allah, filling all that He created! Praise be to Allah, to the number of what is on earth and in the sky. Praise be to Allah, filling what is on earth and in the sky! Praise be to Allah to the number of what is contained within His Book! Praise be to Allah, filling what is contained within His Book! Praise be to Allah to the number of all things. Praise be to Allah, filling all things!

2. Allah is the Greatest, to the number of that which He created! Allah is the Greatest, filling all that He created! Allah is the Greatest, to the number of all that is on earth and in the sky! Allah is the Greatest, filling what is on the earth and in the sky! Allah is the Greatest, to the number of all that is contained within His Book! Allah is the Greatest, filling what is contained within His Book! Allah is the Greatest, to the number of all things! Allah is the Greatest, filling all things!

3. Glory be to Allah! Praise be to Allah! There is no god but Allah; Allah is the Greatest! (100)

4. My Lord! Forgive me, and relent toward me; truly You are the Ever Relenting, the Merciful. (100)

5. I seek Allah's forgiveness. (*Astaghfirullah*) (100)

اَلْحَمْدُ لِلهِ عَدَدَ مَا خَلَقَ، اَلْحَمْدُ لِلهِ مِلْءَ مَا خَلَقَ،

اَلْحَمْدُ لِلهِ عَدَدَ مَا فِي الْأَرْضِ وَالسَّمَاءِ، اَلْحَمْدُ لِلهِ مِلْءَ

مَا فِي الْأَرْضِ وَالسَّمَاءِ، اَلْحَمْدُ لِلهِ عَدَدَ مَا أَحْصَى كِتَابُهُ،

اَلْحَمْدُ لِلهِ مِلْءَ مَا أَحْصَى كِتَابُهُ، اَلْحَمْدُ لِلهِ عَدَدَ كُلِّ

شَيْءٍ، اَلْحَمْدُ لِلهِ مِلْءَ كُلِّ شَيْءٍ ﴿١﴾ اَللهُ أَكْبَرُ عَدَدَ مَا

خَلَقَ، اَللهُ أَكْبَرُ مِلْءَ مَا خَلَقَ، اَللهُ أَكْبَرُ عَدَدَ مَا فِي الْأَرْضِ

وَالسَّمَاءِ، اَللهُ أَكْبَرُ مِلْءَ مَا فِي الْأَرْضِ وَالسَّمَاءِ، اَللهُ أَكْبَرُ

عَدَدَ مَا أَحْصَى كِتَابُهُ، اَللهُ أَكْبَرُ مِلْءَ مَا أَحْصَى كِتَابُهُ، اَللهُ

أَكْبَرُ عَدَدَ كُلِّ شَيْءٍ، اَللهُ أَكْبَرُ مِلْءَ كُلِّ شَيْءٍ ﴿٢﴾

٩- سُبْحَانَ اللهِ وَالْحَمْدُ لِلهِ وَلَا إِلٰهَ إِلَّا اللهُ

وَاللهُ أَكْبَرُ (١٠٠) ﴿٣﴾

١٠- رَبِّ اغْفِرْ لِي وَتُبْ عَلَيَّ إِنَّكَ أَنْتَ التَّوَّابُ

الرَّحِيمُ (١٠٠) ﴿٤﴾

١١- الاستغفار (١٠٠) ﴿٥﴾

1. There is no god but Allah, to the number of all that He created in the sky! There is no god but Allah, to the number of all that He created on earth! There is no god but Allah, to the number of what is between them! There is no god but Allah, to the number of all that He has created!

2. There is no strength or power except in Allah, to the number of all that He created in the sky. There is no strength or power except in Allah, to the number of all that He created on earth. There is no strength or power except in Allah, to the number of what He created on earth. There is no strength or power except in Allah, to the number of what is between them. There is no strength or power except in Allah, to the number of all that He has created.

3. Glory be to Allah, to the number of all that He created! Glory be to Allah, which fills all that He created! Glory be to Allah, to the number of all that is on earth and in the sky! Glory be to Allah, filling all that is on earth and in the sky! Glory be to Allah, to the number of all that is contained within His Book! Glory be to Allah, filling all that is contained within His Book! Glory be to Allah, to the number of all things! Glory be to Allah, filling all things!

لَا إِلٰهَ إِلَّا اللهُ عَدَدَ مَا خَلَقَ فِي السَّمَاءِ، لَا إِلٰهَ إِلَّا

اللهُ عَدَدَ مَا خَلَقَ فِي الْأَرْضِ، لَا إِلٰهَ إِلَّا اللهُ عَدَدَ مَا بَيْنَ

ذٰلِكَ، لَا إِلٰهَ إِلَّا اللهُ عَدَدَ مَا هُوَ خَالِقٌ **(١)**

وَلَا حَوْلَ وَلَا قُوَّةَ إِلَّا بِاللهِ عَدَدَ مَا خَلَقَ فِي السَّمَاءِ،

وَلَا حَوْلَ وَلَا قُوَّةَ إِلَّا بِاللهِ عَدَدَ مَا خَلَقَ فِي الْأَرْضِ،

وَلَا حَوْلَ وَلَا قُوَّةَ إِلَّا بِاللهِ عَدَدَ مَا بَيْنَ ذٰلِكَ، وَلَا حَوْلَ

وَلَا قُوَّةَ إِلَّا بِاللهِ عَدَدَ مَا هُوَ خَالِقٌ **(٢)**

٨ – سُبْحَانَ اللهِ عَدَدَ مَا خَلَقَ، سُبْحَانَ اللهِ مِلْءَ مَا

خَلَقَ، سُبْحَانَ اللهِ عَدَدَ مَا فِي الْأَرْضِ وَالسَّمَاءِ، سُبْحَانَ

اللهِ مِلْءَ مَا فِي الْأَرْضِ وَالسَّمَاءِ، سُبْحَانَ اللهِ عَدَدَ مَاۤ

أَحْصَى كِتَابُهُ، سُبْحَانَ اللهِ مِلْءَ مَاۤ أَحْصَى كِتَابُهُ، سُبْحَانَ

اللهِ عَدَدَ كُلِّ شَيْءٍ، سُبْحَانَ اللهِ مِلْءَ كُلِّ شَيْءٍ **(٣)**

1. Glory be to Allah and to Him be praise to the number of His creations, according to His pleasure, and to the measure of the weight of His Throne and the ink of His words! Glory be to Allah to the number of His creations! Glory be to Allah, according to His pleasure! Glory be to Allah to the measure of the weight of His Throne! Glory be to Allah to the measure of the ink of His words!

2. Glory be to Allah to the number of all that he created in the sky! Glory be to Allah, to the number of all that He created on earth! Glory be to Allah, to the number of what is between them! Glory be to Allah, to the number of all that He has created!

3. Allah is the Greatest, to the number of all that He created in the sky! Allah is the Greatest, to the number of what He created on earth! Allah is the Greatest, to the number of what is between them! Allah is the Greatest, to the number of what He has created!

4. Praise be to Allah, to the number of all that He created in the sky! Praise be to Allah, to the number of all that He created on earth! Praise be to Allah, to the number of what is between them. Praise be to Allah, to the number of all that He has created!

٦- سُبْحَانَ اللهِ وَبِحَمْدِهِ عَدَدَ خَلْقِهِ وَرِضَا نَفْسِهِ وَزِنَةَ عَرْشِهِ وَمِدَادَ كَلِمَاتِهِ، سُبْحَانَ اللهِ عَدَدَ خَلْقِهِ، سُبْحَانَ اللهِ رِضَا نَفْسِهِ، سُبْحَانَ اللهِ زِنَةَ عَرْشِهِ، سُبْحَانَ اللهِ مِدَادَ كَلِمَاتِهِ ﴿١﴾

٧- سُبْحَانَ اللهِ عَدَدَ مَا خَلَقَ فِي السَّمَاءِ، وَسُبْحَانَ اللهِ عَدَدَ مَا خَلَقَ فِي الْأَرْضِ، وَسُبْحَانَ اللهِ عَدَدَ مَا بَيْنَ ذٰلِكَ، وَسُبْحَانَ اللهِ عَدَدَ مَا هُوَ خَالِقٌ ﴿٢﴾

اَللهُ أَكْبَرُ عَدَدَ مَا خَلَقَ فِي السَّمَاءِ، وَاللهُ أَكْبَرُ عَدَدَ مَا خَلَقَ فِي الْأَرْضِ، وَاللهُ أَكْبَرُ عَدَدَ مَا بَيْنَ ذٰلِكَ، وَاللهُ أَكْبَرُ عَدَدَ مَا هُوَ خَالِقٌ ﴿٣﴾

وَالْحَمْدُ للهِ عَدَدَ مَا خَلَقَ فِي السَّمَاءِ، وَالْحَمْدُ للهِ عَدَدَ مَا خَلَقَ فِي الْأَرْضِ، وَالْحَمْدُ للهِ عَدَدَ مَا بَيْنَ ذٰلِكَ، وَالْحَمْدُ للهِ عَدَدَ مَا هُوَ خَالِقٌ ﴿٤﴾

1. The testimony "There is no god but Allah" should be repeated as much as possible especially in the morning and in the evening.

2. There is no god but Allah who is alone without associate. His is the dominion and to Him belongs all praise.

3. I bear witness that there is no god but Allah, and I bear witness that Muhammad is his servant and his Messenger.

4. I bear witness that there is no god but Allah Who is Alone without associate, and I bear witness that Muhammad is His servant and His Messenger. And that Jesus is His servant, the son of His handmaiden, His word that He cast into Mary, and a spirit from Him. I testify that the Garden is true and that Hellfire is true.

5. Glory be to Allah and to Him be praise! Glory be to Allah, the All-Mighty! (*Subhan Allah wa bi-hamdihi, Subhan Allah al-Azim*) (100)

١- يكرر كلمة ''لَاۤ إِلٰهَ إِلَّا اللهُ''، لَا سيما في الصباح والمساء ⟨١⟩

٢- لَاۤ إِلٰهَ إِلَّا اللهُ وَحْدَهُ لَا شَرِيكَ لَهُ، لَهُ الْمُلْكُ وَلَهُ الْحَمْدُ ⟨٢⟩

٣- أَشْهَدُ أَنْ لَاۤ إِلٰهَ إِلَّا اللهُ وَأَشْهَدُ أَنَّ مُحَمَّداً عَبْدُهُ وَرَسُولُهُ ⟨٣⟩

٤- أَشْهَدُ أَنْ لَاۤ إِلٰهَ إِلَّا اللهُ وَحْدَهُ لَا شَرِيكَ لَهُ وَأَشْهَدُ أَنَّ مُحَمَّداً عَبْدُهُ وَرَسُولُهُ وَأَنَّ عِيسٰى عَبْدُ اللهِ وَابْنُ أَمَتِهِ وَكَلِمَتُهُ أَلْقَاهَا إِلٰى مَرْيَمَ وَرُوحٌ مِنْهُ وَأَنَّ الْجَنَّةَ حَقٌّ وَالنَّارَ حَقٌّ ⟨٤⟩

٥- سُبْحَانَ اللهِ وَبِحَمْدِهِ سُبْحَانَ اللهِ الْعَظِيمِ (١٠٠) ⟨٥⟩

١٢٨

أَدْعِيَةٌ لَمْ تُخْتَصَّ بِوَقْتٍ
مِنَ الْأَوْقَاتِ

PRAYERS NOT SPECIFIC TO ANY PARTICULAR OCCASION

After the burial

1. Implore forgiveness for your brother and ask steadfastness (in religion) for him!

   Then one reads the first verses of Surat al-Baqara, and the last verses (2:285-6).

Visiting a cemetery

2. Peace be upon you O believers and Muslims among the indwellers of this abode! Indeed we shall catch up with You if Allah wills. We ask from Allah redemption for us and for you. You are our predecessors and we are your successors; may Allah have mercy on those who went before and those who come after!

يُقَالُ إِذَا فُرِغَ مِنَ الدَّفْنِ:

"اِسْتَغْفِرُوا لِأَخِيكُمْ وَاسْأَلُوا لَهُ التَّثْبُتَ!"

ويقرأ على القبر أول سورة البقرة ﴿الٓمٓ ۝ ذٰلِكَ الْكِتَابُ...﴾ وخاتمتها ﴿ءَامَنَ الرَّسُولُ... الخ﴾ 🌼①

إِذَا زَارَ قَبْراً يَقُولُ:

اَلسَّلَامُ عَلَيْكُمْ أَهْلَ الدِّيَارِ مِنَ الْمُؤْمِنِينَ وَالْمُسْلِمِينَ، وَإِنَّا إِنْ شَاءَ اللهُ بِكُمْ لَلَاحِقُونَ، نَسْأَلُ اللهَ لَنَا وَلَكُمُ الْعَافِيَةَ، أَنْتُمْ لَنَا فَرَطٌ وَنَحْنُ لَكُمْ تَبَعٌ وَيَرْحَمُ اللهُ الْمُسْتَقْدِمِينَ وَالْمُسْتَأْخِرِينَ 🌼②

1. O Allah! Forgive our living and our dead, our male and female, our young and old, and those present and absent!

2. O Allah! Whoever of us You keep alive, let him live by Islam and whoever of us has his soul taken, take it in a state of faith! Privilege this deceased person with refreshment and repose, and with forgiveness and contentment!

3. O Allah! If he acted with excellence, increase him in excellence, and if he behaved badly, overlook that of him! Let him meet with security, good tidings, dignity and nearness [to You], through Your Mercy, Most Merciful of the merciful!

Placing the deceased in his grave

4. "From it (earth) We created you, to it we return you, and from it we bring you forth for another time." (Ta-Ha 55)

In the name of Allah, in the path of Allah, and upon the creed of the Messenger of Allah.

اَللّٰهُمَّ اغْفِرْ لِحَيِّنَا وَمَيِّتِنَا وَذَكَرِنَا وَأُنْثِينَا وَصَغِيرِنَا وَكَبِيرِنَا وَشَاهِدِنَا وَغَائِبِنَا ﴿١﴾

اَللّٰهُمَّ مَنْ أَحْيَيْتَهُ مِنَّا فَأَحْيِهِ عَلَى الْإِسْلَامِ وَمَنْ تَوَفَّيْتَهُ مِنَّا فَتَوَفَّهُ عَلَى الْإِيمَانِ وَخُصَّ هٰذَا الْمَيِّتَ بِالرَّوْحِ وَالرَّاحَةِ وَالْمَغْفِرَةِ وَالرِّضْوَانِ ﴿٢﴾

اَللّٰهُمَّ إِنْ كَانَ مُحْسِناً فَزِدْ فِي إِحْسَانِهِ وَإِنْ كَانَ مُسِيئاً فَتَجَاوَزْ عَنْهُ وَلَقِّهِ الْأَمْنَ وَالْبِشَارَةَ وَالْكَرَامَةَ وَالزُّلْفَى بِرَحْمَتِكَ يَا أَرْحَمَ الرَّاحِمِينَ ﴿٣﴾

يُقَالُ حِينَ وُضِعَ الْمَيِّتُ فِي الْقَبْرِ:
﴿مِنْهَا خَلَقْنَاكُمْ وَفِيهَا نُعِيدُكُمْ وَمِنْهَا نُخْرِجُكُمْ تَارَةً أُخْرَى﴾ بِسْمِ اللّٰهِ وَفِي سَبِيلِ اللّٰهِ وَعَلَى مِلَّةِ رَسُولِ اللّٰهِ ﴿٤﴾

Funeral prayer

When he has prayed over the dead person, magnified Allah's greatness and extolled Him, he says:

1. O Allah! He is Your servant, and the son of Your hand-maiden; he bears witness that there is no god but You, who are alone without associate, and he bears witness that Muhammad is Your servant and Your Messenger. He has become in need of Your mercy, but You are above the need of punishing him. He has retired from this world and its inhabitants. If he was righteous, purify him, and if he was wrongful forgive him!

2. O Allah! Do not deprive us of his reward and do not lead us astray after him!

3. O Allah! Forgive him, have mercy on him, save him and pardon him! Honor his resting place, widen his entrance and wash him with water, snow and hail, purging him of all sins just as a white garment is cleansed of filth.

4. Exchange his house for a better house, his folk for a better folk, his spouse for a better spouse; enter him into Paradise and deliver him from the Hellfire!

اَلصَّلَاةُ عَلَى الْمَيِّتِ:

إِذَا صَلَّى عَلَيْهِ وَكَبَّرَ وَأَثْنَى عَلَى اللهِ يَقُولُ بَعْدَ ذَلِكَ:

اَللّٰهُمَّ إِنَّهُ عَبْدُكَ وَابْنُ أَمَتِكَ يَشْهَدُ أَنْ لَآ إِلٰهَ إِلَّا
أَنْتَ وَحْدَكَ لَا شَرِيكَ لَكَ وَيَشْهَدُ أَنَّ مُحَمَّداً عَبْدُكَ
وَرَسُولُكَ، أَصْبَحَ فَقِيراً إِلَى رَحْمَتِكَ وَأَصْبَحْتَ غَنِيًّا
مِنْ عَذَابِهِ، تَخَلَّى مِنَ الدُّنْيَا وَأَهْلِهَا، إِنْ كَانَ زَاكِياً فَزَكِّهِ
وَإِنْ كَانَ خَاطِئًا فَاغْفِرْ لَهُ ❶

اَللّٰهُمَّ لَا تَحْرِمْنَا أَجْرَهُ وَلَا تُضِلَّنَا بَعْدَهُ ❷

اَللّٰهُمَّ اغْفِرْ لَهُ وَارْحَمْهُ وَعَافِهِ وَاعْفُ عَنْهُ وَأَكْرِمْ
نُزُلَهُ وَأَوْسِعْ مَدْخَلَهُ وَاغْسِلْهُ بِالْمَاءِ وَالثَّلْجِ وَالْبَرَدِ وَنَقِّهِ
مِنَ الْخَطَايَا كَمَا يُنَقَّى الثَّوْبُ الْأَبْيَضُ مِنَ الدَّنَسِ ❸

وَأَبْدِلْهُ دَاراً خَيْراً مِنْ دَارِهِ وَأَهْلاً خَيْراً مِنْ أَهْلِهِ وَزَوْجاً
خَيْراً مِنْ زَوْجِهِ وَأَدْخِلْهُ الْجَنَّةَ وَأَعِذْهُ مِنَ النَّارِ ❹

1. Peace be upon you. I invoke the praise of Allah over you, besides whom there is no other god. To proceed: may Allah, grant you a great reward and inspire you with fortitude! May you and we be blessed with gratitude, for truly our souls, our wealth, our children are wonderful gifts from Allah, Almighty and Majestic is He, and loans entrusted to us to enjoy for a certain period. Then He takes them back at a time known [to Him]. Thus has Allah made gratitude incumbent [upon us] when He bestows [on us], and patience incumbent upon us when He tries us with hardship.

2. And your son/daughter... (names them)/your father/ mother (names them)/your uncle/aunt (names them) [who has died] was among the wonderful gifts [granted by] Allah and the loans that He entrusted to you and allowed you enjoy with joy and felicity, and He took him from you for a great reward. If you count on His reward, [you will receive] blessings, mercy, and guidance. So show fortitude, and let not your grief prevent you from attaining your reward, for then you will fall into regret. And know that your grief will not drive anything away, nor will it take away the cause of sorrow.

سَلَامٌ عَلَيْكَ فَإِنِّي أَحْمَدُ اللهَ إِلَيْكَ الَّذِي لَا إِلٰهَ إِلَّا هُوَ، أَمَّا بَعْدُ، فَأَعْظَمَ اللهُ لَكَ الْأَجْرَ وَأَلْهَمَكَ الصَّبْرَ وَرَزَقَنَا وَإِيَّاكَ الشُّكْرَ فَإِنَّ أَنْفُسَنَا وَأَمْوَالَنَا وَأَوْلَادَنَا مِنْ مَوَاهِبِ اللهِ عَزَّ وَجَلَّ الْهَنِيئَةِ وَعَوَارِيهِ الْمُسْتَوْدَعَةِ يُمَتَّعُ بِهَا إِلَى أَجَلٍ مَعْدُودٍ وَيَقْبِضُهَا بِوَقْتٍ مَعْلُومٍ ثُمَّ افْتَرَضَ اللهُ عَلَيْنَا الشُّكْرَ إِذَا أَعْطَى وَالصَّبْرَ إِذَا ابْتَلَى ﴿١﴾

وَكَانَ (ابْنُكَ.. أَبُوكَ.. عَمُّكَ.. يَعْنِي الْمُتَوَفَّى) مِنْ مَوَاهِبِ اللهِ الْهَنِيئَةِ وَعَوَارِيهِ الْمُسْتَوْدَعَةِ مَتَّعَكَ بِغِبْطَةٍ وَسُرُورٍ وَقَبَضَهُ مِنْكَ بِأَجْرٍ كَثِيرٍ، الصَّلَاةُ وَالرَّحْمَةُ وَالْهُدَى إِنِ احْتَسَبْتَ، وَاصْبِرْ وَلَا يُحْبِطْكَ جَزَعُكَ أَجْرَكَ فَتَنْدَمَ، وَاعْلَمْ أَنَّ الْجَزَعَ لَا يَرُدُّ شَيْئًا وَلَا يَدْفَعُ حُزْنًا ﴿٢﴾

While closing the eyes of the deceased

1. O Allah! Forgive me and forgive... (one mentions his name), raise him rank among the rightly guided, and compensate for those whom he has left behind as they join the company of the departed.

    Forgive us and forgive him, O Lord of the worlds! Make his grave spacious and illuminate it for him!

    Then he reads over him Sura Ya Sin.

Those who are bereaved or have suffered a misfortune

2. "Verily we belong to Allah and verily unto Him is the return." (Baqara 2:156)

    O Allah, reward me for my adversity and compensate me with what is better.

Offering condolence

3. Verily what He has taken back is His and what He has given is His and everything which is His has a determined life-span. (Then He encourages the bereaved to show fortitude and seek their reward from Allah).

وَإِذَا غَمَّضَ الْمَيِّتَ يَدْعُو اللهَ قَائِلاً:

اَللّهُمَّ اغْفِرْ لِي وَلَهُ وَأَعْقِبْنِي مِنْهُ عُقْبَى حَسَنَةً، اَللّهُمَّ اغْفِرْ... (يسمّيه) وَارْفَعْ دَرَجَتَهُ فِي الْمَهْدِيِّينَ وَاخْلُفْهُ فِي عَقِبِهِ فِي الْغَابِرِينَ وَاغْفِرْ لَنَا وَلَهُ يَا رَبَّ الْعَالَمِينَ وَافْسَحْ لَهُ فِي قَبْرِهِ وَنَوِّرْ لَهُ فِيهِ ﴿١﴾

ثم يقرأ عليه سورة يس.

يَقُولُ صَاحِبُ الْمُصِيبَةِ:

﴿إِنَّا للهِ وَإِنَّا إِلَيْهِ رَاجِعُونَ﴾ اَللّهُمَّ أْجُرْنِي فِي مُصِيبَتِي وَأَخْلِفْ لِي خَيْراً مِنْهَا ﴿٢﴾

وَيُقَالُ فِي الْعَزَاءِ:

إِنَّ للهِ مَا أَخَذَ وَلَهُ مَا أَعْطَى وَكُلُّ شَيْءٍ عِنْدَهُ بِأَجَلٍ مُسَمَّىً (ثم يوصي أهل الميت بالصبر والاحتساب) ﴿٣﴾

A sick person who is dying

1. "There is no god but You, glory be to You! Truly I have been among the wrongdoers." (Anbiya 21:87) (40)

2. There is no god but Allah, and Allah is the Greatest. There is no god but Allah, alone without associate. There is no god but Allah, His is the dominion and to Him belongs all praise. There is no god but Allah and there is no strength or power except in Allah.

During the agony of death

3. There is no god but Allah. Truly with death come its pangs of agony. O Allah! Forgive me, have mercy on me, and unite me with the Highest Companion!

4. O Allah! Help me endure the throes of death and its agony!

Prompting another who is dying to say the shahada

5. Somebody who is in the agony of death should be prompted to say: "There is no god but Allah."

يَقْرَأُ فِي مَرَضِ مَوْتِهِ:

﴿لَآ إِلٰهَ إِلَّآ أَنْتَ سُبْحَانَكَ إِنِّي كُنْتُ مِنَ الظَّالِمِينَ﴾ (٤٠) ①

لَا إِلٰهَ إِلَّا اللهُ وَاللهُ أَكْبَرُ، لَآ إِلٰهَ إِلَّا اللهُ وَحْدَهُ لَا شَرِيكَ لَهُ، لَآ إِلٰهَ إِلَّا اللهُ لَهُ الْمُلْكُ وَلَهُ الْحَمْدُ، لَآ إِلٰهَ إِلَّا اللهُ وَلَا حَوْلَ وَلَا قُوَّةَ إِلَّا بِاللهِ ②

يَقُولُ الْمُحْتَضَرُ:

لَا إِلٰهَ إِلَّا اللهُ، إِنَّ لِلْمَوْتِ سَكَرَاتٍ، اَللّٰهُمَّ اغْفِرْ لِي وَارْحَمْنِي وَأَلْحِقْنِي بِالرَّفِيقِ الْأَعْلَى ③ اَللّٰهُمَّ أَعِنِّي عَلَى غَمَرَاتِ الْمَوْتِ وَسَكَرَاتِ الْمَوْتِ ④

تَلْقِينُ الْمُحْتَضَرِ:

وَيُلَقِّنُه مَنْ كَانَ عِنْدَهُ كَلِمَةَ ''لَآ إِلٰهَ إِلَّا اللهُ'' ⑤

١٢١

1. Take away the harm, Lord of men! Heal! For You are the All-Healer; there is no cure save Your cure, and leave him without a trace of sickness!

2. In the name of Allah, I invoke a prayer for protection over you from everything that harms you, from the evil of every soul or envious eye. May Allah cure you! In the name of Allah, I invoke this prayer for your protection.

3. In the name of Allah, I invoke this prayer for your protection. May Allah cure you of every ailment that is within you, and "From the evil of those who blow on knots, ❀ And from the evil of an envier when he envies." (Falaq 113:4-5) (3)

4. O Allah, cure Your servant so he can smite the enemy for Your sake or attend a funeral for Your sake.

5. O Allah, cure him! O Allah, grant him health!

6. O person! (he names them) May Allah forgive you your sins, and grant you health in your religion and your body for the rest of your days!

At the end of the visit he says to the sick person, if they didn't pass away:

7. I ask Allah, the All-Mighty, Lord of the Supreme Throne, to cure you. (7)

اَللّهُمَّ أَذْهِبِ الْبَأْسَ رَبَّ النَّاسِ، اِشْفِ أَنْتَ الشَّافِي لَا شِفَاءَ إِلَّا شِفَاؤُكَ شِفَاءً لَا يُغَادِرُ سَقَماً ﴿١﴾ بِسْمِ اللهِ أَرْقِيكَ مِنْ كُلِّ شَيْءٍ يُؤْذِيكَ وَمِنْ شَرِّ كُلِّ نَفْسٍ أَوْ عَيْنٍ حَاسِدٍ، اَللهُ يَشْفِيكَ، بِسْمِ اللهِ أَرْقِيكَ ﴿٢﴾ بِسْمِ اللهِ أَرْقِيكَ، اَللهُ يَشْفِيكَ مِنْ كُلِّ دَاءٍ فِيكَ ﴿وَمِنْ شَرِّ النَّفَّاثَاتِ فِي الْعُقَدِ ۞ وَمِنْ شَرِّ حَاسِدٍ إِذَا حَسَدَ﴾ (٣) ﴿٣﴾ اَللّهُمَّ اشْفِ عَبْدَكَ يَنْكَأُ لَكَ عَدُوّاً أَوْ يَمْشِي لَكَ إِلَى جَنَازَةٍ ﴿٤﴾ اَللّهُمَّ اشْفِهِ، اَللّهُمَّ عَافِهِ ﴿٥﴾ يَا فُلَانُ (يُسَمِّيهِ) شَفَى اللهُ عُقْمَكَ وَغَفَرَ ذَنْبَكَ وَعَافَاكَ فِي دِينِكَ وَجِسْمِكَ إِلَى مُدَّةِ أَجَلِكَ ﴿٦﴾

يَقُولُ حِينَ عَادَ مَرِيضاً لَمْ يَحْضُرْ أَجَلُهُ:

أَسْأَلُ اللهَ الْعَظِيمَ رَبَّ الْعَرْشِ الْعَظِيمِ أَنْ يَشْفِيَكَ (٧) ﴿٧﴾

Having a fever

1. In the name of Allah, the Great, we take refuge in Allah, the All-Mighty from a throbbing vein, and from the evil of the heat of the Hellfire.

Feeling pain

If a person feels pain, or some discomfort somewhere in their body they put their hand on the area of the complaint and say:

2. In the name of Allah, in the name of Allah, in the name of Allah, I take refuge in the Might of Allah and His Power from the malevolence of this pain that I am experiencing and that is troubling me.

(They repeat this action with the supplication seven times.)

Visiting a sick person

One strokes over the place of sickness or wound with the right hand saying:

3. Let it not be harmful but purifying, if Allah wills. (3)

4. In the name of Allah, the earth of our land mixed with the saliva of one of us is a cure for our sick with the permission of our Lord.

يَقُولُ مَنْ بِهِ حُمَّى:

بِسْمِ اللهِ الْكَبِيرِ، نَعُوذُ بِاللهِ الْعَظِيمِ مِنْ شَرِّ كُلِّ عِرْقٍ نَعَّارٍ، وَمِنْ شَرِّ حَرِّ النَّارِ ❶

إِذَا اشْتَكَى:

إذا اشتكى ألمًا أو شيئًا في جسده يضع يده على الموضع الذي يؤلمه ويقول:

بِسْمِ اللهِ، بِسْمِ اللهِ، بِسْمِ اللهِ، أَعُوذُ بِعِزَّةِ اللهِ وَقُدْرَتِهِ مِنْ شَرِّ مَا أَجِدُ وَأُحَاذِرُ مِنْ وَجَعِي هٰذَا ❷

(يعيد هذا الفعل والدعاء سبعًا)

إِذَا عَادَ مَرِيضًا:

يمسح الموضع العليل أو الجرح بيده اليمنى قائلاً:

لَا بَأْسَ، طَهُورٌ إِنْ شَاءَ اللهُ (٢) ❸ بِسْمِ اللهِ تُرْبَةُ أَرْضِنَا بِرِيقَةِ بَعْضِنَا يُشْفَى بِهِ سَقِيمُنَا بِإِذْنِ رَبِّنَا ❹

١١٩

For somebody who has been burnt

1. Take away the harm, Lord of men! Heal! For You are the Healer; there is no healer except You.

When somebody has an ulcer or wound

The person suffering from the ulcer or wound puts their index finger in the earth and then on raising it says:

2. In the name of Allah, the earth of our land mixed with the saliva of one of us is a cure for our sick with the permission of our Lord.

If somebody suffers from an affliction or illness to the point where life becomes a burden

3. O Allah, keep me alive for as long as life is better for me, and let me die when death is better for me!

Suffering from sore eyes

4. O Allah, let me enjoy my sight and keep this faculty intact and healthy show me the fulfillment of my vengeance upon my enemy and help me against whoever has wronged me!

مَا يُقْرَأُ عَلَى الْمَحْرُوقِ:

أَذْهِبِ الْبَأْسَ رَبَّ النَّاسِ، اشْفِ أَنْتَ الشَّافِي لَا

شَافِيَ إِلَّا أَنْتَ ﴿١﴾

إِذَا كَانَ بِهِ قَرْحَةٌ أَوْ جُرْحٌ:

إذا كان به قرحة أو جرح يضع إصبعه السّبابة في الأرض
ثم يرفعها قائلاً:

بِسْمِ اللهِ تُرْبَةُ أَرْضِنَا بِرِيقَةِ بَعْضِنَا يُشْفَى بِهِ سَقِيمُنَا

بِإِذْنِ رَبِّنَا ﴿٢﴾

وَإِنْ أَصَابَهُ ضُرٌّ فَسَئِمَ مِنَ الْحَيَاةِ يَقُولُ:

اَللّهُمَّ أَحْيِنِي مَا كَانَتِ الْحَيَاةُ خَيْرًا لِي وَتَوَفَّنِي إِذَا

كَانَتِ الْوَفَاةُ خَيْرًا لِي ﴿٣﴾

يَقُولُ مَنْ أَصَابَهُ رَمَدٌ:

اَللّهُمَّ مَتِّعْنِي بِبَصَرِي وَاجْعَلْهُ الْوَارِثَ مِنِّي وَأَرِنِي

فِي الْعَدُوِّ ثَأْرِي وَانْصُرْنِي عَلَى مَنْ ظَلَمَنِي ﴿٤﴾

1. "And [we believe] that He—exalted be the majesty of our Lord!—has taken unto Himself neither spouse nor son." (Jinn 72:3)

2. "Say: He is Allah, the One and Only; ❀ Allah, the Absolute, Eternal; ❀ He begets not, nor is He begotten. ❀ And there is none like unto Him." (Ikhlas 112)

3. "Say: I take refuge with the Lord of the Daybreak, ❀ From the evil of what He created, ❀ From the evil of the darkness as it gathers, ❀ From the evil of those who blow on knots, ❀ And from the evil of an envier when he envies." (Falaq 113)

4. "Say: I take refuge with the Lord of humankind, ❀ The King of humankind, ❀ The God of humankind, ❀ From the evil of the sneaking whisperer, ❀ Who whispers in the breasts of humankind, ❀ From jinn and humankind." (Nas 114)

For a demented (senile) person

He should be treated with invocations of Surat al-Fatiha morning and evening for three days. After reading the Fatiha he expresses quick breaths on a fragment of cloth, which is given to the patient to wear. This process is repeated throughout the period mentioned above.

For someone who has been stung or bitten by a poisonous animal

Surat al-Fatiha is read seven times and then water and salt are rubbed on the place of the bite, after which suras al-Kafirun, al-Falaq, and al-Nas are read over the same place.

﴿وَأَنَّهُ تَعَالَى جَدُّ رَبِّنَا مَا اتَّخَذَ صَاحِبَةً وَلاَ وَلَداً﴾ ﴿١﴾ ﴿قُلْ هُوَ اللهُ أَحَدٌ ۝ اَللهُ الصَّمَدُ ۝ لَمْ يَلِدْ وَلَمْ يُولَدْ ۝ وَلَمْ يَكُنْ لَهُ كُفُواً أَحَدٌ﴾ ﴿٢﴾ ﴿قُلْ أَعُوذُ بِرَبِّ الْفَلَقِ ۝ مِنْ شَرِّ مَا خَلَقَ ۝ وَمِنْ شَرِّ غَاسِقٍ إِذَا وَقَبَ ۝ وَمِنْ شَرِّ النَّفَّاثَاتِ فِي الْعُقَدِ ۝ وَمِنْ شَرِّ حَاسِدٍ إِذَا حَسَدَ﴾ ﴿٣﴾ ﴿قُلْ أَعُوذُ بِرَبِّ النَّاسِ ۝ مَلِكِ النَّاسِ ۝ إِلٰهِ النَّاسِ ۝ مِنْ شَرِّ الْوَسْوَاسِ الْخَنَّاسِ ۝ الَّذِي يُوَسْوِسُ فِي صُدُورِ النَّاسِ ۝ مِنَ الْجِنَّةِ وَالنَّاسِ﴾ ﴿٤﴾

إِذَا أُتِيَ بِمَعْتُوهٍ:

يرقيه بالفاتحة ثلاثة أيام غدوة وعشية، كلما ختمها جمع بصاقه ثم تفله.

مَا يُفْعَلُ بِاللَّدِيغِ:

يقرأ بفاتحة الكتاب سبع مرّات ويمسح اللدغة بماء وملح ويقرأ عليهما سورة الكافرون والمعوذتين.

١١٧

1. "By those who set the ranks, ❂ And those who drive [the clouds], ❂ And those who read the Reminder, ❂ Truly your God is One, ❂ Lord of the heavens and the earth and all that is between them, and Lord of the sun's risings. ❂ Indeed, We have adorned the lowest heaven with the ornament of the stars. ❂ To protect it from every rebellious devil. ❂ They cannot listen to the Sublime Assembly for they are pelted from all sides. ❂ Banished; theirs is a perpetual torment; ❂ Save he who snatches a fragment, and there pursues him a piercing flame." (Saffat 1-10)

2. "He is Allah besides Whom there is no other god; Knower of the Unseen and the visible. He is the All-Merciful, the All-Compassionate. ❂ He is Allah, there is no god but He; the Sovereign, the All-Holy, the Source of Peace, the Source of Security; the Guardian, the All-Mighty; the Compeller, the Majestic. Transcendent is He above all that they ascribe as partner (to Him)! ❂ He is Allah; the Creator, the Producer, the Fashioner (Who has brought His creatures to existence and fashioned them in the best form and perfect harmony, making them undergo different phases). His are the most beautiful names. All that is in the heavens and the earth glorifies Him. He is the All-Mighty, the All-Wise." (Hashr 59:22-4)

﴿وَالصَّافَّاتِ صَفًّا ۞ فَالزَّاجِرَاتِ زَجْرًا ۞ فَالتَّالِيَاتِ ذِكْرًا ۞ إِنَّ إِلَٰهَكُمْ لَوَاحِدٌ ۞ رَبُّ السَّمٰوَاتِ وَالْأَرْضِ وَمَا بَيْنَهُمَا وَرَبُّ الْمَشَارِقِ ۞ إِنَّا زَيَّنَّا السَّمَاءَ الدُّنْيَا بِزِينَةٍ الْكَوَاكِبُ ۞ وَحِفْظًا مِنْ كُلِّ شَيْطَانٍ مَارِدٍ ۞ لَا يَسَّمَّعُونَ إِلَى الْمَلَإِ الْأَعْلَىٰ وَيُقْذَفُونَ مِنْ كُلِّ جَانِبٍ ۞ دُحُورًا وَلَهُمْ عَذَابٌ وَاصِبٌ ۞ إِلَّا مَنْ خَطِفَ الْخَطْفَةَ فَأَتْبَعَهُ شِهَابٌ ثَاقِبٌ ۞ ﴾ ①

﴿هُوَ اللَّهُ الَّذِي لَا إِلَٰهَ إِلَّا هُوَ عَالِمُ الْغَيْبِ وَالشَّهَادَةِ هُوَ الرَّحْمٰنُ الرَّحِيمُ ۞ هُوَ اللَّهُ الَّذِي لَا إِلَٰهَ إِلَّا هُوَ الْمَلِكُ الْقُدُّوسُ السَّلَامُ الْمُؤْمِنُ الْمُهَيْمِنُ الْعَزِيزُ الْجَبَّارُ الْمُتَكَبِّرُ سُبْحَانَ اللَّهِ عَمَّا يُشْرِكُونَ ۞ هُوَ اللَّهُ الْخَالِقُ الْبَارِئُ الْمُصَوِّرُ لَهُ الْأَسْمَاءُ الْحُسْنَىٰ يُسَبِّحُ لَهُ مَا فِي السَّمٰوَاتِ وَالْأَرْضِ وَهُوَ الْعَزِيزُ الْحَكِيمُ﴾ ②

1. "Truly Your Lord is Allah, Who created the heavens and the earth in six days, then established Himself upon the Throne. He envelops the day with the night, which promptly follows it. And the sun, the moon and the stars are all subservient by His command. Are not the creation and the commandment His? Blessed is Allah, the Lord of the worlds. ✿ Call upon your Lord in humble submissiveness and in secret. Truly he loves not those who transgress. ✿ Spread not corruption (mischief) in the earth after it has been put in good order, and call upon Him in fear and hope. Surely. the mercy of Allah is close to the those who do good." (A'raf 7:54-6)

2. "Exalted is Allah, the King, the Truth; there is no god but He, the Lord of the noble Throne. ✿ And whoever calls upon another god along with Allah has no proof. His reckoning is only with his Lord. Certainly the unbelievers do not prosper. ✿ And say: 'My Lord forgive and show mercy, for You are the best of those who show mercy.'" (Mu'minun 23:116-8)

﴿إِنَّ رَبَّكُمُ اللهُ الَّذِي خَلَقَ السَّمَوَاتِ وَالْأَرْضَ فِي سِتَّةِ أَيَّامٍ ثُمَّ اسْتَوَى عَلَى الْعَرْشِ يُغْشِي اللَّيْلَ النَّهَارَ يَطْلُبُهُ حَثِيثاً وَالشَّمْسَ وَالْقَمَرَ وَالنُّجُومَ مُسَخَّرَاتٍ بِأَمْرِهِ أَلَا لَهُ الْخَلْقُ وَالْأَمْرُ تَبَارَكَ اللهُ رَبُّ الْعَالَمِينَ ۞ ادْعُوا رَبَّكُمْ تَضَرُّعاً وَخُفْيَةً إِنَّهُ لَا يُحِبُّ الْمُعْتَدِينَ ۞ وَلَا تُفْسِدُوا فِي الْأَرْضِ بَعْدَ إِصْلَاحِهَا وَادْعُوهُ خَوْفاً وَطَمَعاً إِنَّ رَحْمَتَ اللهِ قَرِيبٌ مِنَ الْمُحْسِنِينَ﴾ ﴿١﴾

﴿فَتَعَالَى اللهُ الْمَلِكُ الْحَقُّ لَا إِلَهَ إِلَّا هُوَ رَبُّ الْعَرْشِ الْكَرِيمِ ۞ وَمَنْ يَدْعُ مَعَ اللهِ إِلَهاً آخَرَ لَا بُرْهَانَ لَهُ بِهِ فَإِنَّمَا حِسَابُهُ عِنْدَ رَبِّهِ إِنَّهُ لَا يُفْلِحُ الْكَافِرُونَ ۞ وَقُلْ رَبِّ اغْفِرْ وَارْحَمْ وَأَنْتَ خَيْرُ الرَّاحِمِينَ﴾ ﴿٢﴾

١١٥

1. "To Allah belongs whatever is in the heavens and the earth. Whether you declare what is in your hearts or conceal it, Allah will bring you to account for it. He forgives whom He wills and He punishes whom he wills, and He has power over all things. ❂ The Messenger believes in what has been sent down to him, and [so do] the believers. All believe in Allah, His angels, His Books, and His messengers—We make no distinction between any of His messengers—and they say: 'We hear and obey. [Grant us] Your forgiveness our Lord! And to You is the journeying.' ❂ Allah does not charge a soul beyond its capacity. It shall be requited only for the [good] it earned and the [evil] it committed. Our Lord! Do not take us to task when we forget or make mistakes! Our Lord! Do not lay on us a burden like that which you laid on those who came before us! Our Lord! Do not charge us with more than we can bear! Pardon us, forgive us, and have mercy on us! You are our Master, grant us victory over the unbelievers." (Baqara 2:284-6)

2. "Allah bears witness that there is no god but He, and (so do) the angels and those endowed with knowledge, maintaining His creation with justice. There is no god but He, the Almighty, the Wise." (Al Imran 3:18)

114

﴿لِلَّهِ مَا فِي السَّمَوَاتِ وَمَا فِي الْأَرْضِ وَإِنْ تُبْدُوا مَا فِي أَنْفُسِكُمْ أَوْ تُخْفُوهُ يُحَاسِبْكُمْ بِهِ اللَّهُ فَيَغْفِرُ لِمَنْ يَشَاءُ وَيُعَذِّبُ مَنْ يَشَاءُ وَاللَّهُ عَلَى كُلِّ شَيْءٍ قَدِيرٌ ۞ آمَنَ الرَّسُولُ بِمَا أُنْزِلَ إِلَيْهِ مِنْ رَبِّهِ وَالْمُؤْمِنُونَ كُلٌّ آمَنَ بِاللَّهِ وَمَلَئِكَتِهِ وَكُتُبِهِ وَرُسُلِهِ لَا نُفَرِّقُ بَيْنَ أَحَدٍ مِنْ رُسُلِهِ وَقَالُوا سَمِعْنَا وَأَطَعْنَا غُفْرَانَكَ رَبَّنَا وَإِلَيْكَ الْمَصِيرُ ۞ لَا يُكَلِّفُ اللَّهُ نَفْسًا إِلَّا وُسْعَهَا لَهَا مَا كَسَبَتْ وَعَلَيْهَا مَا اكْتَسَبَتْ رَبَّنَا لَا تُؤَاخِذْنَا إِنْ نَسِينَا أَوْ أَخْطَأْنَا رَبَّنَا وَلَا تَحْمِلْ عَلَيْنَا إِصْرًا كَمَا حَمَلْتَهُ عَلَى الَّذِينَ مِنْ قَبْلِنَا رَبَّنَا وَلَا تُحَمِّلْنَا مَا لَا طَاقَةَ لَنَا بِهِ وَاعْفُ عَنَّا وَاغْفِرْ لَنَا وَارْحَمْنَا أَنْتَ مَوْلَانَا فَانْصُرْنَا عَلَى الْقَوْمِ الْكَافِرِينَ﴾ ﴿١﴾

﴿شَهِدَ اللَّهُ أَنَّهُ لَا إِلَهَ إِلَّا هُوَ وَالْمَلَئِكَةُ وَأُولُوا الْعِلْمِ قَائِمًا بِالْقِسْطِ لَا إِلَهَ إِلَّا هُوَ الْعَزِيزُ الْحَكِيمُ﴾ ﴿٢﴾

١١٤

1. "Your God is one God; there is no god but He, the All-Merciful, the All-Compassionate. ⊛ Lo! In the creation of the heavens and the earth, the alternation of night and day, the ships which sail across the ocean [with] that which is for the benefit of humankind, the water which Allah sends down from the sky and with which He revives the earth after its death, the animals of all kinds He has scattered therein, the dispatching of the winds and the clouds that are driven between heaven and earth, are signs for people who think." (Baqara 2:163-4)

2. Ayat al-Kursi:

   "Allah! There is no god but He, the All-Living, the Self-Subsistent. Neither does slumber overtake Him nor sleep. To Him belongs whatever is in the heavens and the earth. Who can intercede with Him except by His leave? He knows what is before them and what is behind them, and of His knowledge they comprehend only what He wills. His Throne encompasses the heavens and the earth, and maintaining them both tires Him not. He is the Exalted, the Sublime."

﴿وَإِلَٰهُكُمْ إِلَٰهٌ وَاحِدٌ ۖ لَا إِلَٰهَ إِلَّا هُوَ الرَّحْمَٰنُ الرَّحِيمُ ۝ إِنَّ فِي خَلْقِ السَّمَٰوَاتِ وَالْأَرْضِ وَاخْتِلَافِ اللَّيْلِ وَالنَّهَارِ وَالْفُلْكِ الَّتِي تَجْرِي فِي الْبَحْرِ بِمَا يَنْفَعُ النَّاسَ وَمَا أَنْزَلَ اللَّهُ مِنَ السَّمَاءِ مِنْ مَاءٍ فَأَحْيَا بِهِ الْأَرْضَ بَعْدَ مَوْتِهَا وَبَثَّ فِيهَا مِنْ كُلِّ دَابَّةٍ وَتَصْرِيفِ الرِّيَاحِ وَالسَّحَابِ الْمُسَخَّرِ بَيْنَ السَّمَاءِ وَالْأَرْضِ لَآيَاتٍ لِقَوْمٍ يَعْقِلُونَ ۝١﴾

﴿اللَّهُ لَا إِلَٰهَ إِلَّا هُوَ الْحَيُّ الْقَيُّومُ ۚ لَا تَأْخُذُهُ سِنَةٌ وَلَا نَوْمٌ ۚ لَهُ مَا فِي السَّمَٰوَاتِ وَمَا فِي الْأَرْضِ ۗ مَنْ ذَا الَّذِي يَشْفَعُ عِنْدَهُ إِلَّا بِإِذْنِهِ ۚ يَعْلَمُ مَا بَيْنَ أَيْدِيهِمْ وَمَا خَلْفَهُمْ ۖ وَلَا يُحِيطُونَ بِشَيْءٍ مِنْ عِلْمِهِ إِلَّا بِمَا شَاءَ ۚ وَسِعَ كُرْسِيُّهُ السَّمَٰوَاتِ وَالْأَرْضَ ۖ وَلَا يَؤُودُهُ حِفْظُهُمَا ۚ وَهُوَ الْعَلِيُّ الْعَظِيمُ ۝٢﴾

1. "Let there be no harm! Remove all harm, Lord of men! Heal, for You are the Healer. No one lifts away harm except You and nobody heals except You."

Affliction with a touch of the jinn

He places the person in front of him and reads the following:

I seek refuge in Allah from Satan, the Accursed. In the name of Allah,

the All-Merciful, the All-Compassionate.

2. "All praise belongs to Allah, the Lord of the worlds; ⊛ The All-Merciful, the All-Compassionate; ⊛ Master of the Day of Judgment. ⊛ You alone do we worship and from You alone do we seek help. ⊛ Guide us on the Straight Path. ⊛ The path of those whom You have favored, not of those upon whom is your wrath, nor of those who are astray." (Fatiha 1) Amin.

3. "Alif Lam Mim. ⊛ This is the Book in which there is no doubt, a guidance for the God fearing, ⊛ Who believe in the unseen, establish the prayer, and spend out of what we have provided for them. ⊛ And who believe that which is sent down to you (Muhammad), and that which was sent down before you, and have certainty in the Hereafter. ⊛ These are on true guidance from their Lord, and these are the successful." (Baqara 2:1-5)

لَا بَأْسَ، أَذْهِب الْبَأْسَ رَبَّ النَّاسِ، اشْفِ أَنْتَ الشَّافِي

لَا يَكْشِفُ الضُّرَّ إِلَّا أَنْتَ وَلَا شَافِيَ إِلَّا أَنْتَ ﴿١١﴾

مَا يُفْعَلُ بِالْمُصَابِ بِلَمَّةٍ مِنَ الْجِنِّ:

يضع المصاب بين يديه ثم يقرأ:

أَعُوذُ بِاللهِ مِنَ الشَّيْطَانِ الرَّجِيمِ، بِسْمِ اللهِ الرَّحْمٰنِ

الرَّحِيمِ ﴿الْحَمْدُ للهِ رَبِّ الْعَالَمِينَ ۞ الرَّحْمٰنِ الرَّحِيمِ ۞

مَالِكِ يَوْمِ الدِّينِ ۞ إِيَّاكَ نَعْبُدُ وَإِيَّاكَ نَسْتَعِينُ ۞ اهْدِنَا

الصِّرَاطَ الْمُسْتَقِيمَ ۞ صِرَاطَ الَّذِينَ أَنْعَمْتَ عَلَيْهِمْ غَيْرِ

الْمَغْضُوبِ عَلَيْهِمْ وَلَا الضَّالِّينَ﴾ أمينَ ﴿٢﴾

لا

﴿الٓمٓ ۞ ذٰلِكَ الْكِتَابُ لَا رَيْبَ فِيهِ هُدًى لِلْمُتَّقِينَ

۞ الَّذِينَ يُؤْمِنُونَ بِالْغَيْبِ وَيُقِيمُونَ الصَّلٰوةَ وَمِمَّا

رَزَقْنَاهُمْ يُنْفِقُونَ ۞ وَالَّذِينَ يُؤْمِنُونَ بِمَا أُنْزِلَ إِلَيْكَ وَمَا

أُنْزِلَ مِنْ قَبْلِكَ وَبِالْآخِرَةِ هُمْ يُوقِنُونَ ۞ أُولٰئِكَ عَلٰى

هُدًى مِنْ رَبِّهِمْ وَأُولٰئِكَ هُمُ الْمُفْلِحُونَ﴾ ﴿٣﴾

١١٢

1. O Allah, remover of worry, reliever of distress, the one who answers the prayer of those in dire need, the All-Merciful in this life and the Hereafter and the Beneficent in both [lives]! You have shown mercy toward me. Have mercy on me with a mercy that dispenses me of the need of mercy from all other than You!

2. "O Allah, Owner of Sovereignty! You bestow sovereignty on whom You will and take away sovereignty from whom You will; You exalt whom You will and You abase whom You will. All goodness is in Your hand; indeed You have power over all things." (Al Imran 3:26)

3. All-Merciful in this world and the Hereafter! You grant them to whom You will and You deny them from whom You will. Have mercy on me with a mercy that dispenses me of the need of mercy from all other than You!

For someone who has been afflicted by the evil eye

4. In the name of Allah. O Allah, remove its heat, its cold, and its suffering!

5. Then he says to them: "Get up with the permission of Allah!"

If a beast has been afflicted by the evil eye

He blows in its right nostril four times and in its left three and he says:

اَللّٰهُمَّ فَارِجَ الْهَمِّ كَاشِفَ الْغَمِّ مُجِيبَ دَعْوَةِ الْمُضْطَرِّينَ رَحْمٰنَ الدُّنْيَا وَالْاٰخِرَةِ وَرَحِيمَهُمَا أَنْتَ تَرْحَمُنِي فَارْحَمْنِي بِرَحْمَتِكَ تُغْنِينِي بِهَا عَنْ رَحْمَةِ مَنْ سِوَاكَ ﴿١﴾ ﴿اَللّٰهُمَّ مَالِكَ الْمُلْكِ تُؤْتِي الْمُلْكَ مَنْ تَشَاءُ وَتَنْزِعُ الْمُلْكَ مِمَّنْ تَشَاءُ وَتُعِزُّ مَنْ تَشَاءُ وَتُذِلُّ مَنْ تَشَاءُ بِيَدِكَ الْخَيْرُ إِنَّكَ عَلَى كُلِّ شَيْءٍ قَدِيرٌ﴾ ﴿٢﴾ رَحْمٰنَ الدُّنْيَا وَالْاٰخِرَةِ تُعْطِيهِمَا مَنْ تَشَاءُ وَتَمْنَعُهُمَا مَنْ تَشَاءُ اِرْحَمْنِي رَحْمَةً تُغْنِينِي بِهَا عَنْ رَحْمَةِ مَنْ سِوَاكَ ﴿٣﴾

يَدْعُو لِمَنْ أُصِيبَ بِعَيْنٍ:
بِسْمِ اللهِ، اَللّٰهُمَّ أَذْهِبْ حَرَّهَا وَبَرْدَهَا وَوَصَبَهَا ﴿٤﴾
ثُمَّ يَقُولُ لَهُ: "قُمْ بِإِذْنِ اللهِ" ﴿٥﴾

وَإِنْ كَانَتْ دَابَّةً: يَنْفِثُ فِي مِنْخَرِهَا الْأَيْمَنِ أَرْبَعًا وَفِي الْأَيْسَرِ ثَلَاثًا وَيَقُولُ:

1. "Say: Allah, the One and Only! Allah, the Absolute, Eternal; He begets not, nor is He begotten. And there is none like unto Him." (Ikhlas 112)

   Then one expresses quick breaths to one's left three times.

   If the whisperings come to the person while at worship or in good action

2. I take refuge in Allah from Satan the Accursed. (3)

3. Then they express quick breaths to their left three times and recite:

   "He is the First and the Last, the Manifest and the Hidden, and He is Knower of all things." (Hadid 57:3)

   When someone pays you back for a debt

4. You have paid me back in full, so may Allah fully compensate you and bless you in what is yours!

   If one falls into debt

5. O Allah! Let what You made legitimate suffice me, [so that I have no desire] for what You have forbidden, and through Your bounty make me independent of all other than You!

اَللَّهُ أَحَدٌ، اَللَّهُ الصَّمَدُ، لَمْ يَلِدْ وَلَمْ يُولَدْ، وَلَمْ يَكُنْ لَهُ كُفُوًا أَحَدٌ ﴿١﴾

ثم يتفل عن يساره ثلاثًا.

وَإِنْ كَانَتِ الْوَسْوَسَةُ فِي الْعَمَلِ يَقُولُ:
أَعُوذُ بِاللهِ مِنَ الشَّيْطَانِ الرَّجِيمِ (٣) ﴿٢﴾

ثم يتفل عن يساره ثلاثًا ثم يقرأ: ﴿هُوَ الْأَوَّلُ وَالْآخِرُ وَالظَّاهِرُ وَالْبَاطِنُ وَهُوَ بِكُلِّ شَيْءٍ عَلِيمٌ﴾ ﴿٣﴾

وَإِذَا اسْتَوْفَى دَيْنَهُ يَقُولُ:
أَوْفَيْتَنِي، أَوْفَى اللهُ بِكَ وَبَارَكَ اللهُ لَكَ ﴿٤﴾

إِذَا ابْتُلِيَ بِالدَّيْنِ يَقُولُ:
اَللَّهُمَّ اكْفِنِي بِحَلَالِكَ عَنْ حَرَامِكَ وَأَغْنِنِي بِفَضْلِكَ عَمَّنْ سِوَاكَ ﴿٥﴾

When experiencing dread

1. I seek refuge in the perfect words of Allah from His wrath and punishment, from the evil of His servants, and from the goading of devils, and their approaching me.

In order to drive away devils and demons

2. "Allah! There is no god but He, the All-Living, the Self-Subsistent. Neither does slumber overtake Him nor sleep, and to Him belongs whatever is in the heavens and the earth. Who can intercede with Him except by His leave? He knows what is before them and what is behind them and of His knowledge they comprehend only what He wills. His Throne encompasses the heavens and the earth, and maintaining them both tires Him not. He is the Exalted, the Sublime." (Ayat al-Kursi / Baqara 2:255)

Then one makes the call to prayer.

If one is taunted by [evil] whisperings

3. I seek refuge in Allah from Satan the accursed and from his temptations.

4. I believe in Allah and His messengers.

وَيَقُولُ عِنْدَ الْفَزَعِ:

أَعُوذُ بِكَلِمَاتِ اللهِ التَّامَّةِ مِنْ غَضَبِهِ وَعِقَابِهِ وَشَرِّ عِبَادِهِ وَمِنْ هَمَزَاتِ الشَّيَاطِينِ وَأَنْ يَحْضُرُونِ ﴿١﴾

يَقْرَأُ لِهَرَبِ الشَّيَاطِينِ وَالْغِيلَانِ ج

﴿اللهُ لَا إِلٰهَ إِلَّا هُوَ الْحَيُّ الْقَيُّومُ لَا تَأْخُذُهُ سِنَةٌ وَلَا نَوْمٌ لَهُ مَا فِي السَّمٰوَاتِ وَمَا فِي الْأَرْضِ مَنْ ذَا الَّذِي يَشْفَعُ عِنْدَهُ إِلَّا بِإِذْنِهِ يَعْلَمُ مَا بَيْنَ أَيْدِيهِمْ وَمَا خَلْفَهُمْ وَلَا يُحِيطُونَ بِشَيْءٍ مِنْ عِلْمِهِ إِلَّا بِمَا شَاءَ وَسِعَ كُرْسِيُّهُ السَّمٰوَاتِ وَالْأَرْضَ وَلَا يَؤُودُهُ حِفْظُهُمَا وَهُوَ الْعَلِيُّ الْعَظِيمُ﴾ ﴿٢﴾

ويؤذن.

إِذَا ابْتُلِيَ بِالْوَسْوَسَةِ يَقُولُ:

أَعُوذُ بِاللهِ مِنَ الشَّيْطَانِ الرَّجِيمِ وَمِنْ فِتْنَتِهِ ﴿٣﴾

أٰمَنْتُ بِاللهِ وَرُسُلِهِ ﴿٤﴾

1. O Allah! We take refuge in You from anyone of them (the tyrants) treating us with disregard or persecuting us.

2. O Allah! Lord of the seven heavens and Lord of the Supreme Throne, be my Redeemer!

3. O Allah! God of Gabriel, Mikail, Israfil, and God of Abraham, Ishmael, and Isaac, spare me, and place not anyone of Your creation in authority over me with something that I cannot endure. I am content with Allah as my Lord, with Islam as my religion, with Muhammad as my Prophet and with the Qur'an as my judge and standard.

If one fears Satan or some other being

4. I take refuge in the noble Countenance of Allah, and in the perfect words of Allah that can neither be surpassed by the upright nor by the immoral, from the evil of that which He created, dispersed and originated, from the evil of that which descends from the sky and ascends to it, and from the evil of that which He has dispersed over the earth and that which issues from within it, from the evil of the trials of the night and day, and from the evil of an [unexpected] caller save the caller who brings goodness. O All-Merciful! (*Ya Rahman*).

اَللّٰهُمَّ إِنَّا نَعُوذُ بِكَ أَنْ يَفْرُطَ عَلَيْنَا أَحَدٌ مِنْهُمْ أَوْ أَنْ يَطْغَى ۝ اَللّٰهُمَّ رَبَّ السَّمٰوَاتِ السَّبْعِ وَرَبَّ الْعَرْشِ الْعَظِيمِ كُنْ لِي جَارًا ۝ اَللّٰهُمَّ إِلٰهَ جِبْرِيلَ وَمِيكَائِيلَ وَإِسْرَافِيلَ وَإِلٰهَ إِبْرٰهِيمَ وَإِسْمَاعِيلَ وَإِسْحٰقَ عَافِنِي وَلَا تُسَلِّطَنَّ أَحَدًا مِنْ خَلْقِكَ عَلَيَّ بِشَيْءٍ لَا طَاقَةَ لِي بِهِ، رَضِيتُ بِاللّٰهِ رَبًّا وَبِالْإِسْلَامِ دِينًا وَبِمُحَمَّدٍ نَبِيًّا وَبِالْقُرْآنِ حَكَمًا وَإِمَامًا ۝

وَإِذَا خَافَ شَيْطَانًا أَوْ غَيْرَهُ يَقُولُ:

أَعُوذُ بِوَجْهِ اللّٰهِ الْكَرِيمِ وَبِكَلِمَاتِ اللّٰهِ التَّامَّاتِ الَّتِي لَا يُجَاوِزُهُنَّ بَرٌّ وَلَا فَاجِرٌ مِنْ شَرِّ مَا خَلَقَ وَذَرَأَ وَبَرَأَ وَمِنْ شَرِّ مَا يَنْزِلُ مِنَ السَّمَاءِ وَمِنْ شَرِّ مَا يَعْرُجُ فِيهَا وَمِنْ شَرِّ مَا ذَرَأَ فِي الْأَرْضِ وَمِنْ شَرِّ مَا يَخْرُجُ مِنْهَا وَمِنْ شَرِّ فِتَنِ اللَّيْلِ وَالنَّهَارِ وَمِنْ شَرِّ كُلِّ طَارِقٍ إِلَّا طَارِقًا يَطْرُقُ بِخَيْرٍ يَا رَحْمٰنُ ۝

When one finds difficulty in something

1. O Allah! There is nothing easy except that which You make easy, and You make hardship easy if it be Your will.

If a person is overcome with fatigue from their work, or a demand for sustenance that they cannot meet

They invoke each night before going to sleep: Glory be to Allah! (*Subhan Allah*) (33), Praise be to Allah! (*Al-hamdu li'llah*) (33), and Allah is the Greatest! (*Allahu Akbar*) (33).

Fearing a ruler or tyrant

2. Allah is the Greatest! Allah is the Greatest! Allah is Mightier than all of His creation! Allah is Mightier than all that I fear and am wary of! I take refuge in Allah—besides Whom there is no other god, Who keeps [what is in] the sky from falling onto the earth, save [that it should occur] by His leave—from the mischief of Your servant ... (one names the person). [I take refuge] from his soldiers, his followers and his partisans from amongst jinn and men. O Allah! Be my redeemer from their malevolence. Exalted is Your praise! Honored is Your protégé! There is no god but You. (3)

وَإِذَا اسْتَصْعَبَ عَلَيْهِ شَيْءٌ يَقُولُ:

اَللّٰهُمَّ لَا سَهْلَ إِلَّا مَاجَعَلْتَهُ سَهْلاً وَأَنْتَ تَجْعَلُ الْحَزَنَ إِذَا شِئْتَ سَهْلاً ۞

وَإِذَا أَخَذَهُ إِعْيَاءٌ مِنْ شُغْلٍ أَوْ طَلَبَ زِيَادَةِ قُوتٍ:

يسبّح الله عندما أراد أن ينام كل ليلة (٣٣ مرة)، ويحمد الله (٣٣ مرة)، ويكبر الله (٣٤ مرة).

وَإِذَا خَافَ سُلْطَانًا أَوْ ظَالِماً يَقُولُ:

اَللّٰهُ أَكْبَرُ اَللّٰهُ أَكْبَرُ، اَللّٰهُ أَعَزُّ مِنْ خَلْقِهِ جَمِيعاً، اَللّٰهُ أَعَزُّ مِمَّا أَخَافُ وَأَحْذَرُ، أَعُوذُ بِاللهِ الَّذِي لَآ إِلَهَ إِلَّا هُوَ الْمُمْسِكُ السَّمَاءَ أَنْ تَقَعَ عَلَى الْأَرْضِ إِلَّا بِإِذْنِهِ مِنْ شَرِّ عَبْدِكَ... (يسمي) وَجُنُودِهِ وَأَتْبَاعِهِ وَأَشْيَاعِهِ مِنَ الْجِنِّ وَالْإِنْسِ، اَللّٰهُمَّ كُنْ لِي جَاراً مِنْ شَرِّهِمْ، جَلَّ ثَنَاؤُكَ، وَعَزَّ جَارُكَ، وَلَآ إِلَهَ غَيْرُكَ (٣) ۞

1. (continued) that You make the Qur'an the spring of my heart, the light of my eyes, the reliever of my grief and eraser of my worries and distress. There is no strength or power except in Allah.

And one seeks forgiveness repeatedly.

When afflicted by tribulation or hardship

Whoever is afflicted by tribulation or hardship, waits for the *adhan* to be called, repeats what the muezzin says, and then makes the following supplication:

2. O Allah! Lord of this true call to prayer which is responded to, the call of the Truth, the testimony of piety, let us live by it, die by it. Resurrect us with it, and make us among the best of its people, in life and death!

If one experiences a calamity

3. "Verily we belong to Allah, and verily unto Him we return." (Baqara 2:156)

O Allah! I believe the recompense for my calamity is with You, so reward me by it and substitute for it something better!

Or:

4. "Verily we belong to Allah, and verily unto Him we return." O Allah, reward me for my calamity and replace it with what is better for me!

أَنْ تَجْعَلَ الْقُرْآنَ رَبِيعَ قَلْبِي وَنُورَ بَصَرِي وَجَلَاءَ حُزْنِي وَذَهَابَ هَمِّي وَغَمِّي وَلَا حَوْلَ وَلَا قُوَّةَ إِلَّا بِاللهِ (١)

ويكثر الاستغفار.

إِذَا نَزَلَ بِهِ كَرْبٌ أَوْ شِدَّةٌ:

من نزل به كرب أو شدة يتحين المنادي فيقول كما يقول المؤذن ثم يدعو:

اَللّهُمَّ رَبَّ هٰذِهِ الدَّعْوَةِ الصَّادِقَةِ الْمُسْتَجَابِ لَهَا دَعْوَةِ الْحَقِّ وَكَلِمَةِ التَّقْوَى أَحْيِنَا عَلَيْهَا وَأَمِتْنَا عَلَيْهَا وَابْعَثْنَا عَلَيْهَا وَاجْعَلْنَا مِنْ خِيَارِ أَهْلِهَا أَحْيَاءً وَأَمْوَاتاً (٢)

وَإِذَا أَصَابَتْهُ مُصِيبَةٌ يَقُولُ:

﴿إِنَّا للهِ وَإِنَّا إِلَيْهِ رَاجِعُونَ﴾ اَللّهُمَّ عِنْدَكَ أَحْتَسِبُ مُصِيبَتِي فَأُجُرْنِي فِيهَا وَأَبْدِلْنِي بِهَا خَيْراً مِنْهَا (٣)

''أو'' ﴿إِنَّا للهِ وَإِنَّا إِلَيْهِ رَاجِعُونَ﴾ اَللّهُمَّ أْجُرْنِي فِي مُصِيبَتِي وَأَخْلِفْ لِي خَيْراً مِنْهَا (٤)

1. I have put my trust in the All-Living Who never dies.

2. "Praise belongs to Allah, Who has not taken unto Himself a son, and Who has no partner in sovereignty. Nor has He [need] of an ally due to any weakness. And magnify Him by proclaiming His greatness!" (Isra 17:111)

3. O Allah! It is Your mercy that I hope for, so leave me not to myself for the blinking of an eye, and put right for me all my affairs! There is no god but You - O All-Living, Self-Subsistent [Lord]! (*Ya Hayy, Ya Qayyum*), in Your mercy do I seek relief.

    (One repeats this supplication while in prostration and says also):

4. O All-Living, Self-Subsistent [Lord]! "There is no god but You; glorified are You! Verily I have been one of the wrongdoers." (Anbiya 21:87)

5. O Allah! Verily I am Your servant, the son of Your servant and son of Your handmaiden. I am totally in Your grasp. My past is subject to Your judgment. Whatever You decree I justly deserve. I beseech You by every name with which You have named Yourself, or revealed in Your Book, or taught to one of Your creatures, or kept to Yourself so that it remains in the knowledge of the Unseen,

تَوَكَّلْتُ عَلَى الْحَيِّ الَّذِي لَا يَمُوتُ ﴿١﴾

﴿الْحَمْدُ لله الَّذِي لَمْ يَتَّخِذْ وَلَداً وَلَمْ يَكُنْ لَهُ شَرِيكٌ فِي الْمُلْكِ وَلَمْ يَكُنْ لَهُ وَلِيٌّ مِنَ الذُّلِّ وَكَبِّرْهُ تَكْبِيراً﴾ ﴿٢﴾

اَللَّهُمَّ رَحْمَتَكَ أَرْجُو، فَلَا تَكِلْنِي إِلَى نَفْسِي طَرْفَةَ عَيْنٍ وَأَصْلِحْ لِي شَأْنِي كُلَّهُ لَا إِلَهَ إِلَّا أَنْتَ يَا حَيُّ يَا قَيُّومُ بِرَحْمَتِكَ أَسْتَغِيثُ ﴿٣﴾

(ويكررها وهو ساجد ويقول أيضاً):

يَا حَيُّ يَا قَيُّومُ ﴿لَا إِلَهَ إِلَّا أَنْتَ سُبْحَانَكَ إِنِّي كُنْتُ مِنَ الظَّالِمِينَ﴾ ﴿٤﴾

اَللَّهُمَّ إِنِّي عَبْدُكَ وَابْنُ عَبْدِكَ وَابْنُ أَمَتِكَ، نَاصِيَتِي بِيَدِكَ، مَاضٍ فِيَّ حُكْمُكَ، عَدْلٌ فِيَّ قَضَاؤُكَ، أَسْأَلُكَ بِكُلِّ اسْمٍ هُوَ لَكَ سَمَّيْتَ بِهِ نَفْسَكَ أَوْ أَنْزَلْتَهُ فِي كِتَابِكَ أَوْ عَلَّمْتَهُ أَحَداً مِنْ خَلْقِكَ أَوِ اسْتَأْثَرْتَ بِهِ فِي عِلْمِ الْغَيْبِ عِنْدَكَ ﴿٥﴾

If one is worried about disaster or misfortune

1. There is no god but Allah, the All-Mighty, the All-Clement. There is no god but Allah, Lord of the Supreme Throne.

2. There is no god but Allah, Lord of the heavens, Lord of the earth and Lord of the noble Throne.

3. There is no god but Allah, the All-Clement, the All-Generous.

4. There is no god but Allah, Lord of the Supreme Throne.

5. There is no god but Allah, Lord of the heavens, Lord of the earth and Lord of the noble Throne.

6. Allah is our sufficiency, and what an excellent Guardian! In Allah do we put our trust.

7. There is no god but Allah, the All-Clement, the All-Generous. Glory be to Allah, Lord of the seven heavens and Lord of the Supreme Throne!

8. Praise be to Allah, the Lord of the worlds! O Allah! I seek refuge in You from the mischief of Your servants. Allah is our sufficiency, and what an excellent Guardian! Allah is my sufficiency, and what an excellent Guardian is He!

9. Allah! Allah is my Lord and I don't associate anything with Him. Allah! Allah is my Lord and I don't associate anything with Him. Allah! Allah is my Lord and I don't associate anything with Him.

إِذَا هَمَّ مِنْ عَوَارِضَ وَآفَاتٍ يَقُولُ:

لَآ إِلٰهَ إِلَّا اللهُ الْعَظِيمُ الْحَلِيمُ، لَآ إِلٰهَ إِلَّا اللهُ رَبُّ الْعَرْشِ الْعَظِيمِ ﴿١﴾ لَآ إِلٰهَ إِلَّا اللهُ رَبُّ السَّمٰوَاتِ وَرَبُّ الْأَرْضِ وَرَبُّ الْعَرْشِ الْكَرِيمِ ﴿٢﴾ لَآ إِلٰهَ إِلَّا اللهُ الْحَلِيمُ الْكَرِيمُ ﴿٣﴾ لَآ إِلٰهَ إِلَّا اللهُ رَبُّ الْعَرْشِ الْعَظِيمِ ﴿٤﴾ لَآ إِلٰهَ إِلَّا اللهُ رَبُّ السَّمٰوَاتِ وَربُّ الْأَرْضِ وَرَبُّ الْعَرْشِ الْكَرِيمِ ﴿٥﴾ حَسْبُنَا اللهُ وَنِعْمَ الْوَكِيلُ عَلَى اللهِ تَوَكَّلْنَا ﴿٦﴾ لَآ إِلٰهَ إِلَّا اللهُ الْحَلِيمُ الْكَرِيمُ، سُبْحَانَ اللهِ رَبِّ السَّمٰوَاتِ السَّبْعِ وَرَبِّ الْعَرْشِ الْعَظِيمِ ﴿٧﴾ اَلْحَمْدُ لِلّٰهِ رَبِّ الْعَالَمِينَ، اَللّٰهُمَّ إِنِّي أَعُوذُ بِكَ مِنْ شَرِّ عِبَادِكَ، حَسْبُنَا اللهُ وَنِعْمَ الْوَكِيلُ، حَسْبِيَ اللهُ وَنِعْمَ الْوَكِيلُ ﴿٨﴾ اَللهُ اللهُ رَبِّي لَآ أُشْرِكُ بِهِ شَيْئًا، اللهُ اللهُ رَبِّي لَآ أُشْرِكُ بِهِ شَيْئًا، اَللهُ اَللهُ رَبِّي لَآ أُشْرِكُ بِهِ شَيْئًا ﴿٩﴾

To the person who has embraced Islam

One teaches these words:

1. O Allah, forgive me, have mercy on me, guide me, and provide for me!

When one sneezes

2. Praise be to Allah in every situation, "Praise be to Allah, the Lord of the worlds!"

   Praise be to Allah with a pure and blessed praise from every direction as much as our Lord wishes and according to His good pleasure.

   Other person[s] present respond[s] with

3. May Allah have mercy on you!

   The one who sneezed rejoins with

4. May Allah forgive me and you! May Allah guide you and put your mind at rest!

   Or:

5. May Allah have mercy on us and on you and forgive us and forgive you!

If one hears a ringing in his ear

6. May Allah mention in a good light the person who spoke well of me!

When one gets angry

7. I seek refuge in Allah from Satan, the Accursed.

وَيُعَلِّمُ لِمَنْ أَسْلَمَ:

اَللَّهُمَّ اغْفِرْ لِي وَارْحَمْنِي وَاهْدِنِي وَارْزُقْنِي ﴿١﴾

إِذَا عَطَسَ يَقُولُ:

اَلْحَمْدُ لِلّٰهِ عَلَى كُلِّ حَالٍ ﴿اَلْحَمْدُ لِلّٰهِ رَبِّ الْعَالَمِينَ﴾ اَلْحَمْدُ لِلّٰهِ حَمْدًا كَثِيرًا طَيِّبًا مُبَارَكًا فِيهِ مُبَارَكًا عَلَيْهِ كَمَا يُحِبُّ رَبُّنَا وَيَرْضَى ﴿٢﴾

وَيَقُولُ الْآخَرُ: يَرْحَمُكَ اللّٰهُ ﴿٣﴾

وَيُجِيبُ الْعَاطِسُ: يَغْفِرُ اللّٰهُ لِي وَلَكُمْ، يَهْدِيكُمَا اللّٰهُ وَيُصْلِحُ بَالَكُمْ ﴿٤﴾

''أَوْ'' يَرْحَمُنَا اللّٰهُ وَإِيَّاكُمْ وَيَغْفِرُ اللّٰهُ لَنَا وَلَكُمْ ﴿٥﴾

وَإِذَا طَنَّتْ أُذُنُهُ يَقُولُ:

ذَكَرَ اللّٰهُ بِخَيْرٍ مَنْ ذَكَرَنِي بِخَيْرٍ ﴿٦﴾

وَإِذَا غَضِبَ يَقُولُ:

أَعُوذُ بِاللّٰهِ مِنَ الشَّيْطَانِ الرَّجِيمِ ﴿٧﴾

١٠٣

Receiving good news

One praises Allah, magnifies His greatness and makes prostration.

When a person says: "Truly I love you for the sake of Allah"

1. One replies with "May the One for Whose sake you loved me, love you!"

If somebody says: "May Allah forgive you"

2. One replies with "And you too."

When one is asked "How did your night pass?"

3. "I acknowledge you of my praising Allah."

To the person who has shown one kindness

4. May Allah bless you in your family and in your wealth!

To a person who has done one a favor

5. May Allah reward you with goodness!

وَإِذَا بُشِّرَ بِمَا يَسُرُّهُ:

يحمد ويكبر ويسجد.

وَإِذَا قِيلَ لَهُ: "إِنِّي أُحِبُّكَ فِي اللّٰهِ" يَقُولُ:

أَحَبَّكَ الَّذِيٓ أَحْبَبْتَنِي لَهُ ﴿١﴾

وَإِذَا قَالَ لَهُ أَحَدٌ: "غَفَرَ اللّٰهُ لَكَ" يَقُولُ:

وَلَكَ ﴿٢﴾

وَإِذَا سُئِلَ "كَيْفَ أَصْبَحْتَ؟" يَقُولُ:

أَحْمَدُ اللّٰهَ إِلَيْكَ ﴿٣﴾

وَيَقُولُ لِمَنْ أَحْسَنَ إِلَيْهِ:

بَارَكَ اللّٰهُ لَكَ فِي أَهْلِكَ وَمَالِكَ ﴿٤﴾

وَيَقُولُ لِمَنْ صَنَعَ إِلَيْهِ مَعْرُوفاً:

جَزَاكَ اللّٰهُ خَيْراً ﴿٥﴾

Seeing a fire

One magnifies Allah's greatness making *takbir*.

Hearing the cock crowing

One asks Allah to bestow upon him His favor.

Hearing the bray of a donkey or the barking of dogs

1. I seek refuge in Allah from Satan the Accursed. In the name of Allah, the All-Merciful, the All-Compassionate.

Hearing something displeasing

2. O Allah, there is no goodness except Your goodness, there is no omen except Your omen, and there is no god but You.

3. O Allah! No one produces good deeds except You, no one erases misdeeds except You, and there is no strength or power except in Allah, the Exalted, the All-Mighty.

إِذَا رَأَى الْحَرِيقَ:

يُكَبِّرُ.

إِذَا سَمِعَ صِيَاحَ الدِّيكِ:

يسأل الله من فضله.

وَإِذَا سَمِعَ نَهِيقَ الْحِمَارِ وَنُبَاحَ الْكِلَابِ يَقُولُ:

أَعُوذُ بِاللهِ مِنَ الشَّيْطَانِ الرَّجِيمِ، بِسْمِ اللهِ الرَّحْمٰنِ

الرَّحِيمِ ﴿١﴾

وَإِذَا سَمِعَ مَا يَكْرَهُهُ يَقُولُ:

اَللّٰهُمَّ لَا خَيْرَ إِلَّا خَيْرُكَ وَلَا طَيْرَ إِلَّا طَيْرُكَ وَلَا

إِلٰهَ غَيْرُكَ ﴿٢﴾

اَللّٰهُمَّ لَا يَأْتِي بِالْحَسَنَاتِ إِلَّا أَنْتَ وَلَا يَذْهَبُ

بِالسَّيِّئَاتِ إِلَّا أَنْتَ وَلَا حَوْلَ وَلَا قُوَّةَ إِلَّا بِاللهِ الْعَلِيِّ

الْعَظِيمِ ﴿٣﴾

أَدْعِيَةٌ مُتَعَلِّقَةٌ بِأَحْوَالٍ مُخْتَلِفَةٍ

PRAYERS FOR DIFFERENT OCCASIONS

1. O Allah! Bless us in our fruit, and bless us in our city. Bless us in our *saa'* and bless us in our *mudd*! [5]

When one sees a Muslim laughing

2. May Allah always keep you smiling!

When seeing somebody who is afflicted

3. Praise be to Allah Who has protected me from that with which He has afflicted you and Who has greatly favored me over many of His creation.

---

[5] These are terms of measurement for crops used in the Arab world.

اَللّٰهُمَّ بَارِكْ لَنَا فِي ثَمَرِنَا وَبَارِكْ لَنَا فِي مَدِينَتِنَا وَبَارِكْ لَنَا فِي صَاعِنَا وَبَارِكْ لَنَا فِي مُدِّنَا ﴿١﴾

وَإِذَا رَأَى الْمُسْلِمَ يَضْحَكُ يَقُولُ:
أَضْحَكَ اللّٰهُ سِنَّكَ ﴿٢﴾

وَإِذَا رَأَى مُبْتَلَىً يَقُولُ:
اَلْحَمْدُ لِلّٰهِ الَّذِي عَافَانِي مِمَّا ابْتَلَاكَ بِهِ وَفَضَّلَنِي عَلَى كَثِيرٍ مِمَّنْ خَلَقَ تَفْضِيلاً ﴿٣﴾

If one sees something one loves

1. Praise be to Allah by whose grace righteous deeds are fulfilled!

If one sees something one hates

2. Praise is due to Allah in every situation.

When looking at one's face in the mirror

3. All praise belongs to Allah. O Allah! You granted me a good physical form, so grant me good character and guard my face from the Hellfire![4]

4. All praise is due to Allah who made good my creation, making it proportionate and who gave my creation its form and beautified it. It is He who made me among the Muslims and gave me a fair appearance, beautifying in me what is disfigured in some others.

On seeing the first fruit ripen

5. O Allah! As You have shown us its first [fruit], so also show us the following!

---

[4] Literally "make my face forbidden to the Hellfire!"

إِذَا رَأَى مَا يُحِبُّهُ يَقُولُ:

اَلْحَمْدُ للهِ الَّذِي بِنِعْمَتِهِ تَتِمُّ الصَّالِحَاتُ ﴿١﴾

وَإِذَا رَأَى مَا يَكْرَهُهُ يَقُولُ:

اَلْحَمْدُ للهِ عَلَى كُلِّ حَالٍ ﴿٢﴾

وَإِذَا رَأَى وَجْهَهُ فِي الْمِرْآةِ يَقُولُ:

اَلْحَمْدُ للهِ، اَللَّهُمَّ أَنْتَ حَسَّنْتَ خَلْقِي فَحَسِّنْ خُلُقِي
وَحَرِّمْ وَجْهِي عَلَى النَّارِ ﴿٣﴾ اَلْحَمْدُ للهِ الَّذِي سَوَّى
خَلْقِي فَعَدَّلَهُ وَصَوَّرَ صُورَةَ خَلْقِي فَأَحْسَنَهَا وَجَعَلَنِي
مِنَ الْمُسْلِمِينَ وَأَحْسَنَ صُورَتِي وَزَانَ مِنِّي مَا شَانَ مِنْ
غَيْرِي ﴿٤﴾

وَإِذَا رَأَى بَاكُورَةَ ثَمَرَةٍ يَقُولُ:

اَللَّهُمَّ كَمَآ أَرَيْتَنَا أَوَّلَهُ فَأَرِنَا اٰخِرَهُ ﴿٥﴾

After buying an animal or something similar

The one holds it at the top of its hump (or equivalent) and says:

1. O Allah! Verily I ask of You its goodness, and the goodness that You molded it with, and I seek refuge in You from its evil and the evil that You molded it with.

After being blessed with a child

2. The parent makes the *adhan* (call to prayer) in its ear, chews a piece of date and rubs it around the baby's gums, and then makes the following supplication:

I take refuge in the perfect words of Allah, from all devils and harmful animals, and from every evil eye.

When the child starts to speak

3. Let its first words be: "There is no god but Allah."

If one sees another Muslim wearing a new item of clothing

4. You wore out [your clothes] and then Allah replaced them. Wear them to shreds, then wear them to shreds, then wear them to shreds again.[3]

---

[3] Meaning: "Each time you wear them out may Allah replace them with new clothes, and then may you wear those out, so that Allah may replace them again," and so on. The supplicant is thereby praying for that person to have a long life in a state of grace.

وَإِذَا اشْتَرَى حَيَوَانًا أَوْ مَا يُشَابِهُهُ:

يأخذ بذروة سنامه ويقول:

اَللّهُمَّ إِنِّي أَسْأَلُكَ خَيْرَهَا وَخَيْرَ مَا جَبَلْتَهَا عَلَيْهِ

وَأَعُوذُ بِكَ مِنْ شَرِّهَا وَشَرِّ مَا جَبَلْتَهَا عَلَيْهِ ﴿١﴾

وَإِذَا أُتِيَ بِمَوْلُودٍ:

يؤذّن في أُذنِك ويحنّك له بتمرة ويدعو له بهذه الكلمات:

أَعُوذُ بِكَلِمَاتِ اللهِ التَّامَّةِ مِنْ كُلِّ شَيْطَانٍ وَهَامَّةٍ

وَمِنْ كُلِّ عَيْنٍ لَآمَّةٍ ﴿٢﴾

وَإِذَا أَفْصَحَ الْوَلَدُ:

فلتكن أول كلمة يقولها: "لَا إِلهَ إِلَّا اللهُ" ﴿٣﴾

وَإِذَا رَأَى عَلَى الْمُسْلِمِ ثَوْبًا جَدِيدًا يَقُولُ:

تُبْلِي وَيُخْلِفُ اللهُ، أَبْلِ وَأَخْلِقْ ثُمَّ أَبْلِ وَأَخْلِقْ ثُمَّ

أَبْلِ وَأَخْلِقْ ﴿٤﴾

1. There is no god but Allah, alone without associate. His is the dominion, and all praise is to Him. He gives life and brings death, but He is the All-Living who never dies. All goodness is in His hands, and He has power over all things.

On returning from the market

One reads ten verses of the Holy Qur'an.

When one intends to leave a meeting

2. "Transcendent is Your Lord, Lord of Honor and Might, above all that they ascribe to Him. Peace be upon the Messengers and all praise be to Allah, the Lord of the worlds." (Saffat 37:180-2)

3. Glory be to You, O Allah, and to You be praise! I bear witness that there is no god but You, I seek Your forgiveness, and to You I turn in repentance.(3)

4. I have acted badly, and have wronged myself, so forgive me, for no one forgives sins except You.

If a person sees something that appeals to him

5. O Allah! Bless (me by) this.

لَا إِلٰهَ إِلَّا اللهُ وَحْدَهُ لَا شَرِيكَ لَهُ، لَهُ الْمُلْكُ وَلَهُ الْحَمْدُ يُحْيِي وَيُمِيتُ وَهُوَ حَيٌّ لَا يَمُوتُ بِيَدِهِ الْخَيْرُ وَهُوَ عَلٰى كُلِّ شَيْءٍ قَدِيرٌ ﴿١﴾

وَإِذَا رَجَعَ مِنَ السُّوقِ:

يقرأ عشر آيات من القرآن الكريم.

وَإِذَا أَرَادَ الْخُرُوجَ مِنَ الْمَجْلِسِ يَقُولُ:

﴿سُبْحَانَ رَبِّكَ رَبِّ الْعِزَّةِ عَمَّا يَصِفُونَ ۝ وَسَلَامٌ عَلَى الْمُرْسَلِينَ ۝ وَالْحَمْدُ لِلّٰهِ رَبِّ الْعَالَمِينَ﴾ ﴿٢﴾

سُبْحَانَكَ اللّٰهُمَّ بِحَمْدِكَ أَشْهَدُ أَنْ لَا إِلٰهَ إِلَّا أَنْتَ أَسْتَغْفِرُكَ وَأَتُوبُ إِلَيْكَ (٣) عَمِلْتُ سُوءًا وَظَلَمْتُ نَفْسِي فَاغْفِرْ لِي إِنَّهُ لَا يَغْفِرُ الذُّنُوبَ إِلَّا أَنْتَ ﴿٤﴾

وَإِذَا رَأَى شَيْئًا يُعْجِبُهُ يَقُولُ:

اَللّٰهُمَّ بَارِكْ فِيهِ ﴿٥﴾

Putting on a new garment

1. O Allah! To You is due all praise for You dressed me in it. I ask You for good in it and the good it was made for.

2. And I seek refuge in You from evil in it and the evil it was made for.

3. Praise be to Allah who has provided for me clothing with which to cover my private parts and to adorn myself in my life.

4. Praise be to Allah who dressed me in this, and provided it for me without any strength or power on my part.

Going to the market place

5. There is no god but Allah, alone without associate. His is the dominion, and all praise is to Him. He gives life and brings death, but He is the All-Living who never dies. All goodness is in His hands, and He has power over all things.

6. In the name of Allah, O Allah, I ask of You the good of this market and the goodness within it, and I seek refuge in You from its evil and the evil within it.

7. O Allah! Verily I seek refuge in You from any suffering at this market [that might come about because] of a false oath or a poor deal.

إِذَا لَبِسَ ثَوْباً جَدِيداً يَقُولُ:

اَللّٰهُمَّ لَكَ الْحَمْدُ أَنْتَ كَسَوْتَنِيهِ أَسْأَلُكَ خَيْرَهُ وَخَيْرَ مَاصُنِعَ لَهُ ﴿١﴾ وَأَعُوذُ بِكَ مِنْ شَرِّهِ وَشَرِّ مَا صُنِعَ لَهُ ﴿٢﴾ اَلْحَمْدُ لِلّٰهِ الَّذِي كَسَانِي مَا أُوَارِي بِهِ عَوْرَتِي وَأَتَجَمَّلُ بِهِ فِي حَيَاتِي ﴿٣﴾ اَلْحَمْدُ لِلّٰهِ الَّذِي كَسَانِي هٰذَا وَرَزَقَنِيهِ مِنْ غَيْرِ حَوْلٍ مِنِّي وَلَا قُوَّةٍ ﴿٤﴾

وَإِذَا خَرَجَ إِلَى السُّوقِ يَقُولُ:

لَا إِلٰهَ إِلَّا اللّٰهُ وَحْدَهُ لَا شَرِيكَ لَهُ، لَهُ الْمُلْكُ وَلَهُ الْحَمْدُ يُحْيِي وَيُمِيتُ وَهُوَ حَيٌّ لَا يَمُوتُ بِيَدِهِ الْخَيْرُ وَهُوَ عَلَى كُلِّ شَيْءٍ قَدِيرٌ ﴿٥﴾ بِسْمِ اللّٰهِ اللّٰهُمَّ إِنِّي أَسْأَلُكَ خَيْرَ هٰذِهِ السُّوقِ وَخَيْرَ مَا فِيهَا وَأَعُوذُ بِكَ مِنْ شَرِّهَا وَشَرِّ مَا فِيهَا ﴿٦﴾ اَللّٰهُمَّ إِنِّي أَعُوذُ بِكَ أَنْ أُصِيبَ فِيهَا يَمِيناً فَاجِرَةً أَوْ صَفْقَةً خَاسِرَةً ﴿٧﴾

أَدْعِيَةٌ مُتَعَلِّقَةٌ بِأُمُورِ الشَّخْصِ
وَحَالَاتِهِ الْمُخْتَلِفَةِ

EVERYDAY LIFE SITUATIONS

At the time of a solar eclipse

When one witnesses an eclipse he/she supplicates Allah, magnifies His greatness, performs ritual prayer, makes charitable donations and seeks Allah's forgiveness.

When one sees the new moon

1. Allah is the Greatest! Praise be to Allah! There is no strength or power except in Allah.

2. O Allah! Verily I ask You to grant me the good of this month, and I take refuge in You from the evil of the [Day of] the Gathering.

3. Allah is the Greatest! O Allah! Let this crescent moon shine upon us with prosperity, faith, safety, Islam, and success in what You love and what pleases You! (Addressing the moon): My Lord and Your Lord is Allah, O crescent of goodness and guidance! (3)

4. O Allah! I ask You of the good of this month, and the good that destiny brings, and I seek refuge in You from the evil it may bring. (3)

5. O Allah! Let [this new moon] rise upon us with security, faith, well-being, Islam, the good pleasure of the All-Merciful, and protection from Satan!

When one looks at the moon

6. I seek refuge in Allah from the evil of (the moon of) this dark night.

دُعَاءُ الْكُسُوفِ:

إذا رأى الكسوف يدعو الله ويكبره ويصلي ويتصدق ويستغفر.

إِذَا رَأَى الْهِلاَلَ يَقُولُ:

اَللهُ أَكْبَرُ، اَلْحَمْدُ لله وَلاَ حَوْلَ وَلاَ قُوَّةَ إِلاَّ بِالله ﴿١﴾ اَللّٰهُمَّ إِنِّي أَسْأَلُكَ خَيْرَ هٰذَا الشَّهْرِ وَأَعُوذُ بِكَ مِنْ سُوءِ الْمَحْشَرِ ﴿٢﴾ اَللهُ أَكْبَرُ، اَللّٰهُمَّ أَهِلَّهُ عَلَيْنَا بِالْيُمْنِ وَالْإِيمَانِ وَالسَّلامَةِ وَالْإِسْلامِ وَالتَّوْفِيقِ لِمَا تُحِبُّ وَتَرْضَى، رَبِّي وَرَبُّكَ اللهُ هِلالَ خَيْرٍ وَرُشْدٍ (٣) ﴿٣﴾ اَللّٰهُمَّ إِنِّي أَسْأَلُكَ مِنْ خَيْرِ هٰذَا الشَّهْرِ وَخَيْرِ الْقَدَرِ وَأَعُوذُ بِكَ مِنْ شَرِّهِ (٣) ﴿٤﴾ اَللّٰهُمَّ أَدْخِلْهُ عَلَيْنَا بِالْأَمْنِ وَالْإِيمَانِ وَالسَّلامَةِ وَالْإِسْلامِ وَرِضْوَانٍ مِنَ الرَّحْمٰنِ وَحَذَارٍ مِنَ الشَّيْطَانِ ﴿٥﴾

وَإِذَا نَظَرَ إِلَى الْقَمَرِ يَقُولُ:

أَعُوذُ بِالله مِنْ شَرِّ هٰذَا الْغَاسِقِ ﴿٦﴾

٩٣

When the wind blows up

If the wind blows up he turns his face toward it, kneels down, and stretches out his hands, saying:

1. O Allah! I ask You of its good, the goodness that it contains, and the goodness it was sent with, and I take refuge in You from its evil, the evil it contains and the evil it was sent with.

2. O Allah! Make it a multitude of winds, and not a mere gust! O Allah! Make it a mercy and not a punishment!

If the wind comes with darkness

When the wind comes with darkness he seeks refuge in Allah firstly by reading the suras of refuge (al-Falaq and al-Nas) and then says:

3. O Allah! Verily I ask You of the good of this wind, the goodness it contains, and the good it was sent for.

4. And I take refuge in You from the evil of this wind, the evil it contains, and the evil it was sent for.

5. O Allah! [Let it bring about] germination, not barrenness!

إِذَا هَاجَتِ الرِّيحُ:

إذا هاجت الريح يستقبلها بوجهه ويجثو على ركبتيه ويمدّ يديه ثم يقول:

اَللّٰهُمَّ إِنِّيٓ أَسْأَلُكَ خَيْرَهَا وَخَيْرَ مَا فِيهَا وَخَيْرَ مَآ أُرْسِلَتْ بِهٖ وَأَعُوذُ بِكَ مِنْ شَرِّهَا وَشَرِّ مَا فِيهَا وَشَرِّ مَآ أُرْسِلَتْ بِهٖ ۞

اَللّٰهُمَّ اجْعَلْهَا رِيَاحًا وَلَا تَجْعَلْهَا رِيحًا، اَللّٰهُمَّ اجْعَلْهَا رَحْمَةً وَلَا تَجْعَلْهَا عَذَابًا ۞

وَإِنْ جَاءَ مَعَ الرِّيحِ ظُلْمَةٌ:

وإن جاء مع الريح ظلمة يتعوذ بالمعوذتين ثم يقول:

اَللّٰهُمَّ إِنِّيٓ أَسْأَلُكَ مِنْ خَيْرِ هٰذِهِ الرِّيحِ وَخَيْرِ مَا فِيهَا وَخَيْرِ مَآ أُمِرَتْ بِهٖ ۞ وَأَعُوذُ بِكَ مِنْ شَرِّ هٰذِهِ الرِّيحِ وَشَرِّ مَا فِيهَا وَشَرِّ مَآ أُمِرَتْ بِهٖ ۞ اَللّٰهُمَّ لَقْحًا لَا عَقِيمًا ۞

When one sees a cloud

1. O Allah! Truly we take refuge in You from any evil that may be sent down by it.

   O Allah! [Make it] a rain cloud that brings benefit!

In times of drought

2. O Lord! O Lord!

On seeing some rain

3. O Allah, grant us abundant and beneficial rain! (3)

If the rainfall increases to the point where damage is feared

4. O Allah! Send it down in our vicinity, and not upon us!

   O Allah! [Send it down] on the hills, mountains, high plains and valleys [so that it reaches] the roots of the trees!

When one hears thunder or [sees] lightning

5. O Allah! Don't slay us by Your wrath, or destroy us by Your punishment, but save us before it gets to that point.

6. Glorified be the One whom "the thunder glorifies [with] His praise, and the angels in awe of Him." (Ra'd 13:13)

إِذَا رَأَى سَحَابًا يَقُولُ:

اَللّٰهُمَّ إِنَّا نَعُوذُ بِكَ مِنْ شَرِّ مَا أُرْسِلَ بِهِ، اَللّٰهُمَّ صَيِّبًا نَافِعًا ①

وَإِذَا قَحَطَ الْمَطَرُ يَقُولُ:

يَارَبِّ يَارَبِّ ②

وَإِذَا رَأَى الْمَطَرَ يَقُولُ:

اَللّٰهُمَّ صَيِّبًا نَافِعًا (٣) ③

وَإِذَا كَثُرَ الْمَطَرُ وَخَشِيَ الضَّرَرَ يَقُولُ:

اَللّٰهُمَّ حَوَالَيْنَا وَلاَ عَلَيْنَا، اَللّٰهُمَّ عَلَى الْأَكَامِ وَالْجِبَالِ وَالظِّرَابِ وَالْأَوْدِيَةِ وَمَنَابِتِ الشَّجَرِ ④

وَإِذَا سَمِعَ الرَّعْدَ وَالصَّوَاعِقَ يَقُولُ:

اَللّٰهُمَّ لاَ تَقْتُلْنَا بِغَضَبِكَ وَلاَ تُهْلِكْنَا بِعَذَابِكَ وَعَافِنَا قَبْلَ ذٰلِكَ ⑤ سُبْحَانَ الَّذِي يُسَبِّحُ الرَّعْدُ بِحَمْدِهِ وَالْمَلَئِكَةُ مِنْ خِيفَتِهِ ⑥

٩١

أَدْعِيَةٌ مُتَعَلِّقَةٌ بِالْأُمُورِ الْعُلْوِيَّةِ

PRAYERS RELATED TO
WHAT IS IN THE SKY OR
COMES FROM IT

When the husband moves in with his spouse

1. O Allah, truly I ask You for her good and the goodness You molded her with, and I seek Your protection from her evil, and the evil You molded her with. (Wife prays in the same way as well)

2. O Allah! Truly You have power, but I have none, and You know, but I know not, and You are the Knower of the unseen. So, if You see that such and such a person (the name of the person is mentioned) is good for me in my religion, my life (in this world), and my Hereafter, ordain her/him for me, but if there is somebody else who would be better for me than them in my religion, my life (in this world), and my Hereafter, ordain that person for me (instead).

When they are about to have sexual intercourse

3. In the name of Allah, keep us away from Satan, and keep Satan away from what You grant us [in the way of children].

وَإِذَا دَخَلَ عَلَى أَهْلِهِ يَقُولُ:

اَللَّهُمَّ إِنِّي أَسْأَلُكَ خَيْرَهَا وَخَيْرَ مَا جَبَلْتَهَا عَلَيْهِ وَأَعُوذُ
بِكَ مِنْ شَرِّهَا وَشَرِّ مَا جَبَلْتَهَا عَلَيْهِ ﴿١﴾

اَللَّهُمَّ إِنَّكَ تَقْدِرُ وَلَا أَقْدِرُ وَتَعْلَمُ وَلَا أَعْلَمُ وَأَنْتَ
عَلَّامُ الْغُيُوبِ، فَإِنْ رَأَيْتَ أَنَّ فُلَانَةَ (يسميها باسمها)
خَيْرٌ لِي فِي دِينِي وَدُنْيَايَ وَآخِرَتِي فَاقْدُرْهَا لِي، وَإِنْ
كَانَ غَيْرُهَا خَيْرًا لِي مِنْهَا فِي دِينِي وَدُنْيَايَ وَآخِرَتِي
فَاقْدُرْهَا لِي ﴿٢﴾

وَإِذَا أَرَادَ الْجِمَاعَ يَقُولُ:

بِسْمِ اللهِ، اَللَّهُمَّ جَنِّبْنَا الشَّيْطَانَ وَجَنِّبِ الشَّيْطَانَ مَا
رَزَقْتَنَا ﴿٣﴾

Marriage

The marriage sermon

1. Verily all praise is due to Allah. We praise Him, seek His aid, and beg His forgiveness. And we take refuge in Him from the evil of our selves and from our misdeeds.

2. Whomsoever Allah guides no one can lead astray, and whomsoever He leads astray no one can guide. I bear witness that there is no god but Allah, alone without associate, and I bear witness that Muhammad is His servant and His Messenger.

3. "O you who believe, fear Allah and say what is right." (Ahzab 33:70)

To the one who has got married

4. May Allah bless your (spouse) for you, bless you, and join you in happy union.

اَلنّكَاحُ

خُطْبَةُ النّكَاحِ:

إِنَّ الْحَمْدَ لِلّٰهِ نَحْمَدُهُ وَنَسْتَعِينُهُ وَنَسْتَغْفِرُهُ وَنَعُوذُ بِاللّٰهِ مِنْ شُرُورِ أَنْفُسِنَا وَمِنْ سَيِّئَاتِ أَعْمَالِنَا ﴿١﴾ مَنْ يَهْدِ اللّٰهُ فَلاَ مُضِلَّ لَهُ وَمَنْ يُضْلِلْ فَلاَ هَادِيَ لَهُ، وَأَشْهَدُ أَنْ لَآ إِلٰهَ إِلَّا اللّٰهُ وَحْدَهُ لَا شَرِيكَ لَهُ وَأَشْهَدُ أَنَّ مُحَمَّدًا عَبْدُهُ وَرَسُولُهُ ﴿٢﴾

﴿يَآ أَيُّهَا الَّذِينَ اٰمَنُوا اتَّقُوا اللّٰهَ وَقُولُوا قَوْلًا سَدِيدًا﴾ ﴿٣﴾

وَيُقَالُ لِمَنْ تَزَوَّجَ:

بَارَكَ اللّٰهُ لَكَ وَبَارَكَ عَلَيْكَ وَجَمَعَ بَيْنَكُمَا فِي خَيْرٍ ﴿٤﴾

٨٨

1. O Allah! I ask You for security on the day of fear. O Allah! Truly I seek refuge in You from the evil of that which You have given us, and from the evil of that which You have denied us.

2. O Allah make faith beloved to us, endearing it to our hearts, and make unbelief, impiety and disobedience hateful to us, and make us among the rightly guided!

3. O Allah! Take our souls as Muslims and join us with the righteous without trial or humiliation!

4. O Allah! Slay the unbelievers for they deny the Day of Judgment, Your messengers, and obstruct people from Your path! Send Your affliction and punishment on them, O God of truth! Amin.

اَللّٰهُمَّ إِنِّي أَسْأَلُكَ الْأَمَانَ يَوْمَ الْخَوْفِ، اَللّٰهُمَّ إِنِّي

عَائِذٌ بِكَ مِنْ شَرِّ مَا أَعْطَيْتَنَا وَمِنْ شَرِّ مَا مَنَعْتَنَا ﴿١﴾

اَللّٰهُمَّ حَبِّبْ إِلَيْنَا الْإِيمَانَ وَزَيِّنْهُ فِي قُلُوبِنَا وَكَرِّهْ إِلَيْنَا

الْكُفْرَ وَالْفُسُوقَ وَالْعِصْيَانَ وَاجْعَلْنَا مِنَ الرَّاشِدِينَ ﴿٢﴾

اَللّٰهُمَّ تَوَفَّنَا مُسْلِمِينَ وَأَلْحِقْنَا بِالصَّالِحِينَ غَيْرَ خَزَايَا

وَلَا مَفْتُونِينَ ﴿٣﴾

اَللّٰهُمَّ قَاتِلِ الْكَفَرَةَ الَّذِينَ يُكَذِّبُونَ بِيَوْمِ الدِّينِ

وَيُكَذِّبُونَ بِرُسُلِكَ وَيَصُدُّونَ عَنْ سَبِيلِكَ وَاجْعَلْ عَلَيْهِمْ

رِجْزَكَ وَعَذَابَكَ إِلٰهَ الْحَقِّ. اٰمِينَ ﴿٤﴾

When besieged by the enemy

1. O Allah! Conceal our imperfections and calm our fears!

After victory

The commander straightens the ranks of the troops and then says:

2. O Allah! To You belongs all praise. There is no one who can hold back what You have laid open; and no one can lay open what You have held back. No one can guide those whom You mislead, and no one can mislead those whom You guide. There is no one who can bestow what You have denied, and no one can deny what You have bestowed; no one can bring near one whom You have distanced, and no one can distance one whom You have brought near.

3. O Allah! Shower upon us Your blessings, Your mercy, Your bounty and Your provision!

4. O Allah! Verily I ask You for lasting grace which neither changes nor disappears.

وَإِنْ حَصَرَهُمْ عَدُوٌّ يَقُولُونَ:

اَللّٰهُمَّ اسْتُرْ عَوْرَاتِنَا وَآمِنْ رَوْعَاتِنَا ﴿١﴾

وَإِذَا حَصَلَ النَّصْرُ:

يُسَوِّي الْإِمَامُ الْجُيُوشَ صُفُوفاً ثُمَّ يَقُولُ:

اَللّٰهُمَّ لَكَ الْحَمْدُ كُلُّهُ، لَا قَابِضَ لِمَا بَسَطْتَ وَلَا

بَاسِطَ لِمَا قَبَضْتَ وَلَا هَادِيَ لِمَآ أَضْلَلْتَ وَلَا مُضِلَّ لِمَنْ

هَدَيْتَ وَلَا مُعْطِيَ لِمَا مَنَعْتَ وَلَا مَانِعَ لِمَآ أَعْطَيْتَ وَلَا

مُقَرِّبَ لِمَا بَاعَدْتَ وَلَا مُبَاعِدَ لِمَا قَرَّبْتَ ﴿٢﴾

اَللّٰهُمَّ ابْسُطْ عَلَيْنَا مِنْ بَرَكَاتِكَ وَرَحْمَتِكَ وَفَضْلِكَ

وَرِزْقِكَ ﴿٣﴾

اَللّٰهُمَّ إِنِّيٓ أَسْأَلُكَ النَّعِيمَ الْمُقِيمَ الَّذِي لَا يَحُولُ

وَلَا يَزُولُ ﴿٤﴾

1. "O people! Do not wish to encounter Your enemy, rather ask Allah for preservation [from them]. However, when you meet your enemy show fortitude and know that Paradise is under the shadow of swords."

   Then he makes the following supplication:

2. O Allah, the One who sends down the Book, drives forth the clouds and confounds armies! Vanquish them and grant us victory over them!

If the army look down on the dwelling place of their enemy

3. Allah is the Greatest! May (he names the place) be destroyed!

   Indeed when We descend on the dwelling place of a people, wretched is the morning [after] for those who had been warned. (Saffat 37:177) (3)

Experiencing fear of the enemy

4. O Allah! Verily we leave their defeat to You, and we seek refuge in You from their evil.

''يَا أَيُّهَا النَّاسُ لَا تَمَنَّوْا لِقَاءَ الْعَدُوِّ وَاسْأَلُوا اللهُ الْعَافِيَةَ، فَإِذَا لَقِيتُمُوهُمْ فَاصْبِرُوا وَاعْلَمُوا أَنَّ الْجَنَّةَ تَحْتَ ظِلَالِ السُّيُوفِ'' ①

ثم يدعو هكذا: اَللّٰهُمَّ مُنْزِلَ الْكِتَابِ وَمُجْرِيَ السَّحَابِ وَهَازِمَ الْأَحْزَابِ اِهْزِمْهُمْ وَانْصُرْنَا عَلَيْهِمْ ②

وَإِذَا أَشْرَفَ الْجُنُودُ عَلَى بَلَدِ الْعَدُوِّ يَقُولُونَ: اَللهُ أَكْبَرُ خَرِبَتْ ...(يسمون البلد)، إِنَّا إِذَا نَزَلْنَا بِسَاحَةِ قَوْمٍ فَسَاءَ صَبَاحُ الْمُنْذَرِينَ (٣) ③

وَإِذَا خَافُوا مِنَ الْعَدُوِّ يَقُولُونَ: اَللّٰهُمَّ إِنَّا نَجْعَلُكَ فِي نُحُورِهِمْ وَنَعُوذُ بِكَ مِنْ شُرُورِهِمْ ④

At the Time of War

The prayer made on the occasion of war

When the Muslims are in a situation to engage in war (minor jihad) the commander says:

1. Attack in the name of Allah, and do not commit excesses, act treacherously, mutilate the faces of the dead of your enemy, or kill any children!

Then he makes the following supplication:

2. O Allah! You are my support and my helper to victory. From You I take strength, by You I assail, and by You I fight.

Encountering the enemy

The commander waits for the appropriate moment and then counsels the army with the words of the Prophet (peace and blessings be upon him) or with something similar saying:

اَلْجِهَادُ

دُعَاءُ الْجِهَادِ:

إذا أراد المسلمون الجهاد يقول الأمير:

اُغْزُوا بِسْمِ اللهِ، وَلاَ تَغُلُّوا، وَلاَ تَغْدِرُوا، وَلاَ تَمْثُلُوا، وَلاَ تَقْتُلُوا وَلِيداً ❶

ثم يدعو هكذا: اَللّٰهُمَّ أَنْتَ عَضُدِي وَنَصِيرِي، بِكَ أَحُولُ وَبِكَ أَصُولُ وَبِكَ أُقَاتِلُ ❷

وَعِنْدَ لِقَاءِ الْعَدُوِّ:

ينتظر الأمير الوقت المناسب ثم ينصح كما نصح به النبي ﷺ أو ما يشبهه، مثل:

٨٤

At the time of stoning

One can make whatever supplications one likes during the stoning, apart from at the *Jamra* of 'Aqaba. When the stoning is finished one says:

1. O Allah! Make it a blessed Hajj with sins forgiven.

At the time of sacrifice

2. O Allah! Accept [this sacrifice] from me and from the nation of Muhammad (may Allah bless him and grant him peace)!

3. Allah is the Greatest! (3)

4. O Allah! [This is] from You, and goes back to You, in the name of Allah.

دُعَاءُ الْجِمَارِ:

يدعو عند الجمار ما بدا له سوى العقبة، وإذا فرغ يقول:

اَللّٰهُمَّ اجْعَلْهُ حَجًّا مَبْرُوراً وَذَنْباً مَغْفُوراً ﴿١﴾

وَيَقُولُ فِي الْأُضْحِيَّةِ:

اَللّٰهُمَّ تَقَبَّلْ مِنِّي وَمِنْ أُمَّةِ مُحَمَّدٍ ﷺ ﴿٢﴾

اَللهُ أَكْبَرُ (٣) ﴿٣﴾

اَللّٰهُمَّ مِنْكَ وَإِلَيْكَ بِسْمِ اللهِ ﴿٤﴾

1. O Allah! Open my heart, and make my affairs easy for me! I seek refuge in You from the evil whisperings felt at the heart, from that which disrupts my affairs and from the trial of the grave.

2. O Allah! Truly I seek refuge in You from the evil of what enters the night, the evil of what enters the day, and from the evil that blows in the wind.

While performing waqfa

(pausing at 'Arafat and Muzdalifa)

3. Allah is the Greatest and to Allah be praise! Allah is the Greatest and to Allah be praise! Allah is the Greatest and to Allah be praise!

4. There is no god but Allah, alone without associate. His is the dominion, to Him belongs all praise.

5. O Allah! Lead me with Your guidance, cleanse me with piety, and forgive me in the Hereafter and in this life.

   Then one puts down one's hands, pauses and then raises them up again in supplication and continues with one's supplication as much as one can.

On arrival at the Mash'ar al Haram (the sacred sanctuary)

5. One makes *takbir*, and *tahlil* (*La ilaha illa Allah*) recites the *Labbayk* refrain repeatedly, and remains standing until the sky becomes pale with the dawn.

اَللَّهُمَّ اشْرَحْ لِي صَدْرِي وَيَسِّرْ لِي أَمْرِي وَأَعُوذُ
بِكَ مِنْ وَسَاوِسِ الصَّدْرِ وَشَتَاتِ الْأَمْرِ وَفِتْنَةِ الْقَبْرِ ﴿١﴾
اَللَّهُمَّ إِنِّي أَعُوذُ بِكَ مِنْ شَرِّ مَا يَلِجُ فِي اللَّيْلِ وَشَرِّ مَا
يَلِجُ فِي النَّهَارِ وَشَرِّ مَا تَهُبُّ بِهِ الرِّيَاحُ ﴿٢﴾

وَإِذَا وَقَفَ يَدْعُو هٰكَذَا:
اَللهُ أَكْبَرُ وَللهِ الْحَمْدُ، اَللهُ أَكْبَرُ وَللهِ الْحَمْدُ، اَللهُ أَكْبَرُ
وَللهِ الْحَمْدُ ﴿٣﴾ لَا إِلٰهَ إِلَّا اللهُ وَحْدَهُ لَا شَرِيكَ لَهُ، لَهُ
الْمُلْكُ وَلَهُ الْحَمْدُ ﴿٤﴾ اَللَّهُمَّ اهْدِنِي بِالْهُدٰى وَنَقِّنِي
بِالتَّقْوٰى وَاغْفِرْ لِي فِي الْآخِرَةِ وَالْأُولٰى ﴿٥﴾
ثم يرد يديه فيسكت ثم يرفع ويدعو ويصر بالدعاء.

وَإِذَا أَتَى الْمَشْعَرَ الْحَرَامَ:
يكبر الله ويهلله ويوحده ويلبّي ولا يزال واقفاً حتى يسفر
الصبح جداً.

٨٢

1. O Allah! Verily You have said: "Call on me, and I will answer You." (Baqara 2:186) And for sure You don't break Your promise. Truly I ask You, as You guided me to Islam, don't separate it from me until You take back my soul as a Muslim.

Between Safa and Marwa

2. O Allah! Forgive, and show mercy, for truly You are the Honored with irresistible Might, the All-Generous.

3. O Allah! Forgive, show mercy, and pardon what You know best about, for truly You are the Honored with irresistible Might, the All-Generous.

4. "Our Lord, grant us goodness in this life and in the Hereafter, and save us from the torment of the Hellfire!" (Baqara 2:201)

The supplication of 'Arafat

One recites the *Labbayk* refrain (At Your service!), makes *takbir* and then says the following:

5. There is no god but Allah, alone without associate. His is the dominion, to Him belongs all praise, and He has power over all things.

6. O Allah! Grant me light in my heart, light in my hearing and light in my sight!

اَللّٰهُمَّ إِنَّكَ قُلْتَ ﴿اُدْعُونِي أَسْتَجِبْ لَكُمْ﴾ وَإِنَّكَ لَا
تُخْلِفُ الْمِيعَادَ وَإِنِّي أَسْأَلُكَ كَمَا هَدَيْتَنِي لِلْإِسْلَامِ أَنْ
لَا تَنْزِعَهُ مِنِّي حَتّٰى تَتَوَفّانِي وَأَنَا مُسْلِمٌ ﴿١﴾

وَيَقُولُ بَيْنَ الصَّفَا وَالْمَرْوَةِ:

اَللّٰهُمَّ اغْفِرْ وَارْحَمْ وَأَنْتَ الْأَعَزُّ الْأَكْرَمُ ﴿٢﴾
اَللّٰهُمَّ اغْفِرْ وَارْحَمْ وَاعْفُ عَمَّا تَعْلَمُ إِنَّكَ أَنْتَ
الْأَعَزُّ الْأَكْرَمُ ﴿٣﴾ ﴿رَبَّنَا اٰتِنَا فِي الدُّنْيَا حَسَنَةً وَفِي
الْاٰخِرَةِ حَسَنَةً وَقِنَا عَذَابَ النَّارِ﴾ ﴿٤﴾

دُعَاءُ عَرَفَةَ:

يلبّي ويكبر ثم يقول:

لَا إِلٰهَ إِلَّا اللهُ وَحْدَهُ لَا شَرِيكَ لَهُ، لَهُ الْمُلْكُ وَلَهُ
الْحَمْدُ وَهُوَ عَلٰى كُلِّ شَيْءٍ قَدِيرٌ ﴿٥﴾ اَللّٰهُمَّ اجْعَلْ فِي
قَلْبِي نُوراً وَفِي سَمْعِي نُوراً وَفِي بَصَرِي نُوراً ﴿٦﴾

Then one supplicates with whatever one wishes from the prophetic or other supplications, and when the *tawaf* is completed one prays two *rak'as*. Then one returns to the Hajar al-Aswad, paying one's respects to it, and after that, makes one's way to Safa where one stands facing the *qibla*, proclaims the unity of Allah, magnifies His greatness, and makes the following supplication:

1. O Allah! Protect us through [adherence to] Your religion, through obedience to You and Your Messenger (peace and blessings be upon him); and keep us from [transgressing] the limits You have prescribed!

2. O Allah! Make us love You, and love Your angels, Your prophets, Your messengers, and Your righteous servants!

3. O Allah! Endear us to You, and to Your angels, Your prophets, Your messengers, and Your righteous servants!

4. O Allah! Facilitate our way to ease, and keep us away from hardship! Forgive us in the Hereafter, and in the here and now, and make us among the leaders of the pious!

5. There is no god but Allah, alone without associate. His is the dominion, to Him belongs all praise, and He has power over all things.

6. There is no god but Allah who has fulfilled His promise, supported his servant, and Who alone defeated the troops. There is no god but Allah, and we don't worship anything but Him, devoting ourselves in religion entirely to Him, despite the contempt of the unbelievers.

ثم يدعو ما بدا له من الأدعية المأثورة وغير المأثورة. فإذا فرغ من الطواف يصلي ركعتين ثم يرجع إلى الركن فيستلمه ثم يخرج على الصفا فيستقبل القبلة ويوحد الله ويكبره ثم يدعو هكذا:

اللّٰهُمَّ اعْصِمْنَا بِدِينِكَ وَطَوَاعِيَتِكَ وَطَوَاعِيَةِ رَسُولِكَ ﷺ وَجَنِّبْنَا حُـدُودَكَ ﴿١﴾ اللّٰهُمَّ اجْعَلْنَا نُحِبُّكَ وَنُحِبُّ مَلَائِكَتَكَ وَأَنْبِيَاءَكَ وَرُسُلَكَ وَنُحِبُّ عِبَادَكَ الصَّالِحِينَ ﴿٢﴾ اللّٰهُمَّ حَبِّبْنَا إِلَيْكَ وَإِلَى مَلَائِكَتِكَ وَإِلَى أَنْبِيَائِكَ وَرُسُلِكَ وَإِلَى عِبَادِكَ الصَّالِحِينَ ﴿٣﴾ اللّٰهُمَّ يَسِّرْنَا لِلْيُسْرَى وَجَنِّبْنَا الْعُسْرَى وَاغْفِرْ لَنَا فِي الْآخِرَةِ وَالْأُولَى وَاجْعَلْنَا مِنْ أَئِمَّةِ الْمُتَّقِينَ ﴿٤﴾ لَا إِلٰهَ إِلَّا اللهُ وَحْدَهُ لَا شَرِيكَ لَهُ، لَهُ الْمُلْكُ وَلَهُ الْحَمْدُ وَهُوَ عَلَى كُلِّ شَيْءٍ قَدِيرٌ ﴿٥﴾ لَا إِلٰهَ إِلَّا اللهُ وَحْدَهُ أَنْجَزَ وَعْدَهُ وَنَصَرَ عَبْدَهُ وَهَزَمَ الْأَحْزَابَ وَحْدَهُ، لَا إِلٰهَ إِلَّا اللهُ وَلَا نَعْبُدُ إِلَّا إِيَّاهُ مُخْلِصِينَ لَهُ الدِّينَ وَلَوْ كَرِهَ الْكَافِرُونَ ﴿٦﴾

1. "Our Lord! Grant us goodness in this life and in the Hereafter, and save us from the torment of the Hellfire," (Baqara 2:201) through Your mercy, O Most Merciful of the Merciful!

During tawaf

2. O Allah! Make me content with that with which You have provided me; bless me by it, and recompense those I have left behind with goodness!

3. There is no god but Allah, alone without associate. His is the dominion, to Him belongs all praise, and He has power over all things.

In the first three rounds of tawaf

4. O Allah! Make this a blessed pilgrimage, by which my sins are forgiven, and my efforts are rewarded.

In the last four rounds of tawaf

5. O Allah! Forgive, show mercy, and pardon what You know best about, for truly You are the All-Honored with irresistible Might, the All-Generous.

6. O Allah! "Our Lord! Grant us goodness in this life and goodness in the Hereafter, and save us from the torment of the Hellfire," (Baqara 2:201) through Your mercy, for You are the Most Merciful of the merciful.

﴿رَبَّنَا اٰتِنَا فِي الدُّنْيَا حَسَنَةً وَفِي الْاٰخِرَةِ حَسَنَةً وَقِنَا عَذَابَ النَّارِ﴾ بِرَحْمَتِكَ يَا أَرْحَمَ الرَّاحِمِينَ ﴿١﴾

وَيَدْعُو فِي الطَّوَافِ:

اَللّٰهُمَّ قَنِّعْنِي بِمَا رَزَقْتَنِي وَبَارِكْ لِي فِيهِ وَاخْلُفْ عَلَى كُلِّ غَائِبَةٍ لِي بِخَيْرٍ ﴿٢﴾ لَآ إِلٰهَ إِلَّا اللهُ وَحْدَهُ لَا شَرِيكَ لَهُ، لَهُ الْمُلْكُ وَلَهُ الْحَمْدُ وَهُوَ عَلَى كُلِّ شَيْءٍ قَدِيرٌ ﴿٣﴾

دُعَاءُ الْأَشْوَاطِ الثَّلَاثَةِ الْأُوْلَى:

اَللّٰهُمَّ اجْعَلْهُ حَجًّا مَبْرُورًا وَذَنْبًا مَغْفُورًا وَسَعْيًا مَشْكُورًا ﴿٤﴾

دُعَاءُ الْأَشْوَاطِ الْأَرْبَعَةِ الْاٰخِرَةِ:

اَللّٰهُمَّ اغْفِرْ وَارْحَمْ وَاعْفُ عَمَّا تَعْلَمُ وَأَنْتَ الْأَعَزُّ الْأَكْرَمُ ﴿٥﴾ اَللّٰهُمَّ رَبَّنَا اٰتِنَا فِي الدُّنْيَا حَسَنَةً وَفِي الْاٰخِرَةِ حَسَنَةً وَقِنَا عَذَابَ النَّارِ بِرَحْمَتِكَ يَا أَرْحَمَ الرَّاحِمِينَ ﴿٦﴾

The Hajj

(The Major Pilgrimage)

The pilgrim who intends to travel reads the same supplications as the normal traveler.

Putting on the ihram

(a garment made of two seamless white sheets or towels)

1. At Your beckoning and call, O Allah! At Your service! At Your service! No partner have You. At Your service! Truly praise and grace are Yours, and the dominion; no partner have You.

2. At Your beckoning and call! At Your service, and Your pleasure! All goodness is in Your hands; the aspiring turn to You, and all works are for You. At Your beckoning and call, God of truth! At Your service!

The tawaf

(the circumambulation round the Ka'ba)

The pilgrim circumambulates the Ka'ba, starting at the Hajar al-Aswad (Black Stone) and reads between the first two corners:

اَلْحَجُّ

إذا أراد الحاج السفر يقرأ من الأدعية ما يقرأه المسافر.

وَإِذَا أَحْرَمَ يَقُولُ:

لَبَّيْكَ اللّٰهُمَّ لَبَّيْكَ، لَبَّيْكَ لَا شَرِيكَ لَكَ لَبَّيْكَ، إِنَّ الْحَمْدَ وَالنِّعْمَةَ لَكَ وَالْمُلْكَ، لَا شَرِيكَ لَكَ ﴿١﴾ لَبَّيْكَ، لَبَّيْكَ وَسَعْدَيْكَ وَالْخَيْرُ بِيَدَيْكَ وَالرَّغْبَآءُ إِلَيْكَ وَالْعَمَلُ، لَبَّيْكَ لَبَّيْكَ إِلٰهَ الْحَقِّ لَبَّيْكَ ﴿٢﴾

اَلطَّوَافُ:

يطوف الكعبة ويبدأ الطواف بالركن (أي الحجر الأسود) ويقرأ بين الركنين:

1. There is no god but Allah, alone without associate. His is the dominion, to Him is all praise, and He has power over all things.

2. We return as repentant, worshipping, prostrating servants, our Lord, and You we praise.

3. Allah has fulfilled His promise, supported His servant, and Who alone defeated the troops (this is repeated several times).

Returning home or to the family

4. Repentant, repentant, to our Lord we return again! Leave not a [trace] of sin on us!

Arriving home during the day

5. All praise be to Allah who has sufficed me and granted me shelter!

6. Praise be to Allah, who fed me, and gave me to drink! Praise be to Allah who granted me His favor! I ask You to deliver me from the Hellfire.

Arriving home after a journey

Two *rak'a*s prayed in the normal way.

Returning from a victory

Eight *rak'a*s prayed in the normal way.

لَا إِلٰهَ إِلَّا اللهُ وَحْدَهُ لَا شَرِيكَ لَهُ، لَهُ الْمُلْكُ وَلَهُ الْحَمْدُ وَهُوَ عَلَى كُلِّ شَيْءٍ قَدِيرٌ ﴿١﴾ ايِبُونَ تَائِبُونَ عَابِدُونَ سَاجِدُونَ لِرَبِّنَا حَامِدُونَ ﴿٢﴾ صَدَقَ اللهُ وَعْدَهُ وَنَصَرَ عَبْدَهُ وَهَزَمَ الْأَحْزَابَ وَحْدَهُ (يكررها مرارًا) ﴿٣﴾

وَإِذَا رَجَعَ إِلَى بَيْتِهِ أَوْ أَهْلِهِ يَقُولُ:

تَوْبًا تَوْبًا لِرَبِّنَا أَوْبًا لَا يُغَادِرُ عَلَيْنَا حَوْبًا ﴿٤﴾

وَإِذَا دَخَلَ بَيْتَهُ نَهَارًا يَقُولُ:

اَلْحَمْدُ للهِ الَّذِي كَفَانِي وَاوَانِي ﴿٥﴾ اَلْحَمْدُ للهِ الَّذِي أَطْعَمَنِي وَسَقَانِي وَالْحَمْدُ للهِ الَّذِي مَنَّ عَلَيَّ، أَسْأَلُكَ أَنْ تُجِيرَنِي مِنَ النَّارِ ﴿٦﴾

صَلَاةُ الْقُدُومِ مِنَ السَّفَرِ:

صلاة القدوم ركعتان، تصلى كسائر الصلوات.

صَلَاةُ الْفَتْحِ:

صلاة الفتح ثماني ركعات، تصلى كسائر الصلوات.

٧٧

1. O our Lord (Allah)! Accompany us, and show us Your favor! [We ask this] seeking refuge in Allah from the Hellfire.

When one embarks on a boat

2. "In the name of Allah are its sailing and its mooring. My Lord is indeed the Most Forgiving, the All-Compassionate." (Hud 11:41)

3. "They do not revere Allah as He deserves to be revered. The earth altogether shall be [in] His grasp on the Day of Resurrection, and the heavens shall be rolled up in His right hand. Glory be to Him! Exalted is He above all that they associate with Him." (Zumar 39:67)

If a person intends to stay in a place

4. I take refuge in the perfect words of Allah from the evil of what He created.

5. O earth! My Lord and your Lord is Allah. I seek refuge in Allah from your evil, the evil that is in you, the evil of that which was created on you, and the evil of all that crawls on your surface.

6. O Allah! I seek refuge in You from lions, snakes and scorpions, from the inhabitants of this land, and from those who beget and what they beget.

On returning after a journey

When a person returns from a journey they make the same supplication as when they were about to travel, except that they add:

رَبَّنَا صَاحِبْنَا وَأَفْضِلْ عَلَيْنَا عَائِذاً بِاللهِ مِنَ النَّارِ ﴿١﴾

وَإِذَا رَكِبَ الْبَحْرَ يَقْرَأُ:

﴿بِسم اللهِ مَجْريها وَمُرْسيها إِنَّ رَبِّي لَغَفُورٌ رَحِيمٌ﴾ ﴿٢﴾

﴿وَمَا قَدَرُوا اللهَ حَقَّ قَدْرِه وَالْأَرْضُ جَمِيعاً قَبْضَتُهُ يَوْمَ الْقِيَامَةِ وَالسَّمٰوَاتُ مَطْوِيَّاتٌ بِيَمِينِه سُبْحَانَهُ وَتَعَالَى عَمَّا يُشْرِكُونَ﴾ ﴿٣﴾

وَإِذَا أَقَامَ بِأَرْضٍ يَقُولُ:

أَعُوذُ بِكَلِمَاتِ اللهِ التَّامَّاتِ مِنْ شَرِّ مَا خَلَقَ ﴿٤﴾ يَا أَرْضُ، رَبِّي وَرَبُّكِ اللهُ أَعُوذُ بِاللهِ مِنْ شَرِّكِ وَشَرِّ مَا فِيكِ وَشَرِّ مَا خُلِقَ فِيكِ وَشَرِّ مَا يَدِبُّ عَلَيْكِ ﴿٥﴾ اللّٰهُمَّ أَعُوذُ بِكَ مِنْ أَسَدٍ وَأَسْوَدَ وَمِنَ الْحَيَّةِ وَالْعَقْرَبِ وَمِنْ سَاكِنِ الْبَلَدِ وَمِنْ وَالِدٍ وَمَا وَلَدَ ﴿٦﴾

دُعَاءُ الرُّجُوعِ مِنَ السَّفَرِ:

وإذا رجع من السفر يدعو مثل ما دعا حين أراد الخروج ويزيد:

٧٦

1. I ask of You the good of this town, the good of its people, and the good within it, and I seek refuge in You from its evil, the evil of its people and the evil within it.

2. O Allah! I ask of You the good of this town and the good of whatever You have gathered within it, and I seek refuge in You from its evil and the evil of whatever You have gathered within it.

On entering the town

3. O Allah! Grant us its goodness and protect us from any disease that is in it! Endear us to its folk and endear its righteous folk to us! O Allah, bless us by it! (3)

For a good impression and to receive an increase in provision

They recite the following suras: al-Kafirun, al-Nasr, al-Ikhlas, al-Falaq, and al-Nas.

When going uphill, or downhill on one's journey

Every time one goes up hill one makes *takbir* (magnifies Allah's greatness with the words *Allahu Akbar!*), and when one goes downhill one makes *tasbih* (glorifies Allah with the words *subhan Allah!*).

While traveling at the time shortly before dawn

4. Let every hearer behold our praise of Allah and our [acknowledgement] of the great blessings He has bestowed upon us.

أَسْأَلُكَ خَيْرَ هٰذِهِ الْقَرْيَةِ وَخَيْرَ أَهْلِهَا وَخَيْرَ مَا فِيهَا

وَأَعُوذُ بِكَ مِنْ شَرِّهَا وَمِنْ شَرِّ أَهْلِهَا وَشَرِّ مَا فِيهَا (١)

اَللّٰهُمَّ إِنِّي أَسْأَلُكَ مِنْ خَيْرِ هٰذِهِ الْقَرْيَةِ وَخَيْرِ مَا جَمَعْتَ

فِيهَا وَأَعُوذُ بِكَ مِنْ شَرِّهَا وَشَرِّ مَا جَمَعْتَ فِيهَا (٢)

وَعِنْدَ دُخُوِلهِ الْبَلَدَ يَقُولُ:

اَللّٰهُمَّ ارْزُقْنَا حَيَاهَا وَأَعِذْنَا مِنْ وَبَاهَا وَحَبِّبْنَا إِلٰى أَهْلِهَا

وَحَبِّبْ صَالِحِي أَهْلِهَا إِلَيْنَا اَللّٰهُمَّ بَارِكْ لَنَا فِيهَا (٣)

إِذَا أَرَادَ حُسْنَ هَيْئَتِهِ وَنُمُوَّ زَادِهِ:

يقرأ سور "الكافرون" و "النصر" و "الإخلاص" و "المعوذتين"

إِذَا عَلاَ ثَنِيَّةً فِي سَفَرِهِ وَهَبَطَ مِنْهَا:

كلما علا ثنية في السفر كبّر وإذا هبط سبّح.

وَيَقُولُ وَقْتَ السَّحَرِ فِي سَفَرٍ:

سَمَّعَ سَامِعٌ بِحَمْدِ اللهِ وَحُسْنِ بَلاَئِهِ عَلَيْنَا (٤)

1. Praise be to Allah! "Glory be to He Who subjected this (riding beast/vehicle) to us for otherwise we would not have been able to manage it. ☙ And verily to our Lord we shall be returned." (Zukhruf 43:13-14)

   Glory be to You! Verily I have wronged myself, so forgive me, for no one can forgive sins except You.

2. O Allah! We ask of you on this journey, righteousness, piety, and actions that please You.

3. O Allah! Make our journey easy, and let us not feel its distance! O Allah! You are our Companion on the journey, and the Guardian over our families.

4. O Allah! I take refuge in You from the discomfort of travel, from every unpleasant sight, and from an ill-fated return to my wealth, wife, or children. [I also seek refuge] from deprivation after having plenty, and from the curse of those who are wronged.

On seeing one's destination

5. O Allah! Lord of the seven heavens and what they overshadow, the seven earths and what they bear! Lord of the devils and whomsoever they mislead, and Lord of the winds and that which they disperse!

اَلْحَمْدُ لله ﴿سُبْحَانَ الَّذِي سَخَّرَ لَنَا هٰذَا وَمَا كُنَّا لَهُ مُقْرِنِينَ ● وَإِنَّا إِلَى رَبِّنَا لَمُنْقَلِبُونَ﴾ سُبْحَانَكَ إِنِّي ظَلَمْتُ نَفْسِي فَاغْفِرْ لِي إِنَّهُ لَا يَغْفِرُ الذُّنُوبَ إِلَّا أَنْتَ (١) اَللّٰهُمَّ إِنَّا نَسْأَلُكَ فِي سَفَرِنَا هٰذَا الْبِرَّ وَالتَّقْوٰى وَمِنَ الْعَمَلِ مَا تَرْضٰى (٢) اَللّٰهُمَّ هَوِّنْ عَلَيْنَا سَفَرَنَا هٰذَا وَاطْوِ عَنَّا بُعْدَهُ، اَللّٰهُمَّ أَنْتَ الصَّاحِبُ فِي السَّفَرِ وَالْخَلِيفَةُ فِي الْأَهْلِ (٣) اَللّٰهُمَّ إِنِّي أَعُوذُ بِكَ مِنْ وَعْثَاءِ سَفَرٍ وَكَآبَةِ الْمَنْظَرِ وَسُوءِ الْمُنْقَلَبِ فِي الْمَالِ وَالْأَهْلِ وَالْوَلَدِ وَمِنَ الْحَوْرِ بَعْدَ الْكَوْرِ وَمِنْ دَعْوَةِ الْمَظْلُومِ (٤)

وَإِذَا رَأَى بَلَداً يَقْصِدُهُ يَقُولُ:

اَللّٰهُمَّ رَبَّ السَّمٰوَاتِ السَّبْعِ وَمَا أَظْلَلْنَ وَالْأَرَضِينَ السَّبْعِ وَمَا أَقْلَلْنَ وَرَبَّ الشَّيَاطِينِ وَمَا أَضْلَلْنَ وَرَبَّ الرِّيَاحِ وَمَا ذَرَيْنَ (٥)

1. May Allah increase you in piety, forgive you your sins, and open your way to goodness wherever you may be! May Allah make piety your journey's provision, forgive you your sins and direct goodness to you wherever you turn!

The traveler's prayer

2. I commit you to the care of Allah, whose charges are not forsaken or lost.

3. O Allah! By You I sally forth, from You I take strength, and by You I travel.

If one becomes afraid on his journey

4. He reads Surat al-Quraysh.

Boarding a vehicle or mounting a beast of burden

5. In the name of Allah, the All-Merciful, the All-Compassionate.

When mounted on the riding beast or seated in the vehicle

6. Allah be praised! (3), Allah is the Greatest! (3)

زَوَّدَكَ اللهُ التَّقْوٰى وَغَفَرَ اللهُ ذَنْبَكَ وَيَسَّرَ لَكَ الْخَيْرَ حَيْثُمَا كُنْتَ، جَعَلَ اللهُ التَّقْوٰى زَادَكَ وَغَفَرَ ذَنْبَكَ وَوَجَّهَ لَكَ الْخَيْرَ حَيْثُمَا تَوَجَّهْتَ ﴿١﴾

وَيَقُولُ الْمُسَافِرُ:

أَسْتَوْدِعُكَ اللهَ الَّذِي لَا تَخِيبُ وَلَا تَضِيعُ وَدَائِعُهُ ﴿٢﴾

اَللّٰهُمَّ بِكَ أَصُولُ وَبِكَ أَحُولُ وَبِكَ أَسِيرُ ﴿٣﴾

إِذَا خَافَ فِي سَفَرِهِ:

يَقْرَأُ سُورَةَ ﴿لِإِيلَافِ قُرَيْشٍ﴾ ﴿٤﴾

وَإِذَا وَضَعَ رِجْلَهُ فِي الرِّكَابِ يَقُولُ:

بِسْمِ اللهِ الرَّحْمٰنِ الرَّحِيمِ ﴿٥﴾

وَإِذَا اسْتَوٰى عَلَى ظَهْرِ مَطِيَّتِهِ يَقُولُ:

اَلْحَمْدُ لِلّٰهِ (٣)، اَللهُ أَكْبَرُ (٣) ﴿٦﴾

Zakat
(the obligatory alms)

If one intends to pay the zakat one says:

1. O Allah! Bless Muhammad, Your servant and Messenger, and [bless] the believing men and women, and the Muslim men and women!

Travel

If somebody intends to travel the one bidding him farewell enjoins on him the fear of Allah, and urges him to say the *takbir* (magnify Allah's greatness) at every hill on the way; while saying the following to him on his departure:

1. I consign to Allah the care of your religion, your trust, and your final actions, and I invoke peace over you.
2. O Allah! Make this journey easy so that its distance may be covered quickly!

اَلزَّكَاةُ

إِذَا أَرَادَ أَدَاءَ الزَّكَاةِ يَقُولُ:

اَللّٰهُمَّ صَلِّ عَلَى مُحَمَّدٍ عَبْدِكَ وَرَسُولِكَ وَعَلَى الْمُؤْمِنِينَ وَالْمُؤْمِنَاتِ وَالْمُسْلِمِينَ وَالْمُسْلِمَاتِ ﴿١﴾

اَلسَّفَرُ

إذا أراد أحد سفراً يوصيه المقيم بتقوى الله والتكبير على كل شرف ويقول له عند الخروج:

أَسْتَوْدِعُ اللهَ دِينَكَ وَأَمَانَتَكَ وَخَوَاتِيمَ عَمَلِكَ وَأَقْرَأُ عَلَيْكَ السَّلَامَ ﴿٢﴾ اَللّٰهُمَّ اطْوِ لَهُ الْبَعِيدَ وَهَوِّنْ عَلَيْهِ السَّفَرَ ﴿٣﴾

1. Praise be to Allah who, sufficed us, gave us shelter, and quenched our thirst, without our ever feeling sufficed from need of Him or from acknowledging Him. To You belongs all praise, our Lord, without us feeling sufficiency from need of You, discarding [Your favor] or feeling independence of You.

2. Praise be to Allah who fed us, gave us to drink and made us among the Muslims.

While washing one's hands after a meal

3. Praise be to Allah, who feeds [others], but is not fed. He has showered favor on us by guiding us, feeding us, and giving us to drink, and by every blessing that He has bestowed upon us.

4. Praise be to Allah, who granted us food, gave us to drink, dressed our nakedness, guided us from error, gave us sight instead of blindness, and greatly favored us over many of His creatures.

Praying for the host

5. O Allah! Bless them in what You have provided them, forgive them and have mercy on them!

6. O Allah! Provide food for the one who fed me, and give drink to those who have given me to drink!

اَلْحَمْدُ لِلهِ الَّذِي كَفَانَا وَآوَانَا وَأَرْوَانَا غَيْرَ مَكْفِيٍّ وَلَا مَكْفُورٍ، لَكَ الْحَمْدُ رَبَّنَا غَيْرَ مَكْفِيٍّ وَلَا مُوَدَّعٍ وَلَا مُسْتَغْنًى عَنْهُ ﴿١﴾ اَلْحَمْدُ لِلهِ الَّذِي أَطْعَمَنَا وَسَقَانَا وَجَعَلَنَا مُسْلِمِينَ ﴿٢﴾

حِينَ يَغْسِلُ يَدَيْهِ يَقُولُ:

اَلْحَمْدُ لِلهِ الَّذِي يُطْعِمُ وَلَا يُطْعَمُ مَنَّ عَلَيْنَا فَهَدَانَا وَأَطْعَمَنَا وَسَقَانَا وَكُلَّ بَلَاءٍ حَسَنٍ أَبْلَانَا ﴿٣﴾ اَلْحَمْدُ لِلهِ أَطْعَمَ مِنَ الطَّعَامِ وَسَقَى مِنَ الشَّرَابِ وَكَسَى مِنَ الْعُرْى وَهَدَى مِنَ الضَّلَالِ وَبَصَّرَ مِنَ الْعَمَى وَفَضَّلَ عَلَى كَثِيرٍ مِمَّنْ خَلَقَ تَفْضِيلًا ﴿٤﴾

وَيَدْعُو لِأَهْلِ الطَّعَامِ قَائِلًا:

اَللّهُمَّ بَارِكْ لَهُمْ فِيمَا رَزَقْتَهُمْ وَاغْفِرْ لَهُمْ وَارْحَمْهُمْ ﴿٥﴾ اَللّهُمَّ أَطْعِمْ مَنْ أَطْعَمَنِي وَاسْقِ مَنْ سَقَانِي ﴿٦﴾

Eating with a leper or a handicapped person

1. In the name of Allah, in Him I put my trust and on Him do I rely.

When one finishes eating and drinking

2. All praise be to Allah who provided food and water, caused us to swallow it (food and drink) and made for it a way out.

3. Praise be to Allah who fed me this, and provided it for me with neither power nor strength on my part.

4. O Allah! You have provided food and water in sufficiency, and with some to spare. You have guided, and given life, and to You is due all praise for what You have granted.

5. Praise be to Allah, Who has been gracious to us, and guided us, and Who has satisfied our hunger and quenched our thirst, and has brought us every goodness.

6. O Allah! Bless us by it, and feed us with what is better than it!

7. Praise be to Allah, with abundant, pure, and blessed praise, without our ever feeling sufficed from need of Him, and without our discarding [His favor], or feeling independent of Him, O Lord!

وَإِنْ أَكَلَ مَعَ مَجْذُومٍ أَوْ ذِي عَاهَةٍ يَقُولُ:

بِسْمِ اللهِ ثِقَةً بِاللهِ تَوَكُّلًا عَلَيْهِ ﴿١﴾

وَإِذَا فَرَغَ مِنَ الطَّعَامِ وَالشَّرَابِ يَقُولُ:

اَلْحَمْدُ للهِ الَّذِيَ أَطْعَمَ وَسَقَى وَسَوَّغَهُ وَجَعَلَ لَهُ

مَخْرَجاً ﴿٢﴾ اَلْحَمْدُ للهِ الَّذِيَ أَطْعَمَنِي هٰذَا وَرَزَقَنِيهِ مِنْ

غَيْرِ حَوْلٍ مِنِّي وَلَا قُوَّةٍ ﴿٣﴾ اَللّٰهُمَّ أَطْعَمْتَ وَسَقَيْتَ

وَأَغْنَيْتَ وَأَقْنَيْتَ وَهَدَيْتَ وَأَحْيَيْتَ فَلَكَ الْحَمْدُ عَلَى

مَآ أَعْطَيْتَ ﴿٤﴾ اَلْحَمْدُ للهِ الَّذِي مَنَّ عَلَيْنَا وَهَدَانَا

وَالَّذِيَ أَشْبَعَنَا وَأَرْوَانَا وَكُلَّ الْإِحْسَانِ اٰتَانَا ﴿٥﴾ اَللّٰهُمَّ

بَارِكْ لَنَا فِيهِ وَأَطْعِمْنَا خَيْراً مِنْهُ ﴿٦﴾ اَلْحَمْدُ للهِ حَمْداً

كَثِيراً طَيِّباً مُبَارَكاً فِيهِ غَيْرَ مَكْفِيٍّ وَلَا مُوَدَّعٍ وَلَا

مُسْتَغْنًى عَنْهُ رَبَّنَا ﴿٧﴾

Food

Breaking the fast

1. Thirst has gone, the veins have been moistened, and the reward is assured if Allah wills.

2. May those who are fasting break their fast at your home, the righteous eat of your food, and the angels bless you!

3. O Allah! Verily I ask You by Your mercy which encompasses everything, to forgive me my sins.

4. When the food is served, he begins in the name of Allah, but if he forgets the *basmala* at the beginning of the meal, when he remembers he says:

   In the name of Allah, at its beginning, middle, and end.

اَلطَّعَامُ

دُعَاءُ الْإِفْطَارِ:

يقول الصائم عند الإفطار:

ذَهَبَ الظَّمَأُ وَابْتَلَّتِ الْعُرُوقُ وَثَبَتَ الْأَجْرُ إِنْ شَاءَ اللهُ تَعَالَى ﴿١﴾ أَفْطَرَ عِنْدَكُمُ الصَّائِمُونَ وَأَكَلَ طَعَامَكُمُ الْأَبْرَارُ وَصَلَّتْ عَلَيْكُمُ الْمَلَئِكَةُ ﴿٢﴾ اَللّٰهُمَّ إِنِّي أَسْأَلُكَ بِرَحْمَتِكَ الَّتِي وَسِعَتْ كُلَّ شَيْءٍ أَنْ تَغْفِرَ لِي ذُنُوبِي ﴿٣﴾

وإذا حضر الطعام يبدأ بسم الله وإذا نسي البسملة في أول الطعام يقول إذا ذكر:

بِسْمِ اللهِ أَوَّلَهُ وَأَوْسَطَهُ وَاٰخِرَهُ ﴿٤﴾

أَدْعِيَةٌ مُتَعَلِّقَةٌ بِالطَّعَامِ وَالشَّرَابِ وَالصَّوْمِ
وَالزَّكَاةِ وَالسَّفَرِ وَالْحَجِّ وَالْجِهَادِ وَالنِّكَاحِ

FOOD, DRINK, FASTING, ZAKAT, TRAVEL, THE PILGRIMAGE, WAR, AND MARRIAGE

1. O Allah! Verily I ask You by the pillars of might upholding Your Throne, by the extent of mercy within Your Book, by Your greatest name, by Your most exalted Majesty, and by Your perfect words.

   Then one asks for what one needs, after which one raises one's head and makes the closing salaams (greetings) to the right and left.

The prayer of glorification (tasbih)

2. One prays four rak'as, reciting in each rak'a Surat al-Fatiha and another sura. After finishing the recitation in the first rak'a one invokes the following in the standing position fifteen times:

   Glory be to Allah! Praise be to Allah! There is no god but Allah, and Allah is the Greatest! (*Subhan Allah wa Alhamdu lillah wa La ilaha illallahu wa Allahu Akbar*) Then one bows (*ruku'*) and recites the same invocation in the bowing position ten times. Then one straightens up and recites the invocation in the standing position ten times. Then one prostrates and recites the invocation ten times in prostration (*sajda*). Then one comes up from prostration, and recites it ten times in the sitting position. Then one makes the second prostration and recites it ten times in prostration. Then one comes up from prostration and recites the invocation ten times in the sitting position. One repeats this in all four rak'as.

اَللّٰهُمَّ إِنِّيٓ أَسْأَلُكَ بِمَقَاعِدِ الْعِزِّ مِنْ عَرْشِكَ وَمُنْتَهَى الرَّحْمَةِ مِنْ كِتَابِكَ وَاسْمِكَ الْأَعْظَمِ وَجَدِّكَ الْأَعْلٰى وَكَلِمَاتِكَ التَّامَّةِ ﴿١﴾

ثم يسأل حاجته ثم يرفع رأسه ويسلّم عن يمينه وعن شماله.

صَلَاةُ التَّسْبِيحِ:

يصلي أربع ركعات، يقرأ في كل ركعة فاتحة الكتاب وسورة، فإذا فرغ من القراءة في أول ركعة يقول وهو قائم: ''سُبْحَانَ اللهِ وَالْحَمْدُ لِلهِ وَلَا إِلٰهَ إِلَّا اللهُ وَاللهُ أَكْبَرُ'' خمس عشرة، ثم يركع ويقول وهو راكع عشرًا، ثم يرفع رأسه من الركوع فيقولها عشرًا، ثم يهوي ساجدًا فيقولها عشرًا، ثم يرفع رأسه من السجود فيقولها عشرًا، ثم يسجد فيقولها عشرًا، ثم يرفع رأسه من السجود فيقولها عشرًا، ثم يفعل ذلك في أربع ركعات ﴿٢﴾

1. O Allah! You are the One who judges Your servants concerning their disagreements.

2. There is no god but Allah, the Exalted, the All-Mighty.

3. There is no god but Allah, the All-Clement, the All-Generous.

4. Glory be to the Lord of the seven heavens and the Lord of the Supreme Throne.

5. Praise be to Allah, the Lord of the worlds.

6. O Allah, Alleviator of distress, Reliever of worry, and the One who responds to the prayer of those in dire need if they call on You! O, All-Merciful in this life and the Hereafter, and Beneficent in both! Have mercy on me in this need of mine, by fulfilling it, with a successful outcome, such that I dispense with the mercy of all other than You.

And in another narration:

One prays twelve *rak'as* with a *tashahhud* in every two *rak'as*, and when he sits at the end of his prayer he praises Allah, sends blessings upon the Prophet, then says Allahu Akbar (*takbir*) and goes into prostration. While in prostration one recites the following: al-Fatiha (7), Ayat al-Kursi (7), and Surat al-Ikhlas (7). Then one reads:

7. There is no god but Allah, alone without associate. His is the dominion, all praise is to Him, and He has power over all things. (10)

اَللّٰهُمَّ أَنْتَ تَحْكُمُ بَيْنَ عِبَادِكَ فِيمَا كَانُوا فِيهِ يَخْتَلِفُونَ ﴿١﴾ لَآ إِلٰهَ إِلَّا اللهُ الْعَلِيُّ الْعَظِيمُ ﴿٢﴾ لَا إِلٰهَ إِلَّا اللهُ الْحَلِيمُ الْكَرِيمُ ﴿٣﴾ سُبْحَانَ رَبِّ السَّمٰوَاتِ السَّبْعِ وَرَبِّ الْعَرْشِ الْعَظِيمِ ﴿٤﴾ اَلْحَمْدُ لِلّٰهِ رَبِّ الْعَالَمِينَ ﴿٥﴾ اَللّٰهُمَّ كَاشِفَ الْغَمِّ مُفَرِّجَ الْهَمِّ مُجِيبَ دَعْوَةِ الْمُضْطَرِّينَ إِذَا دَعَوْكَ رَحْمٰنَ الدُّنْيَا وَالْآخِرَةِ وَرَحِيمَهُمَا فَارْحَمْنِي فِي حَاجَتِي هٰذِهِ بِقَضَائِهَا وَنَجَاحِهَا رَحْمَةً تُغْنِينِي بِهَا عَنْ رَحْمَةِ مَنْ سِوَاكَ ﴿٦﴾

وفي رواية: يصلي اثنتي عشرة ركعة ويتشهد بين كل ركعتين وإذا جلس في آخر صلاته يثني على الله ويصلي على النبي ﷺ ثم يكبر ويسجد ويقرأ وهو ساجد فاتحة الكتاب سبع مرات وآية الكرسي سبع مرات وسورة الإخلاص سبع مرات ثم يقول:

لَآ إِلٰهَ إِلَّا اللهُ وَحْدَهُ لَا شَرِيكَ لَهُ، لَهُ الْمُلْكُ وَلَهُ الْحَمْدُ وَهُوَ عَلٰى كُلِّ شَيْءٍ قَدِيرٌ (١٠) ﴿٧﴾

٦٦

The prayer to be said in time of need or affliction

One makes ablution, prays two *rak'as*, and then reads the following supplication:

1. O Allah! Verily I ask You, and turn to You, for the sake of Your Prophet Muhammad, the Prophet of mercy. O Muhammad, I turn to my Lord through you, with my need, so that it may be fulfilled for me. O Allah, grant him (the Prophet, peace and blessings be upon him) intercession for me!

And in another narration:

One prays two *rak'as*, praises Allah and invokes blessings upon the Prophet (peace and blessings be upon him). Then one reads the following supplication:

2. There is no god but Allah, the All-Clement, the All-Generous. Glory be to Allah, the Lord of the Supreme Throne!

3. All praise is due to Allah, Lord of the worlds. I ask You for the means of deserving Your mercy, the means of ascertaining Your forgiveness, protection from every sin, the benefit of every virtue, and freedom from every error. Leave me not with a sin without Your having forgiven it, a worry without Your having relieved it, or a need which has Your approval, without Your having fulfilled it, O Most Merciful of the merciful!

صَلَاةُ الضُّرِّ وَالْحَاجَةِ:

يتوضأ ويصلي ركعتين ثم يدعو:

اَللّٰهُمَّ إِنِّيٓ أَسْأَلُكَ وَأَتَوَجَّهُ إِلَيْكَ بِنَبِيِّكَ مُحَمَّدٍ نَبِيِّ الرَّحْمَةِ، يَا مُحَمَّدُ إِنِّيٓ أَتَوَجَّهُ بِكَ إِلَى رَبِّي فِي حَاجَتِي هَذِهِ لِتُقْضٰى لِي، اَللّٰهُمَّ فَشَفِّعْهُ فِيَّ (١)

وفي رواية: يصلي ركعتين ويثني على الله ويصلي على النبي ﷺ ثم يدعو هذا الدعاء:

لَآ إِلٰهَ إِلَّا اللهُ الْحَلِيمُ الْكَرِيمُ سُبْحَانَ اللهِ رَبِّ الْعَرْشِ الْعَظِيمِ (٢) اَلْحَمْدُ لِلّٰهِ رَبِّ الْعَالَمِينَ أَسْأَلُكَ مُوجِبَاتِ رَحْمَتِكَ وَعَزَآئِمَ مَغْفِرَتِكَ وَالْعِصْمَةَ مِنْ كُلِّ ذَنْبٍ وَالْغَنِيمَةَ مِنْ كُلِّ بِرٍّ وَالسَّلَامَةَ مِنْ كُلِّ إِثْمٍ، لَا تَدَعْ لِي ذَنْبًا إِلَّا غَفَرْتَهُ وَلَا هَمًّا إِلَّا فَرَّجْتَهُ وَلَا حَاجَةً هِيَ لَكَ رِضاً إِلَّا قَضَيْتَهَا يَا أَرْحَمَ الرَّاحِمِينَ (٣)

1. O Allah! Have mercy on me, by enabling me to leave all acts of disobedience forever, as long as You preserve me. Have mercy on me, that I should not burden myself with that which does not concern me, and grant me the ability to look to what earns me Your good pleasure.

2. O Allah, Originator of the heavens and earth, Possessor of Majesty and Bounty, and Unfathomable Might!

3. I ask You, O Allah, All-Merciful, by Your Majesty, and the light of Your Countenance, to enjoin on my heart the memorization of Your Book, as You taught me, and grant me that I should recite it in the way that will earn me Your good pleasure.

4. O Allah, Originator of the heavens and the earth, and Possessor of Majesty and Bounty, and Unfathomable Might!

5. I ask You O Allah, All-Merciful, by Your Majesty and the light of Your Countenance, make Your Book the means of illuminating my vision, enabling my speech, alleviating my heart, expanding my breast, and spurring my body into doing good deeds. For no one helps us in upholding truth save You, and no one grants it (truth) except You. There is no strength or power except in Allah, the Exalted, the All-Mighty. (This should be repeated on three, five or seven consecutive Fridays.)

اَللّٰهُمَّ ارْحَمْنِي بِتَرْكِ الْمَعَاصِي أَبَداً مَا أَبْقَيْتَنِي وَارْحَمْنِي أَنْ أَتَكَلَّفَ مَا لَا يَعْنِينِي وَارْزُقْنِي حُسْنَ النَّظَرِ فِيمَا يُرْضِيكَ عَنِّي ﴿١﴾ اَللّٰهُمَّ بَدِيعَ السَّمٰوَاتِ وَالْأَرْضِ ذَا الْجَلَالِ وَالْإِكْرَامِ وَالْعِزَّةِ الَّتِي لَا تُرَامُ ﴿٢﴾ أَسْأَلُكَ يَآ اَللّٰهُ يَا رَحْمٰنُ بِجَلَالِكَ وَنُورِ وَجْهِكَ أَنْ تُلْزِمَ قَلْبِي حِفْظَ كِتَابِكَ كَمَا عَلَّمْتَنِي وَارْزُقْنِي أَنْ أَتْلُوَهُ عَلَى النَّحْوِ الَّذِي يُرْضِيكَ عَنِّي ﴿٣﴾ اَللّٰهُمَّ بَدِيعَ السَّمٰوَاتِ وَالْأَرْضِ ذَا الْجَلَالِ وَالْإِكْرَامِ وَالْعِزَّةِ الَّتِي لَا تُرَامُ ﴿٤﴾ أَسْأَلُكَ يَآ اَللّٰهُ يَا رَحْمٰنُ بِجَلَالِكَ وَنُورِ وَجْهِكَ أَنْ تُنَوِّرَ بِكِتَابِكَ بَصَرِي وَأَنْ تُطْلِقَ بِهِ لِسَانِي وَأَنْ تُفَرِّجَ بِهِ عَنْ قَلْبِي وَأَنْ تَشْرَحَ بِهِ صَدْرِي وَأَنْ تُعْمِلَ بِهِ بَدَنِي، فَإِنَّهُ لَا يُعِينُنِي عَلَى الْحَقِّ غَيْرُكَ وَلَا يُؤْتِيهِ إِلَّآ أَنْتَ لَا حَوْلَ وَلَا قُوَّةَ إِلَّا بِاللّٰهِ الْعَلِيِّ الْعَظِيمِ ﴿٥﴾ يَفْعَلُ ذٰلِكَ ثَلَاثَ جُمَعٍ أَوْ خَمْساً أَوْ سَبْعاً.

1. "Praise be to Allah who sent down to His servant, the Book" (Kahf 18:1)

2. Glory be to Allah! Praise be to Allah! There is no god but Allah, Allah is the Greatest, and there is no strength or power except in Him. Glory be to Allah and to Him be praise! Glory be to Allah the All-Mighty!

3. O Allah! Send Your blessing, peace and grace upon our master Muhammad and upon his family, to the number of Allah's perfections and in the way that is fitting to His perfection!

4. O Allah! Bless our master Muhammad and the family of our master Muhammad as You blessed Abraham and the family of Abraham, and send Your grace on our master Muhammad and the family of our master Muhammad as You sent grace on Abraham and the family of Abraham. Truly, You are the Owner of Praise, the Glorious.

5. O Allah! Send Your blessing, peace and grace upon our master Muhammad and upon all of his brothers from amongst the prophets and messengers, to the number of what You have created, in accordance with Your pleasure, to the measure of the weight of Your Throne, and the ink of Your words (see Kahf, 18:109), for as long as the dominion of Allah remains.

6. "Our Lord forgive us, and our brothers (and sisters), who preceded us in faith and don't leave in our hearts rancor for those who believe, our Lord truly You are the Tender, the All-Compassionate." (Hashr 59:10)

﴿اَلْحَمْدُ لله الَّذِيّ أَنْزَلَ عَلَى عَبْدِهِ الْكِتَابَ﴾

سُبْحَانَ اللهِ وَالْحَمْدُ لله وَلَاۤ إِلهَ إِلَّا اللهُ وَاللهُ أَكْبَرُ وَلَا

حَوْلَ وَلَا قُوَّةَ إِلَّا بِاللهِ الْعَلِيِّ الْعَظِيمِ ۝١ سُبْحَانَ اللهِ

وَبِحَمْدِهِ سُبْحَانَ اللهِ الْعَظِيمِ ۝٢ اَللّٰهُمَّ صَلِّ وَسَلِّمْ

وَبَارِكْ عَلَى سَيِّدِنَا مُحَمَّدٍ وَعَلَى الِهِ عَدَدَ كَمَالِ اللهِ

وَكَمَا يَلِيقُ بِكَمَالِهِ ۝٣ اَللّٰهُمَّ صَلِّ عَلَى مُحَمَّدٍ وَعَلَى

الِ مُحَمَّدٍ كَمَا صَلَّيْتَ عَلَى إِبْرٰهِيمَ وَعَلَى الِ إِبْرٰهِيمَ

وَبَارِكْ عَلَى مُحَمَّدٍ وَعَلَى الِ مُحَمَّدٍ كَمَا بَارَكْتَ عَلَى

إِبْرٰهِيمَ وَعَلَى الِ إِبْرٰهِيمَ إِنَّكَ حَمِيدٌ مَجِيدٌ ۝٤

اَللّٰهُمَّ صَلِّ وَسَلِّمْ وَبَارِكْ عَلَى سَيِّدِنَا مُحَمَّدٍ وَعَلَى سَآئِرِ

إِخْوَانِهِ مِنَ النَّبِيِّينَ وَالْمُرْسَلِينَ عَدَدَ خَلْقِكَ وَرِضَا نَفْسِكَ

وَزِنَةَ عَرْشِكَ وَمِدَادَ كَلِمَاتِكَ مَا دَامَ مُلْكُ اللهِ تَعَالى ۝٥

﴿رَبَّنَا اغْفِرْ لَنَا وَلِإِخْوَانِنَا الَّذِينَ سَبَقُونَا بِالْإِيمَانِ وَلَا

تَجْعَلْ فِي قُلُوبِنَا غِلاًّ لِلَّذِينَ اٰمَنُوا رَبَّنَا إِنَّكَ رَؤُفٌ رَحِيمٌ﴾ ۝٦

٦٣

1. O Allah! Returner of that which is lost, and Guide of those astray! You it is who guides (people) away from error. Return to me what I have lost through Your power and authority, for truly it is of Your bestowing and from Your bounty.

The prayer for the memorization of the Qur'an

On Thursday night one gets up to pray in the last third of the night, and if one is unable to do that, then during the first third or middle third. Then one makes the ablution and prays four *rak'as* in which after the Fatiha one recites:

In the first *rak'a*: Sura Ya Sin

In the second *rak'a*: Surat al-Dukhan

In the third *rak'a*: Surat al-Sajda

In the fourth *rak'a*: Surat al-Mulk

Then on completion of the last attestation (*tashahhud*) one reads the following supplication:

2. "Praise be to Allah, Lord of the worlds." (Fatiha 1:2)

3. "Praise be to Allah who created the heavens and the earth and made darkness and light." (An'am 6:1)

اَللّٰهُمَّ رَآدَّ الضَّآلَّةِ وَهَادِيَ الضَّلَالَةِ أَنْتَ تَهْدِي مِنَ الضَّلَالَةِ، اُرْدُدْ عَلَيَّ ضَآلَّتِي بِقُدْرَتِكَ وَسُلْطَانِكَ فَإِنَّهَا مِنْ عَطَآئِكَ وَفَضْلِكَ ۝١

دُعَآءُ حِفْظِ الْقُرْاٰنِ وَصَلَاتُهُ:

إذا كانت ليلة الجمعة يقوم في الثلث الأخير، فإن لم يستطع ففي أولها أو أوسطها فيتوضأ ويصلي أربع ركعات يقرأ فيهن بعد فاتحة الكتاب:

في الركعة الأولى: سورة يٰسٓ

وفي الثانية: سورة الدخان

وفي الثالثة: سورة السجدة

وفي الرابعة: سورة الملك

فإذا فرغ من التشهد يقرأ هذا الدعاء:

﴿اَلْحَمْدُ لِلّٰهِ رَبِّ الْعَالَمِينَ﴾ ۝٢

﴿اَلْحَمْدُ لِلّٰهِ الَّذِي خَلَقَ السَّمٰوَاتِ وَالْأَرْضَ وَجَعَلَ الظُّلُمَاتِ وَالنُّورَ﴾ ۝٣

1. O Allah! Truly You have power, but I have none, and You know, but I know not, and You are the Knower of the unseen. So, if You see that such and such a person (the name of the person is mentioned) is good for me in my religion, my life (in this world), and my Hereafter, ordain her/him for me, but if there is somebody else who would be better for me than them in my religion, my life (in this world), and my Hereafter, ordain that person for me (instead).

The prayer of repentance

When one wants to seek forgiveness, one prays two *rak'as*, and says:

2. O Allah! I repent to you for it (the sin I have committed), and I will never go back to it.

3. O Allah! Your forgiveness is vaster than my sins, and Your mercy is of more hope to me than my actions. (3)

On losing something

Whoever loses something makes the ablution, prays two *rak'as* and then says:

4. In the name of Allah, O Guide of those astray, and Returner of that which is lost! Return to me what I have lost, through Your Might and Authority, for truly it is of Your bestowing and from Your bounty.

اَللّٰهُمَّ إِنَّكَ تَقْدِرُ وَلَا أَقْدِرُ وَتَعْلَمُ وَلَا أَعْلَمُ وَأَنْتَ عَلَّامُ الْغُيُوبِ، فَإِنْ رَأَيْتَ أَنَّ فُلَانَةَ (يسميها باسمها) خَيْرٌ لِي فِي دِينِي وَدُنْيَايَ وَاٰخِرَتِي فَاقْدُرْهَا لِي وَإِنْ كَانَ غَيْرُهَا خَيْرًا لِي مِنْهَا فِي دِينِي وَدُنْيَايَ وَاٰخِرَتِي فَاقْدُرْهَا لِي ۝١

صَلَاةُ التَّوْبَةِ:

إذا أراد الاستغفار يصلي ركعتين ثم يستغفر ويقول:

اَللّٰهُمَّ إِنِّي أَتُوبُ إِلَيْكَ مِنْهَا، لَا أَرْجِعُ إِلَيْهَا أَبَدًا ۝٢

اَللّٰهُمَّ مَغْفِرَتُكَ أَوْسَعُ مِنْ ذُنُوبِي وَرَحْمَتُكَ أَرْجٰى عِنْدِي مِنْ عَمَلِي (٣) ۝٣

عِنْدَ ضَيَاعِ شَيْءٍ:

من ضاع له شيء يتوضأ ويصلي ركعتين ثم يقول:

بِسْمِ اللهِ يَا هَادِيَ الضَّالِّ وَرَآدَّ الضَّالَّةِ اُرْدُدْ عَلَيَّ ضَآلَّتِي بِعِزَّتِكَ وَسُلْطَانِكَ فَإِنَّهَا مِنْ عَطَآئِكَ وَفَضْلِكَ ۝٤

Seeking guidance in decision-making (Istikhara)

One performs two *rak'as* of supererogatory prayer and then makes the following supplication:

1. O Allah! I seek Your guidance in my choice, by virtue of Your knowledge, and I seek ability from You by virtue of Your power. I ask You out of Your great favor, for You have power, but I have none, and You know, but I know not, and You are the Knower of the unseen.

2. O Allah! If You know concerning such and such (one names the thing in mind) that this matter is good for me in my religion, my life, my livelihood, the outcome of my affairs, or my immediate and distant affairs, then make it happen for me, and facilitate it for me, and thereafter bless me by it.

3. However, if You know that this matter is bad for me in my religion, my life, my livelihood, the outcome of my affairs, or my immediate and distant affairs, then avert it from me, and avert me from it, and ordain for me the good wherever it may lie and make me content with it.

Prayer (*salat*) and invocation for marriage

When a person intends to marry he prays two *rak'as* and then says:

صَلَاةُ الْاِسْتِخَارَة:

يركع ركعتين من غير الفريضة ثم يدعو:

اَللّٰهُمَّ إِنِّيْ أَسْتَخِيرُكَ بِعِلْمِكَ وَأَسْتَقْدِرُكَ بِقُدْرَتِكَ وَأَسْأَلُكَ مِنْ فَضْلِكَ الْعَظِيمِ، فَإِنَّكَ تَقْدِرُ وَلَا أَقْدِرُ وَتَعْلَمُ وَلَا أَعْلَمُ وَأَنْتَ عَلَّامُ الْغُيُوبِ ﴿١﴾

اَللّٰهُمَّ إِنْ كُنْتَ تَعْلَمُ أَنَّ هٰذَا الْأَمْرَ خَيْرٌ لِي فِي دِينِي وَدُنْيَايَ وَمَعَاشِي وَعَاقِبَةِ أَمْرِي أَوْ عَاجِلِ أَمْرِي وَآجِلِهِ فَاقْدُرْهُ لِي وَيَسِّرْهُ لِي ثُمَّ بَارِكْ لِي فِيهِ ﴿٢﴾ وَإِنْ كُنْتَ تَعْلَمُ أَنَّ هٰذَا الْأَمْرَ شَرٌّ لِي فِي دِينِي وَدُنْيَايَ وَمَعَاشِي وَعَاقِبَةِ أَمْرِي أَوْ عَاجِلِ أَمْرِي وَآجِلِهِ فَاصْرِفْهُ عَنِّي وَاصْرِفْنِي عَنْهُ وَاقْدُرْ لِيَ الْخَيْرَ حَيْثُ كَانَ ثُمَّ رَضِّنِي بِهِ ﴿٣﴾

إِذَا أَرَادَ أَنْ يَتَزَوَّجَ:

إذا أراد أن يتزوج يصلي ركعتين ثم يقول:

٦٠

The prayer for rain (Istisqaa')

For this prayer people go out (in open field or on a hill) when the rim of the sun appears above the horizon and they seek Allah's forgiveness repeatedly. Then the Imam ascends to a high spot and recites:

1. "All praise is due to Allah, the Lord of the worlds ❀ the All-Merciful, the All-Compassionate. ❀ The Master of the Day of Judgment." (Fatiha 1:1-4)

2. Then he raises his hands up high saying: There is no god but Allah and He does what He wills.

3. O Allah! There is no god but You, the Rich Beyond Need, and we are the poor and needy. Send down rain and let what You send down be a source of strength to see us through this spell!

4. O Allah! Give water to Your servants and Your beasts! Spread out Your mercy, and revive this dead land, which is Yours!

5. O Allah! Send down rain that is abundant, wholesome, productive and beneficial, not harmful, promptly and without delay!

   Then he turns his back to the congregation and he turns his robe inside out, raising his hands. Then he descends and prays two *rak'as*.

ذِكْرُ الْاسْتِسْقَاءِ:

يخرجون حين بدا حاجب الشمس ويستغفرون الله كثيراً ثم يصعد الإمام على المنبر فيقول: ﴿اَلْحَمْدُ للهِ رَبِّ الْعَالَمِينَ ۞ اَلرَّحْمٰنِ الرَّحِيمِ ۞ مَالِكِ يَوْمِ الدِّينِ﴾ ۞

ثم يرفع يديه ويبالغ في الرفع قائلاً: لَآ إِلٰهَ إِلَّا اللهُ يَفْعَلُ مَا يُرِيدُ ۞ اَللّٰهُمَّ أَنْتَ اللهُ لَآ إِلٰهَ إِلَّا أَنْتَ الْغَنِيُّ وَنَحْنُ الْفُقَرَاءُ أَنْزِلْ عَلَيْنَا الْغَيْثَ وَاجْعَلْ مَآ أَنْزَلْتَ عَلَيْنَا قُوَّةً وَبَلَاغاً إِلٰى حِينٍ ۞ اَللّٰهُمَّ اسْقِ عِبَادَكَ وَبَهَائِمَكَ وَانْشُرْ رَحْمَتَكَ وَأَحْيِ بَلَدَكَ الْمَيِّتَ ۞ اَللّٰهُمَّ اسْقِنَا غَيْثاً مُغِيثاً مَرِيئًا مَرِيعاً نَافِعاً غَيْرَ ضَآرٍّ عَاجِلاً غَيْرَ أٰجِلٍ ۞

ثم يحول إلى الناس ظهره ويقلب رداءه وهو رافع يديه ثم ينزل من المنبر فيركع ركعتين.

1. In the name of Allah, and there is no god but Him the All-Merciful, the All-Compassionate.

2. O Allah! Free me from worry and grief!

3. O Allah! Truly I take refuge in You from the trial of the Antichrist (*Al Dajjal*).

4. O Allah! Verily I take refuge in You from the punishment of the grave.

5. O Allah! Verily I take refuge in You from the punishment of Hell.

6. O Allah! I take refuge in You from the [burden] of sin and the [yoke] of heavy debt.

7. O Allah! I take refuge in You from the trial of life and death.

8. O Allah! Enter me into Paradise in the company of the righteous!

   Then after saying the *isti'adha* and *basmala*, one recites Ayat al Kursi, surat al-Ikhlas and suras al-Falaq and al-Nas.

   Then one says:

9. Glory be to Allah! (33), Praise be to Allah! (33), Allah is the Greatest (33). There is no god but Allah, alone, without associate, His is the dominion, to Him is all praise, and He has power over all things.

   Then one raises one's hands and makes supplication.

بِسْمِ اللهِ الَّذِي لَا إِلَهَ إِلَّا هُوَ الرَّحْمَنُ الرَّحِيمُ ﴿١﴾ اَللّهُمَّ أَذْهِبْ عَنِّي الْهَمَّ وَالْحَزَنَ ﴿٢﴾ اَللّهُمَّ إِنِّي أَعُوذُ بِكَ مِنْ فِتْنَةِ الْمَسِيحِ الدَّجَالِ ﴿٣﴾ اَللّهُمَّ إِنِّي أَعُوذُ بِكَ مِنْ عَذَابِ الْقَبْرِ ﴿٤﴾ اَللّهُمَّ إِنِّي أَعُوذُ بِكَ مِنْ عَذَابِ جَهَنَّمَ ﴿٥﴾ اَللّهُمَّ إِنِّي أَعُوذُ بِكَ مِنَ الْمَأْثَمِ وَالْمَغْرَمِ ﴿٦﴾ اَللّهُمَّ إِنِّي أَعُوذُ بِكَ مِنْ فِتْنَةِ الْمَحْيَا وَالْمَمَاتِ ﴿٧﴾ اَللّهُمَّ أَدْخِلْنِي الْجَنَّةَ مَعَ الْأَبْرَارِ ﴿٨﴾

ثم يقرأ بعد الاستعاذة والبسملة سورة الفاتحة وآية الكرسي وسورة الإخلاص والمعوذتين.

ثم يقول: سُبْحَانَ اللهِ (٣٣) اَلْحَمْدُ لِلهِ (٣٣) اَللهُ أَكْبَرُ (٣٣)، لَا إِلَهَ إِلَّا اللهُ وَحْدَهُ لَا شَرِيكَ لَهُ، لَهُ الْمُلْكُ وَلَهُ الْحَمْدُ وَهُوَ عَلَى كُلِّ شَيْءٍ قَدِيرٌ ﴿٩﴾

ثم يرفع يديه ويدعو.

1. O Allah! Save me from Your punishment on the day Your servants are resurrected!

2. O Allah, Lord of Gabriel, Mikail, Israfil and Lord of Muhammad! Shield me from the heat of the Hellfire and from the punishment of the grave!

3. O Allah! Help me to remember You, give thanks to You and to worship You properly!

4. O Allah! Forgive me for my misdeeds, unintentional or deliberate! O Allah! Guide me to righteous actions and morals, for no one guides to them, and gets rid of their opposites (bad actions and morals) except You.

5. O Allah! Forgive me for all my errors and sins! O Allah! Refresh me, restore me, provide for me, and guide me to righteous actions and morals, for no one guides to them except You and no one gets rid of their opposites except You.

6. O Allah! Rectify for me my religion, make my home spacious, and bless me in my provision!

"Transcendent is Your Lord, Lord of Honor and Might, above all that they ascribe to Him. Peace be upon the Messengers and all praise be to Allah, the Lord of the worlds." (Saffat 37:180-2)

رَبِّ قِنِي عَذَابَكَ يَوْمَ تَبْعَثُ عِبَادَكَ ﴿١﴾ اَللّٰهُمَّ
رَبَّ جِبْرِيلَ وَمِيكَائِيلَ وَإِسْرَافِيلَ وَرَبَّ مُحَمَّدٍ أَعِذْنِي مِنْ
حَرِّ النَّارِ وَعَذَابِ الْقَبْرِ ﴿٢﴾ اَللّٰهُمَّ أَعِنِّي عَلَى ذِكْرِكَ
وَشُكْرِكَ وَحُسْنِ عِبَادَتِكَ ﴿٣﴾ اَللّٰهُمَّ اغْفِرْ لِي خَطَايَاىَ
وَعَمْدِي، اَللّٰهُمَّ اهْدِنِي لِصَالِحِ الْأَعْمَالِ وَالْأَخْلَاقِ لَا
يَهْدِي لِصَالِحِهَا وَلَا يَصْرِفُ سَيِّئَهَا إِلَّا أَنْتَ ﴿٤﴾ اَللّٰهُمَّ
اغْفِرْ لِي خَطِيئَي وَذُنُوبِي كُلَّهَا، اللّٰهُمَّ انْعِشْنِي وَاجْبُرْنِي
وَارْزُقْنِي وَاهْدِنِي لِصَالِحِ الْأَعْمَالِ وَالْأَخْلَاقِ لَا يَهْدِي
لِصَالِحِهَا إِلَّا أَنْتَ وَلَا يَصْرِفُ سَيِّئَهَا إِلَّا أَنْتَ ﴿٥﴾

اَللّٰهُمَّ أَصْلِحْ لِي دِينِي وَوَسِّعْ لِي فِي دَارِي
وَبَارِكْ لِي فِي رِزْقِي ﴿سُبْحَانَ رَبِّكَ رَبِّ الْعِزَّةِ عَمَّا
يَصِفُونَ ۞ وَسَلَامٌ عَلَى الْمُرْسَلِينَ ۞ وَالْحَمْدُ للهِ رَبِّ
الْعَالَمِينَ﴾ ﴿٦﴾

After the sunna prayer of Fajr is completed

1. O Allah! Lord of Gabriel, Mikail, Israfil and Muhammad the Prophet, peace and blessings be upon him, save me from the Hellfire!

2. O All-Living Self-Subsistent [Lord]! There is no god save You. (40)

After the Fajr and Maghrib prayers

3. There is no god but Allah, alone, without associate, His is the dominion, to Him is all praise, He gives life and death, and He has power over all things. (10)

4. O Allah! Deliver me from the Hellfire! (7)

5. O Allah! Enter us into Paradise! O Allah! Make the best part of my life the last part, make the best of my actions my final action, and make my best day the day I meet You!

6. O Allah! I seek refuge in You from unbelief, poverty, and the punishment of the grave.

7. O Allah! I take refuge in You from cowardice, and I take refuge in You from declining to the age of decrepitude. I take refuge in You from the trial of this life, and I take refuge in You from the punishment of the grave.

وَيَقْرَأُ بَعْدَ سُنَّةِ الصُّبْحِ:

اَللّٰهُمَّ رَبَّ جِبْرِيلَ وَمِيكَائِيلَ وَإِسْرَافِيلَ وَمُحَمَّدٍ النَّبِيِّ ﷺ أَجِرْنِي مِنَ النَّارِ ﴿١﴾

يَا حَيُّ يَا قَيُّومُ لَا إِلٰهَ إِلَّا أَنْتَ (٤٠) ﴿٢﴾

وَبَعْدَ صَلَاتَي الصُّبْحِ وَالْمَغْرِبِ يَقُولُ:

لَا إِلٰهَ إِلَّا اللهُ وَحْدَهُ لَا شَرِيكَ لَهُ، لَهُ الْمُلْكُ وَلَهُ الْحَمْدُ يُحْيِي وَيُمِيتُ وَهُوَ عَلٰى كُلِّ شَيْءٍ قَدِيرٌ (١٠) ﴿٣﴾

اَللّٰهُمَّ أَجِرْنِي مِنَ النَّارِ (٧) ﴿٤﴾

اَللّٰهُمَّ أَدْخِلْنَا الْجَنَّةَ، اَللّٰهُمَّ اجْعَلْ خَيْرَ عُمُرِي اٰخِرَهُ وَخَيْرَ عَمَلِي خَوَاتِمَهُ وَاجْعَلْ خَيْرَ أَيَّامِي يَوْمَ أَلْقَاكَ ﴿٥﴾ اَللّٰهُمَّ إِنِّي أَعُوذُ بِكَ مِنَ الْكُفْرِ وَالْفَقْرِ وَعَذَابِ الْقَبْرِ ﴿٦﴾ اَللّٰهُمَّ إِنِّي أَعُوذُ بِكَ مِنَ الْجُبْنِ وَأَعُوذُ بِكَ أَنْ أُرَدَّ إِلٰى أَرْذَلِ الْعُمُرِ وَأَعُوذُ بِكَ مِنْ فِتْنَةِ الدُّنْيَا وَأَعُوذُ بِكَ مِنْ عَذَابِ الْقَبْرِ ﴿٧﴾

During the sajdat al tilawa (a prostration prescribed after the reading or hearing of certain verses of the Qur'an)

1. My face is prostrated to the One Who created and formed it, and gave it openings for hearing and sight through His strength and power. (several times).

2. O Allah, record for me a reward for it (the *sajda*; prostration), and lift a burden [of sin] off my shoulders. Keep the reward for it with You as a deposit for me, and accept it from me, as You accepted it from Your servant David, peace be upon him.

3. "Glory be to our Lord, as the promise of our Lord was certainly fulfilled." (Isra 17:108)

During the two rak'as (cycles) of the sunna of the Fajr prayer

4. First *rak'a*: Surat al-Kafirun. (Qur'an 109)
   Second *rak'a*; Surat al-Ikhlas (Qur'an 112)
   Or

5. First *rak'a*: Surat Al Imran (3:84).
   Second *rak'a*; Surat Al Imran (3:64).

وَفِي سَجْدَةِ التِّلَاوَةِ يَقُولُ:

سَجَدَ وَجْهِيَ لِلَّذِي خَلَقَهُ وَصَوَّرَهُ وَشَقَّ سَمْعَهُ

وَبَصَرَهُ بِحَوْلِهِ وَقُوَّتِهِ (دفعات) ﴿١﴾

اَللَّهُمَّ اكْتُبْ لِي بِهَا أَجْراً وَضَعْ عَنِّي بِهَا وِزْراً

وَاجْعَلْهَا لِي عِنْدَكَ ذُخْراً وَتَقَبَّلْهَا مِنِّي كَمَا تَقَبَّلْتَهَا مِنْ

عَبْدِكَ دَاوُدَ عَلَيْهِ السَّلَامْ ﴿٢﴾

﴿سُبْحَانَ رَبِّنَا إِنْ كَانَ وَعْدُ رَبِّنَا لَمَفْعُولاً﴾ ﴿٣﴾

يَقْرَأُ فِي رَكْعَتَيْ سُنَّةِ الْفَجْرِ:

سُورَة ﴿قُلْ يَا أَيُّهَا الْكَافِرُونَ... الخ﴾

وسُورَة ﴿قُلْ هُوَ اللهُ أَحَدْ... الخ﴾ ﴿٤﴾

أو ﴿قُلْ آمَنَّا بِاللهِ وَمَا أُنْزِلَ... الخ﴾

و ﴿قُلْ يَا أَهْلَ الْكِتَابِ تَعَالَوْا إِلَى كَلِمَةٍ سَوَاءٍ...

الخ﴾ ﴿٥﴾

1. O Allah! No one can withhold what You have bestowed, and no one can bestow what You have withheld. Nor is the possessor of fortune availed against You by his fortune.

2. There is no strength or power except in Allah. There is no god but Allah, and we worship only Him. To Him belongs all bounty, to Him belongs all favor, and to Him belongs the most beautiful praise. (We say) There is no god but Allah, and we sincerely devote ourselves to Him in religion despite the contempt of the unbelievers.

Qunut: A special supplication recited during the witr prayer

3. O Allah, Lord of Gabriel, Mikail, Israfil, and Muhammad! I seek refuge in You from the Hellfire. (3)

4. O Allah, guide me along with those You have guided, and grant me health along with those whom You have granted health. Take me into Your care along with those whom You have taken into Your care, and bless me in what You have given me. Save me from the evil of what You have decreed, for verily You are the One Who decrees, and You are not subject to any decree. For sure, the one You have befriended cannot be humiliated, and the one You take as an enemy will not find honor. Blessed are You, O Allah, our Lord, and Exalted! May Allah bless the Prophet!

اَللّٰهُمَّ لَا مَانِعَ لِمَا أَعْطَيْتَ وَلَا مُعْطِيَ لِمَا مَنَعْتَ وَلَا يَنْفَعُ ذَا الْجَدِّ مِنْكَ الْجَدُّ ﴿١﴾ لَا حَوْلَ وَلَا قُوَّةَ إِلَّا بِاللّٰهِ، لَآ إِلٰهَ إِلَّا اللّٰهُ وَلَا نَعْبُدُ إِلَّآ إِيَّاهُ، لَهُ النِّعْمَةُ وَلَهُ الْفَضْلُ وَلَهُ الثَّنَاءُ الْحَسَنُ، لَآ إِلٰهَ إِلَّا اللّٰهُ مُخْلِصِينَ لَهُ الدِّينَ وَلَوْ كَرِهَ الْكَافِرُونَ ﴿٢﴾

وَإِذَا قَنَتَ يَقُولُ:

اَللّٰهُمَّ رَبَّ جِبْرِيلَ وَمِيكَآئِيلَ وَإِسْرَافِيلَ وَمُحَمَّدٍ أَعُوذُ بِكَ مِنَ النَّارِ (٣) ﴿٣﴾

اَللّٰهُمَّ اهْدِنِي فِيمَنْ هَدَيْتَ، وَعَافِنِي فِيمَنْ عَافَيْتَ، وَتَوَلَّنِي فِيمَنْ تَوَلَّيْتَ، وَبَارِكْ لِي فِيمَآ أَعْطَيْتَ، وَقِنِي شَرَّ مَا قَضَيْتَ، فَإِنَّكَ تَقْضِي وَلَا يُقْضَى عَلَيْكَ وَإِنَّهُ لَا يَذِلُّ مَنْ وَالَيْتَ وَلَا يَعِزُّ مَنْ عَادَيْتَ تَبَارَكْتَ اللّٰهُمَّ رَبَّنَا وَتَعَالَيْتَ وَصَلَّى اللّٰهُ عَلَى النَّبِيِّ ﴿٤﴾

1. O Allah! Forgive me for what I have done and for what I will do, for what I have concealed, and what I have declared, and what I committed excess in, and for what You know best about from me. You are the Hastener, You are the Postponer, and there is no god but You.

2. O Allah! I take refuge in You from the punishment of the grave. I take refuge in You from the trial of the Antichrist (*Al Dajjal*), and I take refuge in You from the trial of life and death.

3. O Allah! I take refuge in You from the [yoke] of debt and the [burden] of sin.

4. O Allah! Truly I take refuge in You from the punishment of Hell, from the punishment of the grave, from the trial of life and death, and from the trial of the Antichrist.

After the salaam which terminates the ritual prayer

5. I seek forgiveness from Allah, the All-Mighty. (3)

6. O Allah! You are the Source of Peace (and well-being), and from You comes peace, blessed and Exalted are You, Possessor of Majesty and Bounty!

7. There is no god but Allah, alone, without associate. His is the dominion, His is the praise, and He has power over all things.

اَللُّهُمَّ اغْفِرْ لِي مَا قَدَّمْتُ وَمَا أَخَّرْتُ وَمَا أَسْرَرْتُ

وَمَا أَعْلَنْتُ وَمَا أَسْرَفْتُ وَمَا أَنْتَ أَعْلَمُ بِهِ مِنِّي، أَنْتَ

الْمُقَدِّمُ وَأَنْتَ الْمُؤَخِّرُ لَا إِلهَ إِلَّا أَنْتَ ۝١ اَللُّهُمَّ إِنِّي

أَعُوذُ بِكَ مِنْ عَذَابِ الْقَبْرِ وَأَعُوذُ بِكَ مِنْ فِتْنَةِ الْمَسِيحِ

الدَّجَّالِ وَأَعُوذُ بِكَ مِنْ فِتْنَةِ الْمَحْيَا وَالْمَمَاتِ ۝٢

اَللُّهُمَّ إِنِّي أَعُوذُ بِكَ مِنَ الْمَغْرَمِ وَالْمَأْثَمِ ۝٣

اَللُّهُمَّ إِنِّي أَعُوذُ بِكَ مِنْ عَذَابِ جَهَنَّمَ وَمِنْ عَذَابِ الْقَبْرِ

وَمِنْ فِتْنَةِ الْمَحْيَا وَالْمَمَاتِ وَمِنْ فِتْنَةِ الْمَسِيحِ الدَّجَّالِ ۝٤

وَبَعْدَ السَّلَامِ يَقُولُ:

أَسْتَغْفِرُ اللهَ الْعَظِيمَ (٣) ۝٥

اَللُّهُمَّ أَنْتَ السَّلَامُ وَمِنْكَ السَّلَامُ تَبَارَكْتَ يَا ذَا

الْجَلَالِ وَالْإِكْرَامِ ۝٦ لَا إِلهَ إِلَّا اللهُ وَحْدَهُ لَا شَرِيكَ لَهُ،

لَهُ الْمُلْكُ وَلَهُ الْحَمْدُ وَهُوَ عَلَى كُلِّ شَيْءٍ قَدِيرٌ ۝٧

٥٣

When making the attestation (tashahhud)

1. All worship (*tahiyya*; the worship offered by all the living beings through their lives), prayers, good words and deeds belong to Allah. Peace be upon you O Prophet, and the mercy of Allah and His blessings! Peace be upon us and upon the righteous servants of Allah! I bear witness that there is no god but Allah and I bear witness that Muhammad is His servant and Messenger.

2. O Allah! Bless our master Muhammad and the family of our master Muhammad as You blessed Abraham and the family of Abraham, and send Your grace on our master Muhammad and the family of our master Muhammad as You sent grace on Abraham and the family of Abraham. Truly You are the Owner of Praise, the Glorious.

3. O Allah! Truly I have greatly wronged my soul, and no one forgives sins except You, so forgive me with Your forgiveness, and have mercy on me, for You are the All-Forgiving, the All-Compassionate.

وَفِي التَّشَهُّدِ يَقْرَأُ:

اَلتَّحِيَّاتُ للهِ والصَّلَوَاتُ والطَّيِّبَاتُ، اَلسَّلَامُ عَلَيْكَ
أَيُّهَا النَّبِيُّ وَرَحْمَةُ اللهِ وَبَرَكَاتُهُ، اَلسَّلَامُ عَلَيْنَا وَعَلَى عِبَادِ
اللهِ الصَّالِحِينَ أَشْهَدُ أَنْ لَا إِلَهَ إِلَّا اللهُ وَأَشْهَدُ أَنَّ مُحَمَّداً
عَبْدُهُ وَرَسُولُهُ ﴿١﴾

اَللَّهُمَّ صَلِّ عَلَى سَيِّدِنَا مُحَمَّدٍ وَعَلَى اٰلِ سَيِّدِنَا
مُحَمَّدٍ كَمَا صَلَّيْتَ عَلَى إِبْرٰهِيمَ وَعَلَى اٰلِ إِبْرٰهِيمَ وَبَارِكْ
عَلَى سَيِّدِنَا مُحَمَّدٍ وَعَلَى اٰلِ سَيِّدِنَا مُحَمَّدٍ كَمَا بَارَكْتَ
عَلَى إِبْرٰهِيمَ وَعَلَى اٰلِ إِبْرٰهِيمَ إِنَّكَ حَمِيدٌ مَجِيدٌ ﴿٢﴾

اَللَّهُمَّ إِنِّي ظَلَمْتُ نَفْسِي ظُلْماً كَثِيراً وَلَا يَغْفِرُ
الذُّنُوبَ إِلَّا أَنْتَ فَاغْفِرْ لِي مَغْفِرَةً مِنْ عِنْدِكَ وَارْحَمْنِي
إِنَّكَ أَنْتَ الْغَفُورُ الرَّحِيمُ ﴿٣﴾

1. O Allah! To You I prostrate myself, in You I believe, and in You have I placed my trust. My face is prostrated to the One Who created and formed it, and gave it openings for hearing and sight; blessed is Allah the Best of creators!

2. Humbled before You are my hearing, my sight, my blood, my flesh, my bones, my nerves and what is borne on my two feet for the sake of Allah, the Lord of the worlds.

3. Transcendent and Holy is the Lord of the angels and the Spirit.

4. O Allah! Forgive me for all my sins, the greater and the minor, the first and the last, and the openly known and those kept secret!

5. Glory be to the Owner of the world of Names and Attributes (*jabarut*, or the intermediary world) and heavenly kingdom (*malakut*; the realm of spirits, the veiled reality beyond), Possessor of Greatness and Absolute Might.

In the sitting position between the two prostrations

6. O Allah! Forgive me, have mercy on me, grant me health, guide me, provide for me, restore me, and raise me up!

7. O Lord! Grant me a pious heart, clean from association (*shirk*), and righteous, not disbelieving nor wretched!

8. O Lord, forgive and show mercy, and overlook what You know best about, for truly You are the Honorable with irresistible Might, the All-Generous.

اَللّٰهُمَّ لَكَ سَجَدْتُ وَبِكَ اٰمَنْتُ وَلَكَ أَسْلَمْتُ، سَجَدَ

وَجْهِي لِلَّذِي خَلَقَهُ وَصَوَّرَهُ وَشَقَّ سَمْعَهُ وَبَصَرَهُ تَبَارَكَ اللهُ

أَحْسَنُ الْخَالِقِينَ ﴿١﴾ خَشَعَ سَمْعِي وَبَصَرِي وَدَمِي وَلَحْمِي

وَعَظْمِي وَعَصَبِي وَمَا اسْتَقَلَّتْ بِهِ قَدَمَيَّ لِلهِ رَبِّ الْعَالَمِينَ ﴿٢﴾

سُبُّوحٌ قُدُّوسٌ رَبُّ الْمَلٰئِكَةِ وَالرُّوحِ ﴿٣﴾

اَللّٰهُمَّ اغْفِرْ لِي ذَنْبِي كُلَّهُ دِقَّهُ وَجِلَّهُ وَأَوَّلَهُ وَاٰخِرَهُ

وَعَلَانِيَتَهُ وَسِرَّهُ ﴿٤﴾ سُبْحَانَ ذِي الْجَبَرُوتِ وَالْمَلَكُوتِ

وَالْكِبْرِيَاءِ وَالْعَظَمَةِ ﴿٥﴾

وَفِي الْجُلُوسِ بَيْنَ السَّجْدَتَيْنِ يَقُولُ:

اَللّٰهُمَّ اغْفِرْ لِي وَارْحَمْنِي وَعَافِنِي وَاهْدِنِي وَارْزُقْنِي

وَاجْبُرْنِي وَارْفَعْنِي ﴿٦﴾ رَبِّ هَبْ لِي قَلْبًا تَقِيًّا نَقِيًّا مِنَ

الشِّرْكِ بَرِيًّا لَا كَافِرًا وَلَا شَقِيًّا ﴿٧﴾ رَبِّ اغْفِرْ وَارْحَمْ

وَتَجَاوَزْ عَمَّا تَعْلَمُ إِنَّكَ أَنْتَ الْأَعَزُّ الْأَكْرَمُ ﴿٨﴾

1. O Allah! To You belongs praise that fills the heavens, the earth, that which is between them, and fills whatever You wish beyond that. O Owner of glory and praise! The most truthful words spoken by a servant—and all of us are Your servants—are: "No one can deny the one to whom You have given, no one can give to the one whom You have denied, and the possessor of fortune is not availed against You by his fortune."

2. O Allah! Purify me with snow, hail, and cold water!

3. O Allah! Purify me from sin and error as the white garment is cleansed from filth.

In prostration

4. Glory be to my Lord, Most High! (3-9)

5. Glory be to You, O Allah, our Lord, and to You be all praise! O Allah, forgive me!

6. O Allah, truly I seek refuge in Your good pleasure from Your anger, in Your exemption from Your punishment, and I seek refuge in You from You. I admit that I am unable to praise You as You have praised Yourself.

اَللّٰهُمَّ لَكَ الْحَمْدُ مِلْءَ السَّمٰوَاتِ وَمِلْءَ الْأَرْضِ وَمِلْءَ
مَا بَيْنَهُمَا وَمِلْءَ مَا شِئْتَ مِنْ شَيْءٍ بَعْدُ، أَهْلَ الْمَجْدِ وَالثَّنَاءِ
أَحَقُّ مَا قَالَ الْعَبْدُ وَكُلُّنَا لَكَ عَبْدٌ، لَا مَانِعَ لِمَا أَعْطَيْتَ
وَلَا مُعْطِيَ لِمَا مَنَعْتَ وَلَا يَنْفَعُ ذَا الْجَدِّ مِنْكَ الْجَدُّ ﴿١﴾
اَللّٰهُمَّ طَهِّرْنِي بِالثَّلْجِ وَالْبَرَدِ وَالْمَاءِ الْبَارِدِ ﴿٢﴾

اَللّٰهُمَّ طَهِّرْنِي مِنَ الذُّنُوبِ وَالْخَطَايَا كَمَا يُنَقَّى
الثَّوْبُ الْأَبْيَضُ مِنَ الدَّنَسِ ﴿٣﴾

وَفِي السُّجُودِ يَقُولُ:

سُبْحَانَ رَبِّيَ الْأَعْلٰى (٣-٩) ﴿٤﴾

سُبْحَانَكَ اللّٰهُمَّ رَبَّنَا وَبِحَمْدِكَ اللّٰهُمَّ اغْفِرْ لِي ﴿٥﴾
اَللّٰهُمَّ إِنِّي أَعُوذُ بِرِضَاكَ مِنْ سَخَطِكَ وَبِمُعَافَاتِكَ مِنْ
عُقُوبَتِكَ وَأَعُوذُ بِكَ مِنْكَ لَا أُحْصِي ثَنَاءً عَلَيْكَ أَنْتَ
كَمَا أَثْنَيْتَ عَلٰى نَفْسِكَ ﴿٦﴾

In ruku' (the bowing position)

1. Glory be to the Owner of the world of Names and Attributes (*jabarut*, or the intermediary world) and heavenly kingdom (*malakut*; the realm of spirits, the veiled reality beyond), Possessor of Greatness and Absolute Might.

2. Glory be to my Lord, the All-Mighty! (3-9)

3. Glory be to You O Allah, our Lord! And to You is all praise. O Allah, forgive me!

4. Glory be to Allah, and to Him be praise! (3)

5. Transcendent and Holy is You, the Lord of the angels and the Spirit.

6. O Allah! To You I bow, in You I believe, and to You I submit. Humbled before You are my hearing, my sight, my brain, my bones, my nerves and what is borne on my two feet for the sake of Allah, the Lord of the worlds.

Raising one's head from ruku'

(according to some Imams):

7. Allah is the Greatest of the great, and praise be to Allah, manifold! Glory be to Allah, in the early morning and in the evening.

8. O Allah, our Lord! To You belongs all praise, praise manifold, pure and blessed.

وَفِي الرُّكُوعِ يَقُولُ:

سُبْحَانَ ذِي الْجَبَرُوتِ وَالْمَلَكُوتِ وَالْكِبْرِيَاءِ

وَالْعَظَمَةِ ﴿١﴾ سُبْحَانَ رَبِّيَ الْعَظِيمِ (٣-٩) ﴿٢﴾

سُبْحَانَكَ اللّٰهُمَّ رَبَّنَا وَبِحَمْدِكَ اللّٰهُمَّ اغْفِرْ لِي ﴿٣﴾

سُبْحَانَ اللهِ وَبِحَمْدِهِ (٣) ﴿٤﴾ سُبُّوحٌ قُدُّوسٌ رَبُّ

الْمَلَئِكَةِ وَالرُّوحِ ﴿٥﴾

اَللّٰهُمَّ لَكَ رَكَعْتُ وَبِكَ آمَنْتُ وَلَكَ أَسْلَمْتُ، خَشَعَ

لَكَ سَمْعِي وَبَصَرِي وَمُخِّي وَعَظْمِي وَعَصَبِي وَمَا

اسْتَقَلَّتْ بِهِ قَدَمِيَّ لِلّٰهِ رَبِّ الْعَالَمِينَ ﴿٦﴾

وَإِذَا رَفَعَ رَأْسَهُ مِنَ الرُّكُوعِ يَقُولُ:

(عند بعض الأئمة:)

اَللهُ أَكْبَرُ كَبِيرًا وَالْحَمْدُ لِلّٰهِ كَثِيرًا وَسُبْحَانَ اللهِ بُكْرَةً

وَأَصِيلاً ﴿٧﴾ اَللّٰهُمَّ رَبَّنَا وَلَكَ الْحَمْدُ حَمْدًا كَثِيرًا طَيِّبًا

مُبَارَكًا فِيهِ ﴿٨﴾

٤٩

1. O Allah! You are the Sovereign, there is no god but You. You are my Lord and I am Your servant. I have wronged my soul, and I confess my sin, so forgive me for all my sins, for truly there is no one who forgives sins except You. Guide me to the best morals, for no one guides to them except You, and rid me of bad characteristics for no one can get rid of them except You.

2. At Your beckoning and Your pleasure! All goodness is in Your hands, and evil is not attributed to You. I seek shelter in Your grace and turn to You. Blessed are You, O our Lord, and exalted! I seek forgiveness from You in repentance.

3. O Allah! Distance me from my misdeeds as You have distanced the East from the West!

4. O Allah! Wash away my sins with water, snow and hail!

5. O Allah! Cleanse me of my sins as the white garment is cleaned of filth.

6. Glory be to You O Allah, and to You is all praise! Blessed is Your name, exalted is Your majesty. There is no god but You.

اَللّٰهُمَّ أَنْتَ الْمَلِكُ لَا إِلٰهَ إِلَّا أَنْتَ، أَنْتَ رَبِّي وَأَنَا عَبْدُكَ ظَلَمْتُ نَفْسِي وَاعْتَرَفْتُ بِذَنْبِي فَاغْفِرْ لِي ذُنُوبِي جَمِيعاً إِنَّهُ لَا يَغْفِرُ الذُّنُوبَ إِلَّا أَنْتَ، وَاهْدِنِي لِأَحْسَنِ الْأَخْلَاقِ لَا يَهْدِي لِأَحْسَنِهَا إِلَّا أَنْتَ، وَاصْرِفْ عَنِّي سَيِّئَهَا لَا يَصْرِفُ سَيِّئَهَا إِلَّا أَنْتَ ﴿١﴾ لَبَّيْكَ وَسَعْدَيْكَ وَالْخَيْرُ كُلُّهُ فِي يَدَيْكَ وَالشَّرُّ لَيْسَ إِلَيْكَ أَنَا بِكَ وَإِلَيْكَ، تَبَارَكْتَ رَبَّنَا وَتَعَالَيْتَ أَسْتَغْفِرُكَ وَأَتُوبُ إِلَيْكَ ﴿٢﴾ اَللّٰهُمَّ بَاعِدْ بَيْنِي وَبَيْنَ خَطَايَايَ كَمَا بَاعَدْتَ بَيْنَ الْمَشْرِقِ وَالْمَغْرِبِ ﴿٣﴾ اَللّٰهُمَّ اغْسِلْ خَطَايَايَ بِالْمَاءِ وَالثَّلْجِ وَالْبَرَدِ ﴿٤﴾ اَللّٰهُمَّ نَقِّنِي مِنْ خَطَايَايَ كَمَا يُنَقَّى الثَّوْبُ الْأَبْيَضُ مِنَ الدَّنَسِ ﴿٥﴾

سُبْحَانَكَ اللّٰهُمَّ وَبِحَمْدِكَ وَتَبَارَكَ اسْمُكَ وَتَعَالٰى جَدُّكَ وَلَا إِلٰهَ غَيْرُكَ ﴿٦﴾

1. O Allah! Grant Muhammad the highest and most virtuous ranks in Paradise, make his love and remembrance among the chosen ones You made nearest to You.

2. O Allah! Bless Muhammad, raise him to the rank of intercession in Your presence, and include us in his intercession on the Day of Judgment!

Ritual Prayer (*Salat*)

After the reciting of "Allahu Akbar" (Takbirat al-Ihram) which initiates the ritual prayer

3. (According to some Imams) Allah is the Greatest of the great, and praise be to Allah, manifold!

   I seek refuge in Allah from the blowing, spitting and goading of Satan the accursed. Glory be to Allah, in the early morning and in the evening!

4. I have directed my face to the One Who produced the heavens and the earth, as a true Muslim and I am not among those who associate partners with Him.

5. Truly my prayer, my rites, my life, and my death are for Allah, Lord of the Worlds.

   No associate has He, and this is what I have been commanded, for I am among the Muslims.

اَللّٰهُمَّ أَعْطِ مُحَمَّداً الْوَسِيلَةَ وَالْفَضِيلَةَ وَاجْعَلْ فِي أَعْلَيْنَ دَرَجَتِهِ وَفِي الْمُصْطَفَيْنَ مَحَبَّتَهُ وَفِي الْمُقَرَّبِينَ ذِكْرَهُ ﴿١﴾

اَللّٰهُمَّ صَلِّ عَلَى مُحَمَّدٍ وَبَلِّغْهُ دَرَجَةَ الْوَسِيلَةِ عِنْدَكَ وَاجْعَلْنَا فِي شَفَاعَتِهِ يَوْمَ الْقِيَامَةِ ﴿٢﴾

دُعَاءُ الْافْتِتَاحِ بَعْدَ تَكْبِيرَةِ الْإِحْرَامِ:

(عند بعض الأئمة:)

اَللهُ أَكْبَرُ كَبِيراً وَالْحَمْدُ لله كَثِيراً، أَعُوذُ بِاللهِ مِنَ الشَّيْطَانِ الرَّجِيمِ مِنْ نَفْخِهِ وَنَفْثِهِ وَهَمْزِهِ فَسُبْحَانَ اللهِ بُكْرَةً وَأَصِيلاً ﴿٣﴾

﴿وَجَّهْتُ وَجْهِيَ لِلَّذِي فَطَرَ السَّمٰوَاتِ وَالْأَرْضَ حَنِيفاً مُسْلِماً وَمَآ أَنَا مِنَ الْمُشْرِكِينَ﴾ ﴿٤﴾ ﴿إِنَّ صَلَاتِي وَنُسُكِي وَمَحْيَايَ وَمَمَاتِي لله رَبِّ الْعَالَمِينَ، لَا شَرِيكَ لَهُ وَبِذٰلِكَ أُمِرْتُ وَأَنَا مِنَ الْمُسْلِمِينَ﴾ ﴿٥﴾

The Call to Prayer (Adhan)

1. It is *sunna* to make the call to prayer (*adhan*), and so is
    the *iqama*. On hearing the *adhan* one repeats what the
    muezzin says, except that instead of "Come to the prayer"
    and "Come to salvation" one says: "There is no strength
    or power except in Allah."

    ### Hearing the adhan for the evening prayer

2. O Allah! Now is [the time of] the advancing of Your night
    and the retreating of Your day, the voices of Your suppli-
    cants, and the coming of Your prayer times, so forgive me!

    ### The prayer after the adhan

3. I bear witness that there is no god but Allah, alone, with-
    out associate, and that Muhammad is His servant and His
    Messenger.

4. I am content with Allah as my Lord, with Muhammad as
    my Messenger and with Islam as my religion.

    O Allah! Lord of this call [to prayer] that has been com-
    pleted, and the ritual prayer that is about to be performed,
    grant our master Muhammad nearness to You, reaching
    Paradise and beyond, and exalt him to the praised station
    of intercession that You promised him.

اَلْأَذَانُ

وَيُسَنُّ الأذان كما عرف والإقامة كذلك؛ وإذا سمع الأذان يقول مثلما قال المؤذن إلا أنه يقول بدل ''حَيَّ عَلَى الصَّلَاةِ'' و''حَيَّ عَلَى الفَلَاحِ'': (لَاحَوْلَ وَلَا قُوَّةَ إِلَّا بِاللهِ) ﴿١﴾

وَإِذَا سَمِعَ أَذَانَ الْمَغْرِبِ يَقُولُ:

اَللّٰهُمَّ هٰذَا إِقْبَالُ لَيْلِكَ وَإِدْبَارُ نَهَارِكَ وَأَصْوَاتُ دُعَاتِكَ وَحُضُورُ صَلَوَاتِكَ فَاغْفِرْ لِي ﴿٢﴾

اَلدُّعَاءُ بَعْدَ الْأَذَانِ:

أَشْهَدُ أَنْ لَا إِلٰهَ إِلَّا اللهُ وَحْدَهُ لَا شَرِيكَ لَهُ وَأَنَّ مُحَمَّدًا عَبْدُهُ وَرَسُولُهُ، رَضِيتُ بِاللهِ رَبًّا وَبِمُحَمَّدٍ رَسُولًا وَبِالْإِسْلَامِ دِينًا ﴿٣﴾

اَللّٰهُمَّ رَبَّ هٰذِهِ الدَّعْوَةِ التَّامَّةِ وَالصَّلَاةِ الْقَائِمَةِ أتِ سَيِّدَنَا مُحَمَّدٍ الْوَسِيلَةَ وَالْفَضِيلَةَ وَابْعَثْهُ مَقَامًا مَحْمُودًا الَّذِي وَعَدْتَهُ ﴿٤﴾

1. In the name of Allah, and blessings and peace be upon the Messenger of Allah.
2. I seek refuge in Allah, the All-Mighty, in His Greatness, and in His pre-eternal Authority, from Satan the accursed.
3. O Allah! Open for me the gates of Your mercy!

Leaving the mosque

One leaves the mosque with one's left foot first and says:

4. O Allah! Bless Muhammad and the family of Muhammad.

   In the name of Allah, and blessings and peace be upon the Messenger of Allah.
5. O Allah! Forgive me for my sins and open for me the gates of Your favor.
6. O Allah! Grant me protection from Satan. O Allah! I ask of You Your favor.

To someone buying and selling in the mosque

7. May your trade not prosper!

To someone calling out for something he has lost

8. May Allah not return it to you!

بِسْمِ اللهِ وَالصَّلَاةُ وَ السَّلَامُ عَلَى رَسُولِ اللهِ ﴿١﴾

أَعُوذُ بِاللهِ الْعَظِيمِ وَبِوَجْهِهِ الْكَرِيمِ وَبِسُلْطَانِهِ الْقَدِيمِ

مِنَ الشَّيْطَانِ الرَّجِيمِ ﴿٢﴾

اَللّٰهُمَّ افْتَحْ لِي أَبْوَابَ رَحْمَتِكَ ﴿٣﴾

وَعِنْدَ خُرُوجِهِ مِنَ الْمَسْجِدِ:

يخرج من المسجد برجله اليسرى ويقول:

اَللّٰهُمَّ صَلِّ عَلَى مُحَمَّدٍ وَعَلَى اٰلِ مُحَمَّدٍ، بِسْمِ اللهِ

وَالصَّلَاةُ وَالسَّلَامُ عَلَى رَسُولِ اللهِ ﴿٤﴾

اَللّٰهُمَّ اغْفِرْ لِي ذَنْبِي وَافْتَحْ لِي أَبْوَابَ فَضْلِكَ ﴿٥﴾ اَللّٰهُمَّ

اعْصِمْنِي مِنَ الشَّيْطَانِ، اَللّٰهُمَّ إِنِّي أَسْأَلُكَ مِنْ فَضْلِكَ

﴿٦﴾

وَ إِذَا رَأَى مَنْ يَبِيعُ وَيَشْتَرِي فِي الْمَسْجِدِ يَقُولُ لَهُ:

لَا أَرْبَحَ اللهُ تِجَارَتَكَ ﴿٧﴾

وَإِذَا سَمِعَ مَنْ يَنْشُدُ ضَالَّةً فِي الْمَسْجِدِ يَقُولُ لَهُ:

لَا رَدَّهَا اللهُ عَلَيْكَ ﴿٨﴾

٤٥

Mosque

On setting out for the mosque

1. In the name of Allah, I believe in Allah and put my trust in Him, there is no strength or power except in Allah. O Allah! By the inviolability of those who petition You, and by this departure of mine—for truly I do not go out with insolence, or arrogance, or in ostentation, or seeking esteem, but rather I have set out seeking Your good pleasure, and in fear of Your wrath—I ask You to deliver me from the Hellfire and bring me into Paradise.

2. O Allah! Grant for me light in my heart, light on my tongue, light in my sight, light in my hearing, light on my right, light behind me, light in front of me, light above me, and light beneath me!

   Grant me light! Grant me light in my nerves, light in my blood, light in my hair, light in my skin, and light in my soul, and magnify my light. O Allah! Give me light!

Entering the mosque

One enters the mosque with one's right foot first and says:

وَإِذَا تَوَجَّهَ إِلَى الْمَسْجِدِ يَقُولُ:

بِسْمِ اللهِ، اٰمَنْتُ بِاللهِ، تَوَكَّلْتُ عَلَى اللهِ، لَا حَوْلَ وَلَا
قُوَّةَ إِلَّا بِاللهِ، اَللّٰهُمَّ بِحُرْمَةِ السَّآئِلِينَ عَلَيْكَ وَبِمَخْرَجِي
هٰذَا فَإِنِّي لَمْ أَخْرُجْهُ أَشَرًا وَلَا بَطَرًا وَلَا رِيَآءً وَلَا
سُمْعَةً، خَرَجْتُ ابْتِغَآءَ مَرْضَاتِكَ وَاتِّقَآءَ سَخَطِكَ،
أَسْأَلُكَ أَنْ تُعِيذَنِي مِنَ النَّارِ وَأَنْ تُدْخِلَنِي الْجَنَّةَ ﴿١﴾

اَللّٰهُمَّ اجْعَلْ فِي قَلْبِي نُورًا وَفِي لِسَانِي نُورًا وَفِي
بَصَرِي نُورًا وَفِي سَمْعِي نُورًا وَمِنْ يَمِينِي نُورًا وَمِنْ خَلْفِي
نُورًا وَمِنْ أَمَامِي نُورًا وَاجْعَلْ مِنْ فَوْقِي نُورًا وَمِنْ تَحْتِي
نُورًا وَاجْعَلْ لِي نُورًا وَفِي عَصَبِي نُورًا وَفِي لَحْمِي نُورًا
وَفِي دَمِي نُورًا وَفِي شَعْرِي نُورًا وَفِي بَشَرِي نُورًا وَاجْعَلْ
فِي نَفْسِي نُورًا وَأَعْظِمْ لِي نُورًا، اَللّٰهُمَّ أَعْطِنِي نُورًا ﴿٢﴾

وَعِنْدَ دُخُولِهِ الْمَسْجِدَ:

يدخل المسجد برجله اليمنى ويقول:

٤٤

After completing the ablution

1. I bear witness that there is no god but Allah and that Muhammad is His servant and His Messenger.

2. O Allah! Make me of those who are penitent and make me of those who purify themselves.

3. Glory be to You Allah, and to You is all praise! I bear witness that there is no god but You. I seek Your forgiveness, and turn to You in repentance. May Allah bless our master, Muhammad, his family and his companions and grant them peace!

4. In the name of Allah, the Merciful, the Compassionate "Verily we sent it down on the night of Power ❀ And what will convey to you what the night of Power is? ❀ The night of Power is better than a thousand months ❀ During which the angels descend and the Spirit by permission of their Lord with every decree ❀ Peace then reigns until the rise of dawn." (Qadr 97) (3)

5. O Allah! Forgive me for my sins, make my home spacious, bless my provision and don't make what You have kept from me a cause for temptation!

وَإِذَا فَرَغَ مِنَ الْوُضُوءِ يَقُولُ:

أَشْهَدُ أَنْ لَا إِلٰهَ إِلَّا اللهُ وَحْدَهُ لَا شَرِيكَ لَهُ وَأَشْهَدُ أَنَّ مُحَمَّداً عَبْدُهُ وَرَسُولُهُ ﴿١﴾

اَللّٰهُمَّ اجْعَلْنِي مِنَ التَّوَّابِينَ وَاجْعَلْنِي مِنَ الْمُتَطَهِّرِينَ ﴿٢﴾

سُبْحَانَكَ اللّٰهُمَّ وَبِحَمْدِكَ أَشْهَدُ أَنْ لَا إِلٰهَ إِلَّا أَنْتَ أَسْتَغْفِرُكَ وَأَتُوبُ إِلَيْكَ وَصَلَّى اللهُ عَلَى سَيِّدِنَا مُحَمَّدٍ وَعَلَى اٰلِهِ وَصَحْبِهِ وَسَلَّمَ ﴿٣﴾

بِسْمِ اللهِ الرَّحْمٰنِ الرَّحِيمِ ﴿إِنَّا أَنْزَلْنَاهُ فِي لَيْلَةِ الْقَدْرِ ۝ وَمَا أَدْرَاكَ مَا لَيْلَةُ الْقَدْرِ ۝ لَيْلَةُ الْقَدْرِ خَيْرٌ مِنْ أَلْفِ شَهْرٍ ۝ تَنَزَّلُ الْمَلٰئِكَةُ وَالرُّوحُ فِيهَا بِإِذْنِ رَبِّهِمْ مِنْ كُلِّ أَمْرٍ ۝ سَلَامٌ هِيَ حَتَّى مَطْلَعِ الْفَجْرِ﴾ (٣) ﴿٤﴾

اَللّٰهُمَّ اغْفِرْ لِي ذَنْبِي وَوَسِّعْ لِي فِي دَارِي وَبَارِكْ لِي فِي رِزْقِي وَلَا تَفْتِنِّي بِمَا زَوَيْتَ عَنِّي ﴿٥﴾

٤٣

Purification

Before entering the bathroom

1. O Allah! Verily I seek refuge in You from the filthy, impure, wicked, malevolent, Satan the accursed.

2. In the name of Allah, verily I seek refuge in You from male and female devils which are filthy from head to toe.

After leaving the bathroom

3. Your forgiveness I beseech! Praise is due to Allah Who let me taste its (the food's) delight, Who kept within me its nourishment, and ridded me of its harm.

4. (Or) Praise be to Allah Who has ridded me of its harm and kept me healthy.

5. O Allah! Purify my heart from hypocrisy and safeguard my private parts from all indecency.

When beginning the ablution (wudu)

6. In the name of Allah, the Merciful, the Compassionate. O Allah! Forgive me for my sins, make my home spacious, and bless my provision!

7. I bear witness that there is no god but Allah and that Muhammad is the Messenger of Allah.

إِذَا أَرَادَ أَنْ يَدْخُلَ الْخَلَاءَ يَقُولُ:

اَللّٰهُمَّ إِنِّيٓ أَعُوذُ بِكَ مِنَ الرِّجْسِ وَالنَّجَسِ الْخَبِيثِ الْمُخْبِثِ الشَّيْطَانِ الرَّجِيمِ ﴿١﴾

بِسْمِ اللهِ اَللّٰهُمَّ إِنِّيٓ أَعُوذُ بِكَ مِنَ الْخُبْثِ وَالْخَبَائِثِ ﴿٢﴾

وَإِذَا خَرَجَ مِنَ الْخَلَاءِ يَقُولُ:

غُفْرَانَكَ، اَلْحَمْدُ لِلّٰهِ الَّذِي أَذَاقَنِي لَذَّتَهُ وَأَبْقٰى فِيَّ قُوَّتَهُ وَأَذْهَبَ عَنِّي أَذَاهُ ﴿٣﴾

(أَوْ) اَلْحَمْدُ لِلّٰهِ الَّذِي أَذْهَبَ عَنِّي الْأَذٰى وَعَافَانِي ﴿٤﴾

اَللّٰهُمَّ طَهِّرْ قَلْبِي مِنَ النِّفَاقِ وَحَصِّنْ فَرْجِي مِنَ الْفَوَاحِشِ ﴿٥﴾

وَإِذَا تَوَضَّأَ يَقُولُ:

بِسْمِ اللهِ الرَّحْمٰنِ الرَّحِيمِ، اَللّٰهُمَّ اغْفِرْ لِي ذَنْبِي وَوَسِّعْ لِي فِي دَارِي وَبَارِكْ لِي فِي رِزْقِي ﴿٦﴾

أَشْهَدُ أَنْ لَآ إِلٰهَ إِلَّا اللهُ وَأَنَّ مُحَمَّداً رَسُولُ اللهِ ﴿٧﴾

أَدْعِيَةٌ مُتَعَلِّقَةٌ بِالطُّهُورِ وَالْمَسْجِدِ
وَالْأَذَانِ وَالصَّلَاةِ

PURIFICATION, THE MOSQUE,
THE CALL TO PRAYER (*ADHAN*)
AND THE RITUAL PRAYER (*SALAT*)

During the witr prayer after Surat al-Fatiha

In the first *rak'a* (cycle): Surat al-A'la.

In the second *rak'a*: Surat al-Kafirun.

In the third *rak'a*: Surat al-Ikhlas.

After witr

1. I seek refuge in Allah from the blowing and goading of Satan, the accursed.

2. Glory be to the Owner of the earthly (*mulk*; unveiled reality possessing a space) and heavenly (*malakut*; the realm of spirits, the veiled reality beyond) kingdoms, the world of Names and Attributes (*jabarut*,[2] or the intermediary world), Possessor of Greatness and Absolute Might.

3. Glory be to the Sovereign, the All-Holy! (3)

4. (Aloud) Lord of the angels and Spirit (Gabriel)!

   O Allah! Truly I seek refuge in Your good pleasure from Your anger, in Your exemption from Your punishment, and I seek refuge in You from You. I admit that I am unable to praise You as You have praised Yourself.

---

[2] *Jabarut* cannot be translated fully in one or two words. It refers to the universal and absolute influence of the manifestation of the Divine names on all created things.

وَيَقْرَأُ فِي الْوِتْرِ بَعْدَ فَاتِحَةِ الْكِتَابِ:

في الركعة الأولى: سورة الأعلى

و في الركعة الثانية: سورة الكافرون

و في الركعة الثالثة: سورة الإخلاص

وَيَقْرَأُ بَعْدَهُ:

أَعُوذُ بِاللهِ مِنَ الشَّيْطَانِ الرَّجِيمِ مِنْ نَفْخِهِ وَنَفْثِهِ
وَهَمْزِهِ ﴿١﴾

سُبْحَانَ ذِي الْمُلْكِ وَالْمَلَكُوتِ وَالْعِزَّةِ وَالْجَبَرُوتِ
وَالْكِبْرِيَاءِ وَالْعَظَمَةِ ﴿٢﴾

سُبْحَانَ الْمَلِكِ الْقُدُّوسِ (٣) ﴿٣﴾

وَيَرْفَعُ صَوْتَهُ قَائِلًا: رَبُّ الْمَلَئِكَةِ وَالرُّوحِ ﴿٤﴾

اَللّٰهُمَّ إِنِّي أَعُوذُ بِرِضَاكَ مِنْ سَخَطِكَ وَبِمُعَافَاتِكَ
مِنْ عُقُوبَتِكَ وَأَعُوذُ بِكَ مِنْكَ، لَا أُحْصِي ثَنَاءً عَلَيْكَ
أَنْتَ كَمَا أَثْنَيْتَ عَلَى نَفْسِكَ ﴿٥﴾

When one has got up and prayed for a portion of the night

1. O Allah! To You is due all praise for You are the Sustainer of the heavens and the earth and all that is within them. All praise is Yours, for You are the King of the heavens and the earth and all that is within them. All praise is Yours, for You are the Light of the heavens and the earth and all that is within them. All praise is Yours, for You are the Truth, Your promise is true, the meeting with You is true and Your word is true.

   Paradise is true, the Hellfire is true, the Prophets are true, Muhammad (peace and blessings be upon him) is true, and the Last Hour is true.

   O Allah! To You I have submitted, in You do I believe, in You have I put my trust, and unto You I turn in repentance. For Your sake I have disputed, and from You I seek judgment, so forgive me for what I have done and for what I will do, for what I have concealed and what I have declared, and for that [in me] that You know best about.

   You are the Hastener and the Postponer, there is no god but You, and there is no strength or power except in Allah.

وَيَدْعُو إِذَا قَامَ مِنَ اللَّيْلِ:

اَللّٰهُمَّ لَكَ الْحَمْدُ أَنْتَ قَيُّومُ السَّمٰوَاتِ وَالْأَرْضِ وَمَنْ فِيهِنَّ، وَلَكَ الْحَمْدُ أَنْتَ مَلِكُ السَّمٰوَاتِ وَالْأَرْضِ وَمَنْ فِيهِنَّ، وَلَكَ الْحَمْدُ أَنْتَ نُورُ السَّمٰوَاتِ وَالْأَرْضِ وَمَنْ فِيهِنَّ، وَلَكَ الْحَمْدُ أَنْتَ الْحَقُّ وَوَعْدُكَ الْحَقُّ وَلِقَاؤُكَ حَقٌّ وَقَوْلُكَ حَقٌّ وَالْجَنَّةُ حَقٌّ وَالنَّارُ حَقٌّ وَالنَّبِيُّونَ حَقٌّ وَمُحَمَّدٌ ﷺ حَقٌّ وَالسَّاعَةُ حَقٌّ، اَللّٰهُمَّ لَكَ أَسْلَمْتُ وَبِكَ اٰمَنْتُ وَعَلَيْكَ تَوَكَّلْتُ وَإِلَيْكَ أَنَبْتُ وَبِكَ خَاصَمْتُ وَإِلَيْكَ حَاكَمْتُ فَاغْفِرْ لِي مَا قَدَّمْتُ وَمَا أَخَّرْتُ وَمَا أَسْرَرْتُ وَمَا أَعْلَنْتُ وَمَا أَنْتَ أَعْلَمُ بِهِ مِنِّي، أَنْتَ الْمُقَدِّمُ وَأَنْتَ الْمُؤَخِّرُ لَا إِلٰهَ إِلَّا أَنْتَ وَلَا حَوْلَ وَلَا قُوَّةَ إِلَّا بِالله ﴿١﴾

٣٩

Tahajjud

The Prophet (peace and blessings be upon him) used to get up at night to pray, and would pray eleven *rak'as* (cycles) (three witr, and eight tahajjud). When he got up he would say:

Allah is the Greatest! (*Allahu Akbar*) (10)

Praise be to Allah! (*Alhamdulillah*) (10)

Glory be to Allah! (*Subhan Allah*) (10)

There is no god but Allah. (*La ilaha illallah*) (10)

I seek forgiveness from Allah, the All-Mighty (*astaghfirullah al-'Azim*) (10)

O Allah! Forgive me, guide me, provide for me, and keep me healthy. (10)

O Allah! I seek refuge in You from a straightening space on the Day of Resurrection. (10)

اَلتَّهَجُّدُ

كان النبي ﷺ إذا قام من الليل يصلي إحدى عشرة ركعة

ويوتر؛ ويقول إذا قام:

اَللهُ أَكْبَرُ (١٠)

اَلْحَمْدُ للهِ (١٠)

سُبْحَانَ اللهِ (١٠)

لَا إِلهَ إِلَّا اللهُ (١٠)

أَسْتَغْفِرُ اللهَ الْعَظِيمَ (١٠)

اَللّهُمَّ اغْفِرْ لِي وَاهْدِنِي وَارْزُقْنِي وَعَافِنِي (١٠)

اَللّهُمَّ إِنِّي أَعُوذُ بِكَ مِنْ ضِيقِ الْمَقَامِ يَوْمَ الْقِيَامَةِ (١٠)

In the name of Allah, the Merciful, the Compassionate. (10)

Glory be to Allah! (10)

I believe in Allah and reject all idols. (10)

On waking up

1. Praise be to Allah who has revived us after death, and unto Him is the Resurrection. There is no god but You, Glorified are You, O Allah! I seek Your forgiveness for my sins, and I ask You for Your mercy.

2. O Allah! Increase my knowledge, and let not my heart stray after You have guided me, and grant me Your mercy, for truly You are the One Who bestows.

بِسْمِ اللهِ الرَّحْمٰنِ الرَّحِيمِ (١٠)

سُبْحَانَ اللهِ (١٠)

اٰمَنْتُ بِاللهِ وَكَفَرْتُ بِالطَّاغُوتِ (١٠)

وَإِذَا انْتَبَهَ يَقُولُ:

اَلْحَمْدُ للهِ الَّذِيٓ أَحْيَانَا بَعْدَ مَا أَمَاتَنَا وَإِلَيْهِ النُّشُورُ ﴿١﴾
لَاۤ إِلٰهَ إِلَّاۤ أَنْتَ سُبْحَانَكَ اللّٰهُمَّ أَسْتَغْفِرُكَ لِذَنْبِي وَأَسْأَلُكَ
رَحْمَتَكَ، اَللّٰهُمَّ زِدْنِي عِلْمًا وَلَا تُزِغْ قَلْبِي بَعْدَ إِذْ هَدَيْتَنِي
وَهَبْ لِي مِنْ لَدُنْكَ رَحْمَةً إِنَّكَ أَنْتَ الْوَهَّابُ ﴿٢﴾

1. O Allah, Lord of the seven heavens and what they overshadow, Lord of the earth and what it bears, and Lord of the devils and those they mislead! Be my Redeemer from the evil of all that You created, against anyone of them that commit an excess against me or oppress me! Mighty is the one under Your protection, blessed is Your name, exalted is Your praise, there is no god other than You, and there is no god but You.

2. O Allah! The stars have faded, eyes have come to rest, and You are the All-Living, the Self-Subsistent, [Who is] neither overtaken by slumber nor sleep. O All-Living, Self-Subsistent [Lord]! (*Ya Hayyu, Ya Qayyum*) Calm my night, and let me sleep (in peace)!

   (Abdullah ibn 'Amr ibn 'As (a Companion of the Prophet) used to teach these words to those of his children that had reached the age of reasoning, and for those who were younger than that he would write the words on a piece of paper which would be hung around their necks.)

When one turns in his bed

3. There is no god but Allah, the One, the Subduer, Lord of the heavens and the earth and what is between them. He is the Almighty, the Forgiving.

اَللّٰهُمَّ رَبَّ السَّمٰوَاتِ السَّبْعِ وَمَاۤ أَظَلَّتْ وَرَبَّ الْأَرَضِينَ وَمَاۤ أَقَلَّتْ وَرَبَّ الشَّيَاطِينِ وَمَاۤ أَضَلَّتْ كُنْ لِي جَارًا مِنْ شَرِّ خَلْقِكَ أَجْمَعِينَ أَنْ يَفْرُطَ عَلَيَّ أَحَدٌ مِنْهُمْ وَأَنْ يَطْغٰى، عَزَّ جَارُكَ وَتَبَارَكَ اسْمُكَ وَجَلَّ ثَنَاؤُكَ وَلَاۤ إِلٰهَ غَيْرُكَ وَلَاۤ إِلٰهَ إِلَّاۤ أَنْتَ ﴿١﴾

اَللّٰهُمَّ غَارَتِ النُّجُومُ وَهَدَأَتِ الْعُيُونُ وَأَنْتَ حَيٌّ قَيُّومٌ لَا تَأْخُذُهُ سِنَةٌ وَلَا نَوْمٌ يَا حَيُّ يَا قَيُّومُ أَهْدِئْ لَيْلِي وَأَنِمْ عَيْنِي ﴿٢﴾

(كان عبد الله بن عمرو بن العاص يلقنها من عقل من ولده، ومن لم يعقل منهم يكتبها له في صَكّ ثم يعلقها في عنقه)

وَإِذَا تَحَرَّكَ فِي الْفِرَاشِ يَقُولُ:

لَاۤ إِلٰهَ إِلَّا اللهُ الْوَاحِدُ الْقَهَّارُ رَبُّ السَّمٰوَاتِ وَالْأَرْضِ وَمَا بَيْنَهُمَا الْعَزِيزُ الْغَفَّارُ ﴿٣﴾

After having a good dream

If one has a good dream one praises Allah for it and does not speak about the dream to anyone except those whom one loves.

After having an unpleasant dream

After seeing something unpleasant in a dream one expresses quick breaths three times to the left side and seeks refuge in Allah from Satan. Then one turns over (to go back to sleep) or gets up to pray.

Feeling afraid or lonely

1. I take refuge in the perfect words of Allah from His wrath and punishment, from the evil of His servants and from the goading of devils and their approaching me.

2. I take refuge in the perfect words of Allah that cannot be surpassed either by the upright or by the immoral, from any evil that descends from the sky and any that ascends to it, and from any evil that He dispersed over the earth and that issues from within it, and from the evil of the trials of the night and day. And from the evil of unexpected callers at night or during the day, except for one who brings goodness, O All-Merciful One! (*ya Rahman*)

إِذَا رَأَى مِنْ نَومِهِ مَا يُحِبُّ:

إذا رأى من نومه ما يحب يحمد الله عليه ولا يحدّث بما
رأى إلا من يحب.

إِذَا رَأَى مِنْ نَوْمِهِ مَا يَكْرَهُ:

إذا رأى من نومه ما يكره يتفل أو ينفث ثلاثًا عن يساره
ويتعوذ بالله من الشيطان ويتحول أو يقوم فيصلي.

إِذَا فَزِعَ أَو وَجَدَ وَحْشَةً يَقُولُ:

أَعُوذُ بِكَلِمَاتِ اللهِ التَّامَّةِ مِنْ غَضَبِهِ وَعِقَابِهِ وَشَرِّ
عِبَادِهِ وَمِنْ هَمَزَاتِ الشَّيَاطِينِ وَأَنْ يَحْضُرُونِي ﴿١﴾ أَعُوذُ بِكَلِمَاتِ اللهِ التَّامَّاتِ الَّتِي لَا يُجَاوِزُهُنَّ بَرٌّ وَلَا
فَاجِرٌ مِنْ شَرِّ مَا يَنْزِلُ مِنَ السَّمَاءِ وَمَا يَعْرُجُ فِيهَا وَمِنْ
شَرِّ مَا ذَرَأَ فِي الْأَرْضِ وَمَا يَخْرُجُ مِنْهَا وَمِنْ شَرِّ فِتَنِ
اللَّيْلِ وَفِتَنِ النَّهَارِ، وَمِنْ شَرِّ طَوَارِقِ اللَّيْلِ وَالنَّهَارِ إِلَّا
طَارِقًا يَطْرُقُ بِخَيْرٍ يَا رَحْمٰنُ ﴿٢﴾

1. O Allah! Grant me the enjoyment of my hearing and sight, and let me bequeath them (those faculties) to You intact. Grant me victory over my enemy and realize for me my vengeance on them!

2. O Allah! I take refuge in You from the imposition of debt and from hunger, for truly it is a wretched companion.

3. All praise is due to Allah Who has fed us, and given us to drink, sated our hunger, and quenched our thirst, for many are those who do not have anybody to meet their needs or provide them shelter.

4. All praise is due to Allah who met my needs, Who provided shelter for me, Who fed me and gave me to drink; Who bestowed on me graciously, favored me, and gave to me in abundance. Praise is due to Allah whatever the situation.

   O Allah, Lord, Owner and God of everything! I seek refuge in You from the hellfire.

5. In Your name, my Lord, have I laid down on my side, and in Your name I raise it up. If You take back my soul forgive it and have mercy on it, and if You send it back, protect it with the protection You accord Your righteous servants.

6. O Allah! Save me from Your punishment as You save the righteous on the day that You resurrect Your servants. (3)

اَللّٰهُمَّ أَمْتِعْنِي بِسَمْعِي وَبَصَرِي وَاجْعَلْهُمَا الْوَارِثَ مِنِّي وَانْصُرْنِي عَلٰى عَدُوِّي وَأَرِنِي مِنْهُ ثَأْرِي ﴿١﴾

اَللّٰهُمَّ إِنِّيْ أَعُوذُ بِكَ مِنْ غَلَبَةِ الدَّيْنِ وَمِنَ الْجُوعِ فَإِنَّهُ بِئْسَ الضَّجِيعُ ﴿٢﴾

اَلْحَمْدُ للهِ الَّذِيْ أَطْعَمَنَا وَسَقَانَا وَكَفَانَا وَاٰوَانَا، فَكَمْ مِمَّنْ لَا كَافِيَ لَهُ وَلَا مُؤْوِيَ لَهُ ﴿٣﴾

اَلْحَمْدُ للهِ الَّذِي كَفَانِي وَاٰوَانِي وَأَطْعَمَنِي وَسَقَانِي وَالَّذِي مَنَّ عَلَيَّ فَأَفْضَلَ وَالَّذِيْ أَعْطَانِي فَأَجْزَلَ وَالْحَمْدُ للهِ عَلٰى كُلِّ حَالٍ، اَللّٰهُمَّ رَبَّ كُلِّ شَيْءٍ وَمَلِيكَهُ وَإِلٰهَ كُلِّ شَيْءٍ أَعُوذُ بِكَ مِنَ النَّارِ ﴿٤﴾

بِاسْمِكَ رَبِّي وَضَعْتُ جَنْبِي وَبِكَ أَرْفَعُهُ، إِنْ أَمْسَكْتَ نَفْسِي فَاغْفِرْ لَهَا وَارْحَمْهَا وَإِنْ أَرْسَلْتَهَا فَاحْفَظْهَا بِمَا تَحْفَظُ بِهِ عِبَادَكَ الصَّالِحِينَ ﴿٥﴾

اَللّٰهُمَّ قِنِي عَذَابَكَ يَوْمَ تَبْعَثُ عِبَادَكَ (٣) ﴿٦﴾

٣٤

1. O Allah! Save me from Your punishment on the day when You resurrect Your servants. In Your name I die and live.

2. There is no god but Allah, alone without associate, His is the dominion, His is the praise, and He has power over all things.

   There is no strength or power except in Allah, the All-High, the All-Mighty.

   Glory be to Allah! Praise be to Allah! There is no god but Allah. Allah is the Greatest. There is no strength or power except in Allah, the All-High, the All-Mighty.

3. O Allah! I seek refuge in You and in Your perfect words from the evil of all that is in Your charge. O Allah! You are the One Who removes the [yoke of debt] and [burden] of sin. O Allah! Your soldier is not defeated, Your promise is not broken, and the owner of a fortune is not availed against You by his fortune.

4. Glory be to You Allah, and to You be praise! In the name of Allah I have laid down on my side. O Allah! Forgive me my sins and drive away the devil inside me; release me from my dependency (on others), and place me in the highest assembly!

5. O Allah! in Your name have I laid down on my side, so forgive me for my sins!

اَللّٰهُمَّ قِنِي عَذَابَكَ يَوْمَ تَبْعَثُ عِبَادَكَ، بِاسْمِكَ أَمُوتُ وَأَحْيَا ﴿١﴾

لَآ إِلٰهَ إِلَّا اللهُ وَحْدَهُ لَا شَرِيكَ لَهُ، لَهُ الْمُلْكُ وَلَهُ الْحَمْدُ وَهُوَ عَلٰى كُلِّ شَيْءٍ قَدِيرٌ، لَا حَوْلَ وَلَا قُوَّةَ إِلَّا بِاللهِ الْعَلِيِّ الْعَظِيمِ، سُبْحَانَ اللهِ وَالْحَمْدُ للهِ وَلَاإِلٰهَ إِلَّا اللهُ وَاللهُ أَكْبَرُ وَلَا حَوْلَ وَلَا قُوَّةَ إِلَّا بِاللهِ الْعَلِيِّ الْعَظِيمِ ﴿٢﴾

اَللّٰهُمَّ إِنِّي أَعُوذُ بِوَجْهِكَ الْكَرِيمِ وَكَلِمَاتِكَ التَّامَّةِ مِنْ شَرِّ مَآ أَنْتَ اٰخِذٌ بِنَاصِيَتِهِ، اَللّٰهُمَّ أَنْتَ تَكْشِفُ الْمَغْرَمَ وَالْمَأْثَمَ، اَللّٰهُمَّ لَا يُهْزَمُ جُنْدُكَ وَلَا يُخْلَفُ وَعْدُكَ وَلَا يَنْفَعُ ذَا الْجَدِّ مِنْكَ الْجَدُّ، سُبْحَانَكَ اللّٰهُمَّ وَبِحَمْدِكَ ﴿٣﴾

بِسْمِ اللهِ وَضَعْتُ جَنْبِي، اَللّٰهُمَّ اغْفِرْ لِي ذَنْبِي وَأَخْسِئْ شَيْطَانِي وَفُكَّ رِهَانِي وَاجْعَلْنِي فِي النَّدِيِّ الْأَعْلٰى ﴿٤﴾

اَللّٰهُمَّ بِاسْمِكَ رَبِّي وَضَعْتُ جَنْبِي فَاغْفِرْ لِي ذَنْبِي ﴿٥﴾

٣٣

1. O Allah! You created my soul and You will take it back, its death and life are in Your hands. If You return it alive protect it, and if you take it back forgive it.

   O Allah! I ask You for well-being.

2. O Allah! Lord of the heavens, Lord of the earth, and Lord of the Supreme Throne, our Lord and Lord of everything, Cleaver of the grain and the kernel, and the One who sent down the Torah, the Gospel and the Criterion (*al-Furqan*—the Qur'an)! I take refuge in You from the evil of everything, for everything is in Your grasp.

   O Allah! You are the First and there is nothing before You, You are the Last and there is nothing after You, You are the Manifest (Who owns and rules everything from outside) and there is nothing above You,[1] You are the Hidden (Who owns and rules everything from within) and there is nothing beyond You. Settle for us our debts, and keep us free from poverty.

3. O Allah! Truly I have submitted myself to You, turned my face to You, entrusted my affairs to You, relied on You, there is no refuge or security except in You. O Allah! I believe in the Book that You revealed, and in the Prophet that You sent.

---

[1] The presence of Allah is free from any associations related with occupying space. Here, "above" signifies "beyond" in the sense of what is manifest. Thus He is at the heart of things without being encompassed by anything.

اَللّٰهُمَّ أَنْتَ خَلَقْتَ نَفْسِي وَأَنْتَ تَتَوَفَّاهَا، لَكَ مَمَاتُهَا وَمَحْيَاهَا إِنْ أَحْيَيْتَهَا فَاحْفَظْهَا وَإِنْ أَمَتَّهَا فَاغْفِرْ لَهَا، اَللّٰهُمَّ إِنِّي أَسْأَلُكَ الْعَافِيَةَ ۝

اَللّٰهُمَّ رَبَّ السَّمٰوَاتِ وَرَبَّ الْأَرْضِ وَرَبَّ الْعَرْشِ الْعَظِيمِ رَبَّنَا وَرَبَّ كُلِّ شَيْءٍ فَالِقَ الْحَبِّ وَالنَّوَى وَمُنْزِلَ التَّوْرَاةِ وَالْإِنْجِيلِ وَالْفُرْقَانِ أَعُوذُ بِكَ مِنْ شَرِّ كُلِّ شَيْءٍ أَنْتَ اٰخِذٌ بِنَاصِيَتِهِ، اَللّٰهُمَّ أَنْتَ الْأَوَّلُ فَلَيْسَ قَبْلَكَ شَيْءٌ وَأَنْتَ الْاٰخِرُ فَلَيْسَ بَعْدَكَ شَيْءٌ وَأَنْتَ الظَّاهِرُ فَلَيْسَ فَوْقَكَ شَيْءٌ وَأَنْتَ الْبَاطِنُ فَلَيْسَ دُونَكَ شَيْءٌ اقْضِ عَنَّا الدَّيْنَ وَأَغْنِنَا مِنَ الْفَقْرِ ۝

اَللّٰهُمَّ إِنِّي أَسْلَمْتُ نَفْسِي إِلَيْكَ وَوَجَّهْتُ وَجْهِي إِلَيْكَ وَفَوَّضْتُ أَمْرِي إِلَيْكَ وَأَلْجَأْتُ ظَهْرِي إِلَيْكَ رَغْبَةً وَرَهْبَةً إِلَيْكَ لَا مَلْجَأَ وَلَا مَنْجٰى مِنْكَ إِلَّا إِلَيْكَ، اَللّٰهُمَّ اٰمَنْتُ بِكِتَابِكَ الَّذِي أَنْزَلْتَ وَنَبِيِّكَ الَّذِي أَرْسَلْتَ ۝

1. The Verse of the Throne (Ayat al-Kursi):
   "Allah! There is no god but He, the All-Living, the Self-Subsistent. Neither does slumber overtake Him nor sleep, and to Him belongs whatever is in the heavens and the earth. Who can intercede with Him except by His leave? He knows what is before them and what is behind them and they only comprehend of His knowledge only that which He wills. His Throne encompasses the heavens and the earth, and maintaining them both tires Him not. He is the Exalted, the Sublime." (Baqara 2:255)

2. Then he reads the suras Ya Sin, al-Sajda, al-Mulk, and al-Kafirun.

3. Then he joins his palms, reads into them the suras al-Ikhlas, al-Falaq, and al-Nas, blows into them and then wipes them over as much of his body as he can, starting with his head and face. (3)

Retiring to bed

4. They ask for forgiveness then read the following: Allah is the Greatest! (33) Glory be to Allah! (33), Allah be praised! (33).

﴿اَللّٰهُ لَآ إِلٰهَ إِلَّا هُوَ الْحَيُّ الْقَيُّومُ لَا تَأْخُذُهُ سِنَةٌ وَلَا نَوْمٌ لَهُ مَا فِي السَّمٰوَاتِ وَمَا فِي الْأَرْضِ مَنْ ذَا الَّذِي يَشْفَعُ عِنْدَهُ إِلَّا بِإِذْنِهِ يَعْلَمُ مَا بَيْنَ أَيْدِيهِمْ وَمَا خَلْفَهُمْ وَلَا يُحِيطُونَ بِشَيْءٍ مِنْ عِلْمِهِ إِلَّا بِمَا شَاءَ وَسِعَ كُرْسِيُّهُ السَّمٰوَاتِ وَالْأَرْضَ وَلَا يَؤُودُهُ حِفْظُهُمَا وَهُوَ الْعَلِيُّ الْعَظِيمُ﴾ (١)

ويقرأ سورة يٰسٓ وسورة السجدة وسورة الملك وسورة

﴿قُلْ يَآ أَيُّهَا الْكَافِرُونَ﴾ (٢)

ثم يجمع كفيه فيقرأ سُوَرَ ﴿قُلْ هُوَ اللّٰهُ أَحَدٌ﴾ والفلق والناس فينفث فيهما ثم يمسح بهما ما استطاع من جسده يبدأ بهما على رأسه ووجهه (٣) (٣)

إِذَا أَوٰى إِلٰى فِرَاشِهِ:

يستغفر ثم يقول: اَللّٰهُ أَكْبَرُ (٣٣) سُبْحَانَ اللّٰهِ (٣٣) اَلْحَمْدُ لِلّٰهِ (٣٣) (٤)

٣١

Before going to sleep

1. "Alif Lam Mim. ❀ This is the Book in which there is no doubt, within it is guidance for the God-revering and pious. ❀ Who believe in the unseen, establish the prayer and spend out of what we have provided them. ❀ And who believe in that which is sent down to you (Muhammad), and that which was sent down before you, and have certainty in the Hereafter. ❀ These are on true guidance from their Lord, and these are the successful." (Baqara 2:1-5)

2. "The Messenger believes in what has been sent down to him, and so do the believers. All believe in Allah, His angels, His Books, and His messengers—We make no distinction between any of His messengers—and they say: 'We hear and obey. Your forgiveness, O our Lord! And to You is the journeying. ❀ Allah does not charge a soul beyond its capacity. It shall be requited only for the good it earned and the evil it committed. Our Lord! Do not take us to task when we forget or make mistakes! Our Lord! Do not lay on us a burden like that which you laid on those who came before us! Our Lord! Do not charge us with more than we can bear! Pardon us, forgive us, and have mercy on us! You are our Master, grant us victory over the unbelievers." (Baqara 2:285-286)

إِذَا أَرَادَ أَنْ يَنَامَ يَقْرَأُ:

﴿الٓمٓ ۝ ذٰلِكَ الْكِتَابُ لَا رَيْبَ فِيهِ هُدًى لِلْمُتَّقِينَ ۝ الَّذِينَ يُؤْمِنُونَ بِالْغَيْبِ وَيُقِيمُونَ الصَّلٰوةَ وَمِمَّا رَزَقْنَاهُمْ يُنْفِقُونَ ۝ وَالَّذِينَ يُؤْمِنُونَ بِمَا أُنْزِلَ إِلَيْكَ وَمَا أُنْزِلَ مِنْ قَبْلِكَ وَبِالْآخِرَةِ هُمْ يُوقِنُونَ ۝ أُولٰئِكَ عَلٰى هُدًى مِنْ رَبِّهِمْ وَأُولٰئِكَ هُمُ الْمُفْلِحُونَ ۝﴾ (١)

﴿آمَنَ الرَّسُولُ بِمَا أُنْزِلَ إِلَيْهِ مِنْ رَبِّهِ وَالْمُؤْمِنُونَ كُلٌّ آمَنَ بِاللهِ وَمَلٰئِكَتِهِ وَكُتُبِهِ وَرُسُلِهِ لَا نُفَرِّقُ بَيْنَ أَحَدٍ مِنْ رُسُلِهِ وَقَالُوا سَمِعْنَا وَأَطَعْنَا غُفْرَانَكَ رَبَّنَا وَإِلَيْكَ الْمَصِيرُ ۝ لَا يُكَلِّفُ اللهُ نَفْساً إِلَّا وُسْعَهَا لَهَا مَا كَسَبَتْ وَعَلَيْهَا مَا اكْتَسَبَتْ رَبَّنَا لَا تُؤَاخِذْنَا إِنْ نَسِينَا أَوْ أَخْطَأْنَا رَبَّنَا وَلَا تَحْمِلْ عَلَيْنَا إِصْراً كَمَا حَمَلْتَهُ عَلَى الَّذِينَ مِنْ قَبْلِنَا رَبَّنَا وَلَا تُحَمِّلْنَا مَا لَا طَاقَةَ لَنَا بِهِ وَاعْفُ عَنَّا وَاغْفِرْ لَنَا وَارْحَمْنَا أَنْتَ مَوْلٰينَا فَانْصُرْنَا عَلَى الْقَوْمِ الْكَافِرِينَ﴾ (٢)

O Lord! I ask You for the goodness of this night, and the goodness of the nights thereafter and I seek refuge in You from the evil of this night and the evil of the nights thereafter.

1. O Lord! I take refuge in You from sloth and the troubles of old age. O Lord! I seek refuge in You from torment in the hellfire, and torment of the grave. 1. O Allah! I take refuge in You from sloth, decrepitude, the troubles of old age, the temptation of this world and the punishment of the Hereafter. The evening has fallen upon us and upon the creation, and all belongs to Allah, the Lord of the worlds.

2. O Allah! I ask from You the goodness of this night, the triumph, the support, the light, the grace, and the guidance therein, and I seek refuge in You from the evil of this night and the evil thereafter.

3. O Allah! Make faith beloved to us, endearing it to our hearts, and make unbelief, impiety and disobedience hateful to us, and make us among the rightly guided.

4. O Allah! Verily I ask You for a soul that is at peace with You, believing in the meeting with You, content with Your decree, and satisfied with whatever You bestow.

شَيْءٍ قَدِيرٌ، رَبِّ إِنِّي أَسْأَلُكَ خَيْرَ مَا فِي هٰذِهِ اللَّيْلَةِ وَخَيْرَ مَا بَعْدَهَا وَأَعُوذُ بِكَ مِنْ شَرِّ مَا فِي هٰذِهِ اللَّيْلَةِ وَشَرِّ مَا بَعْدَهَا، رَبِّ أَعُوذُ بِكَ مِنَ الْكَسَلِ وَسُوءِ الْكِبَرِ رَبِّ أَعُوذُ بِكَ مِنْ عَذَابٍ فِي النَّارِ وَعَذَابٍ فِي الْقَبْرِ ﴿٤﴾

اَللّٰهُمَّ إِنِّي أَعُوذُ بِكَ مِنَ الْكَسَلِ وَالْهَرَمِ وَسُوءِ الْكِبَرِ وَفِتْنَةِ الدُّنْيَا وَعَذَابِ الْقَبْرِ، أَمْسَيْنَا وَأَمْسَى الْمُلْكُ لِلّٰهِ رَبِّ الْعَالَمِينَ ﴿١﴾

اَللّٰهُمَّ إِنِّي أَسْأَلُكَ خَيْرَ هٰذِهِ اللَّيْلَةِ وَفَتْحَهَا وَنَصْرَهَا وَنُورَهَا وَبَرَكَتَهَا وَهُدَاهَا وَأَعُوذُ بِكَ مِنْ شَرِّ مَا فِيهَا وَشَرِّ مَا بَعْدَهَا ﴿٢﴾

اَللّٰهُمَّ حَبِّبْ إِلَيْنَا الْإِيمَانَ وَزَيِّنْهُ فِي قُلُوبِنَا وَكَرِّهْ إِلَيْنَا الْكُفْرَ وَالْفُسُوقَ وَالْعِصْيَانَ وَاجْعَلْنَا مِنَ الرَّاشِدِينَ ﴿٣﴾

اَللّٰهُمَّ إِنِّي أَسْأَلُكَ نَفْسًا بِكَ مُطْمَئِنَّةً تُؤْمِنُ بِلِقَائِكَ وَتَرْضَى بِقَضَائِكَ وَتَقْنَعُ بِعَطَائِكَ ﴿٤﴾

1. I seek refuge in the perfect words of Allah from the evil of what He created. (3)

2. "So glorify Allah when you enter the night and when you enter the morning. ❂ To Him belongs all praise in the heavens and the earth, at the close of day and at noon-tide. ❂ He brings forth the living from the dead, and He brings forth the dead from the living; even so shall you be brought forth." (Rum 30:17-19)

3. The Verse of the Throne (Ayat al-Kursi):

   "Allah! There is no god but He, the All-Living, the Self-Subsistent. Neither does slumber overtake Him nor sleep, and to Him belongs whatever is in the heavens and the earth. Who can intercede with Him except by His leave? He knows what is before them and what is behind them and they comprehend of His knowledge only that which He wills. His Throne encompasses the heavens and the earth, and maintaining them both tires Him not. He is the Exalted, the Sublime." (Baqara 2:255)

4. Evening has fallen upon us and upon creation—all belongs to Allah, and all praise is due to Him. There is no god but Allah, alone, without associate, His is the dominion, to Him is all praise, and He has power over all things.

أَعُوذُ بِكَلِمَاتِ اللهِ التَّامَّاتِ مِنْ شَرِّ مَا خَلَقَ (٣) ﴿١﴾

﴿فَسُبْحَانَ اللهِ حِينَ تُمْسُونَ وَحِينَ تُصْبِحُونَ ۞ وَلَهُ الْحَمْدُ فِي السَّمٰوَاتِ وَالْأَرْضِ وَعَشِيّاً وَحِينَ تُظْهِرُونَ ۞ يُخْرِجُ الْحَيَّ مِنَ الْمَيِّتِ وَيُخْرِجُ الْمَيِّتَ مِنَ الْحَيِّ وَيُحْيِي الْأَرْضَ بَعْدَ مَوْتِهَا وَكَذٰلِكَ تُخْرَجُونَ ﴿٢﴾

﴿ اَللهُ لَا إِلٰهَ إِلَّا هُوَ اَلْحَيُّ الْقَيُّومُ لَا تَأْخُذُهُ سِنَةٌ وَلَا نَوْمٌ لَهُ مَا فِي السَّمٰوَاتِ وَمَا فِي الْأَرْضِ مَنْ ذَا الَّذِي يَشْفَعُ عِنْدَهُ إِلَّا بِإِذْنِهِ يَعْلَمُ مَا بَيْنَ أَيْدِيهِمْ وَمَا خَلْفَهُمْ وَلَا يُحِيطُونَ بِشَيْءٍ مِنْ عِلْمِهِ إِلَّا بِمَا شَاءَ وَسِعَ كُرْسِيُّهُ السَّمٰوَاتِ وَالْأَرْضَ وَلَا يَؤُودُهُ حِفْظُهُمَا وَهُوَ الْعَلِيُّ الْعَظِيمُ ﴿٣﴾

أَمْسَيْنَا وَأَمْسَى الْمُلْكُ للهِ وَالْحَمْدُ للهِ لَا إِلٰهَ إِلَّا اللهُ وَحْدَهُ لَا شَرِيكَ لَهُ، لَهُ الْمُلْكُ وَلَهُ الْحَمْدُ وَهُوَ عَلَى كُلِّ

1. Allah is my sufficiency, there is no god but Him. In Him have I put my trust and He is the Lord of the Supreme Throne. (Tawba 9:129) (7)

2. O Allah! You are my Lord, there is no god but You. You created me, I am Your servant and I have tried to keep my oath and promise to You as much as I can. I seek refuge in You from the evil of what I have done. I acknowledge the grace You have bestowed upon me, and I acknowledge my sin. So, forgive me, for truly no one forgives sins except You.

3. There is no god but Allah and Allah is the Greatest, there is no god but Allah alone, there is no god but Allah without associate, there is no god but Allah. His is the dominion and all praise is due to Him. There is no god but Allah and there is no strength or power except in Allah.

4. O Allah! Verily I ask You for good health with faith, faith with good character, success followed by salvation, I ask You for Your mercy, for well-being, for Your forgiveness and good pleasure.

5. In the name of Allah with [the protection of] Whose name nothing on earth or in heaven can do harm, and He is the All- Hearing, the All-Knowing. (3)

﴿حَسْبِيَ اللهُ لَا إِلَهَ إِلَّا هُوَ عَلَيْهِ تَوَكَّلْتُ وَهُوَ رَبُّ الْعَرْشِ الْعَظِيمِ﴾ (٧) ①

اَللّٰهُمَّ أَنْتَ رَبِّي لَا إِلَهَ إِلَّا أَنْتَ خَلَقْتَنِي وَأَنَا عَبْدُكَ وَأَنَا عَلَى عَهْدِكَ وَوَعْدِكَ مَا اسْتَطَعْتُ أَعُوذُ بِكَ مِنْ شَرِّ مَا صَنَعْتُ أَبُوءُ لَكَ بِنِعْمَتِكَ عَلَيَّ وَأَبُوءُ لَكَ بِذَنْبِي فَاغْفِرْ لِي فَإِنَّهُ لَا يَغْفِرُ الذُّنُوبَ إِلَّا أَنْتَ ②

لَا إِلَهَ إِلَّا اللهُ وَاللهُ أَكْبَرُ لَا إِلَهَ إِلَّا اللهُ وَحْدَهُ لَا إِلَهَ إِلَّا اللهُ لَا شَرِيكَ لَهُ لَا إِلَهَ إِلَّا اللهُ لَهُ الْمُلْكُ وَلَهُ الْحَمْدُ لَا إِلَهَ إِلَّا اللهُ وَلَا حَوْلَ وَلَا قُوَّةَ إِلَّا بِاللهِ ③

اَللّٰهُمَّ إِنِّي أَسْأَلُ لَكَ صِحَّةً فِي إِيمَانٍ وَإِيمَانًا فِي حُسْنِ خُلُقٍ وَنَجَاحًا يَتْبَعُهُ فَلَاحٌ وَرَحْمَةً مِنْكَ وَعَافِيَةً وَمَغْفِرَةً مِنْكَ وَرِضْوَانًا ④

بِسْمِ اللهِ الَّذِي لَا يَضُرُّ مَعَ اسْمِهِ شَيْءٌ فِي الْأَرْضِ وَلَا فِي السَّمَاءِ وَهُوَ السَّمِيعُ الْعَلِيمُ (٣) ⑤

٢٧

1.   O Allah! You are the most worthy of remembrance and the most worthy of worship. You are the best helper of all those who are sought [for help]. You are the most compassionate of owners, the most generous of those who are petitioned, and the most liberal of givers. You are the King without associate, Alone without peer. Everything perishes except You. You are not obeyed except by Your leave and You are not disobeyed except in Your knowledge. When You are obeyed You show gratitude and when You are disobeyed You are forgiving. You are the closest Witness and the Guardian most nigh. You come between (humankind) and their own souls, and You have them completely in Your grasp. You have recorded their actions and set down their life spans. Hearts reach You and with You all that which is secret is open to view. The legitimate is only that which You have made legitimate, and the forbidden is only that which You have forbidden. Religion is what You have prescribed, and the command is what You have decreed. The creation is Your creation and every servant is Your servant. You are Allah, the Compassionate, the Beneficent. I ask You by the light of Your Countenance by which the heavens and the earth became illuminated, by every right that is Yours and by the right of those who ask of You, to support me through this day and night and to save me from the' hellfire through Your Power.

اَللّٰهُمَّ أَنْتَ أَحَقُّ مَنْ ذُكِرَ وَأَحَقُّ مَنْ عُبِدَ وَأَنْصَرَ مَنِ ابْتُغِيَ وَأَرْأَفُ مَنْ مَلَكَ وَأَجْوَدُ مَنْ سُئِلَ وَأَوْسَعُ مَنْ أَعْطَى، أَنْتَ الْمَلِكُ لَا شَرِيكَ لَكَ وَالْفَرْدُ لَا نِدَّ لَكَ كُلُّ شَيْءٍ هَالِكٌ إِلَّا وَجْهَكَ إِلَّا لَنْ تُطَاعَ إِلَّا بِإِذْنِكَ وَلَنْ تُعْصَى إِلَّا بِعِلْمِكَ تُطَاعُ فَتَشْكُرُ وَتُعْصَى فَتَغْفِرُ أَقْرَبُ شَهِيدٍ وَأَدْنَى حَفِيظٍ حُلْتَ دُونَ النُّفُوسِ وَأَخَذْتَ بِالنَّوَاصِي وَكَتَبْتَ الْآثَارَ وَنَسَخْتَ الْآجَالَ، الْقُلُوبُ لَكَ مُفْضِيَةٌ وَالسِّرُّ عِنْدَكَ عَلَانِيَةٌ، الْحَلَالُ مَا أَحْلَلْتَ وَالْحَرَامُ مَا حَرَّمْتَ وَالدِّينُ مَا شَرَعْتَ وَالْأَمْرُ مَا قَضَيْتَ الْخَلْقُ خَلْقُكَ وَالْعَبْدُ عَبْدُكَ وَأَنْتَ اللهُ الرَّؤُوفُ الرَّحِيمُ، أَسْأَلُكَ بِنُورِ وَجْهِكَ الَّذِي أَشْرَقَتْ لَهُ السَّمٰوَاتُ وَالْأَرْضُ وَبِكُلِّ حَقٍّ هُوَ لَكَ وَبِحَقِّ السَّائِلِينَ عَلَيْكَ أَنْ تُقِيلَنِي فِي هٰذِهِ الْغَدَاةِ وَفِي هٰذِهِ الْعَشِيَّةِ وَأَنْ تُجِيرَنِي مِنَ النَّارِ بِقُدْرَتِكَ ۞ ١١

٢٦

1. We are content with Allah as our Lord, with Islam as our religion and with Muhammad as our Messenger. I am content with Allah as my Lord, with Islam as my religion, and with Muhammad as my prophet. (3)

2. O Allah! I take refuge in You from unbelief and poverty. O Allah! I take refuge in You from the punishment of the grave, there is no god but You. (3)

3. O Allah! Grant me health in my body and health in my hearing. O Allah! Grant me health in my sight, there is no god but You. (3)

4. Glory be to Allah, and to Him be praise, there is no strength except in Allah. Whatever He wills comes to be, and what He wills not does not come to pass. I know that Allah has power over all things and that His knowledge encompasses everything.

5. We have reached the evening with the pristine way of Islam, with the testimony of sincerity, with the religion of our Prophet Muhammad (peace and blessings be upon him) and with the faith of our forefather Abraham the pure Muslim who was not among the idolaters.

6. O All-Living, Self-Subsistent [Lord]! In your mercy I seek relief. Rectify for me all my affairs and leave me not to my self even for the blinking of an eye.

رَضِينَا بِاللهِ رَبَّاً وَبِالْإِسْلَامِ دِيناً وَبِمُحَمَّدٍ رَسُولاً،
رَضِيتُ بِاللهِ رَبَّاً وَبِالْإِسْلام دِيناً وَبِمُحَمَّدٍ نَبِيّاً (٣) ﴿١﴾

اَللّهُمَّ إِنِّي أَعُوذُ بِكَ مِنَ الْكُفْرِ وَالْفَقْرِ، اَللّهُمَّ إِنِّي
أَعُوذُ بِكَ مِنْ عَذَابِ الْقَبْرِ لَا إِلَهَ إِلَّا أَنْتَ (٣) ﴿٢﴾

اَللّهُمَّ عَافِنِي فِي بَدَنِي، اَللّهُمَّ عَافِنِي فِي سَمْعِي،
اَللّهُمَّ عَافِنِي فِي بَصَرِي لَا إِلَهَ إِلَّا أَنْتَ (٣) ﴿٣﴾

سُبْحَانَ اللهِ وَبِحَمْدِه لَا قُوَّةَ إِلَّا بِاللهِ مَا شَاءَ اللهُ كَانَ
وَمَا لَمْ يَشَأْ لَمْ يَكُنْ أَعْلَمُ أَنَّ اللهَ عَلَى كُلِّ شَيْءٍ قَدِيرٌ
وَأَنَّ اللهَ قَدْ أَحَاطَ بِكُلِّ شَيْءٍ علْماً ﴿٤﴾

أَمْسَيْنَا عَلَى فِطْرَةِ الْإِسْلامِ وَكَلِمَةِ الْإِخْلَاصِ وَعَلَى
دِينِ نَبِيِّنَا مُحَمَّدٍ ﷺ وَعَلَى مِلَّةِ أَبِينَا إِبْرَاهِيمَ حَنِيفاً
مُسْلِماً وَمَا كَانَ مِنَ الْمُشْرِكِينَ ﴿٥﴾

يَا حَيُّ يَا قَيُّومُ بِرَحْمَتِكَ أَسْتَغِيثُ أَصْلِحْ لِي شَأْنِي
كُلَّهُ وَلَا تَكِلْنِي إِلَى نَفْسِي طَرْفَةَ عَيْنٍ ﴿٦﴾

٢٥

1. O Allah! Originator of the heavens and earth, Knower of the unseen and the manifest, and Lord and Owner of everything. I bear witness that there is no god but You. I seek refuge in You from the evil of my self, the evil of Satan and his helpers and from wronging myself or another Muslim. (3)

2. O Allah! As evening falls I do bear witness before You, before the bearers of Your Throne, Your angels, and before all of Your creation, that You are Allah besides whom there is no other god and that Muhammad is Your servant and Messenger. (3)

3. O Allah! Grant me well-being in this life and the Hereafter!

   O Allah! I ask You for pardon and for preservation in my religion, in my life in this world, in my family and in my wealth. O Allah! Conceal my imperfections and calm all my fears!

   O Allah! Protect me (against dangers) from in front, from behind, from my right, from my left, and from above, and I take refuge in Your greatness from being swallowed by the earth beneath me.

اَللّٰهُمَّ فَاطِرَ السَّمٰوَاتِ وَالْأَرْضِ عَالِمَ الْغَيْبِ وَالشَّهَادَةِ رَبَّ كُلِّ شَيْءٍ وَمَلِيكَهُ أَشْهَدُ أَنْ لَاۤ إِلٰهَ إِلَّاۤ أَنْتَ أَعُوذُ بِكَ مِنْ شَرِّ نَفْسِي وَشَرِّ الشَّيْطَانِ وَشِرْكِهِ وَأَنْ أَقْتَرِفَ عَلٰى نَفْسِي سُوۤءًا أَوْ أَنْ أَجُرَّهُ عَلٰى مُسْلِمٍ (٣) ﴿١﴾

اَللّٰهُمَّ إِنِّيۤ أَمْسَيْتُ أُشْهِدُكَ وَأُشْهِدُ حَمَلَةَ عَرْشِكَ وَمَلٰئِكَتَكَ وَجَمِيعَ خَلْقِكَ بِأَنَّكَ أَنْتَ اللهُ الَّذِي لَاۤ إِلٰهَ إِلَّاۤ أَنْتَ وَحْدَكَ لَا شَرِيكَ لَكَ وَأَنَّ مُحَمَّدًا عَبْدُكَ وَرَسُولُكَ (٣) ﴿٢﴾

اَللّٰهُمَّ إِنِّيۤ أَسْأَلُكَ الْعَافِيَةَ فِي الدُّنْيَا وَالْاٰخِرَةِ، اَللّٰهُمَّ إِنِّيۤ أَسْأَلُكَ الْعَفْوَ وَالْعَافِيَةَ فِي دِينِي وَدُنْيَايَ وَأَهْلِي وَمَالِي، اَللّٰهُمَّ اسْتُرْ عَوْرَاتِي وَاٰمِنْ رَوْعَاتِي، اَللّٰهُمَّ احْفَظْنِي مِنْ بَيْنِ يَدَيَّ وَمِنْ خَلْفِي وَعَنْ يَمِينِي وَعَنْ شِمَالِي وَمِنْ فَوْقِي وَأَعُوذُ بِعَظَمَتِكَ أَنْ أُغْتَالَ مِنْ تَحْتِي ﴿٣﴾

٢٤

1. Then one says:
   Glory be to Allah! (33) Praise be to Allah! (33) Allah is the Greatest. (33).

2. Then one supplicates with what comes to his heart from Allah after which he invokes a hundred times:
   There is no god but Allah. (100)

3. Then he says: O Allah, Turner of hearts! Bind our hearts to Your religion.

4. I seek refuge in Allah from Satan the accursed. In the name of Allah, the Merciful, the Compassionate. (10)

5. Evening has fallen upon us and upon the creation, and all belongs to Allah. He has no associate, there is no god but He and to Him is the journeying. The evening has come upon us and the creation, and all belongs to Allah. I seek refuge in Allah who by His leave keeps what is in the sky from falling onto the earth, from the evil of what He created and dispersed and originated perfectly.

6. O Allah! Verily I ask You for good health with faith, faith with good character, success followed by salvation, and for Your mercy, well-being, Your forgiveness and good pleasure.

ثم يقول: سُبْحَانَ اللهِ (٣٣)، اَلْحَمْدُ للهِ (٣٣)، اَللهُ أَكْبَرُ (٣٣) ❪١❫

ثم يدعو ما شاء الله... ثم يقول مائة مرة ''لَآ إِلَهَ إِلَّا اللهُ'' ❪٢❫

ثم يقول: اَللّهُمَّ يَا مُقَلِّبَ الْقُلُوبِ ثَبِّتْ قُلُوبَنَا عَلَى دِينِكَ ❪٣❫

أَعُوذُ بِاللهِ مِنَ الشَّيْطَانِ الرَّجِيمِ، بِسْمِ اللهِ الرَّحْمٰنِ الرَّحِيمِ (١٠) ❪٤❫

أَمْسَيْنَا وَأَمْسَى الْمُلْكُ للهِ لَا شَرِيكَ لَهُ لَآ إِلَهَ إِلَّا هُوَ وَإِلَيْهِ الْمَصِيرُ، أَمْسَيْنَا وَأَمْسَى الْمُلْكُ للهِ أَعُوذُ بِاللهِ الَّذِي يُمْسِكُ السَّمَاءَ أَنْ تَقَعَ عَلَى الْأَرْضِ إِلَّا بِإِذْنِهِ مِنْ شَرِّ مَا خَلَقَ وَذَرَأَ وَبَرَأَ ❪٥❫

اَللّهُمَّ إِنِّيٓ أَسْأَلُكَ صِحَّةً فِي إِيمَانٍ وَإِيمَانًا فِي حُسْنِ خُلُقٍ وَنَجَاحًا يَتْبَعُهُ فَلَاحٌ وَرَحْمَةً مِنْكَ وَعَافِيَةً وَمَغْفِرَةً مِنْكَ وَرِضْوَانًا ❪٦❫

٢٣

Evening Prayers

After the evening (maghrib) ritual prayer:

1. O Allah! You are the Source of Peace and all peace comes from You. Blessed are You and exalted, O Lord of infinite goodness and bounty!

    Then one says:

2. Glory be to Allah who is exempt from all shortcomings, and all praise be to Him, Lord of the worlds; there is no god but Allah, and Allah is the Greatest; there is no strength or power except in Allah, the All-High, the All-Mighty.

3. Then the following is read (Ayat al-Kursi):

    Allah! There is no god but He, the All-Living, the Self-Subsistent. Neither does slumber overtake Him nor sleep, and to Him belongs whatever is in the heavens and the earth. Who can intercede with Him except by His leave? He knows what is before them and what is behind them and they comprehend of His knowledge only that which He wills. His Throne encompasses the heavens and the earth, and maintaining them both tires Him not. He is the Exalted, the Sublime. (Baqara 2:255)

أَذْكَارُ الْمَسَاءِ

يَقُولُ بَعْدَ الْمَغْرِبِ:

اَللّٰهُمَّ أَنْتَ السَّلَامُ وَمِنْكَ السَّلَامُ تَبَارَكْتَ وَتَعَالَيْتَ يَا ذَا الْجَلَالِ وَالْإِكْرَامِ ﴿١﴾

ويقول بعد ذلك: سُبْحَانَ اللهِ وَالْحَمْدُ للهِ وَلَا إِلٰهَ إِلَّا اللهُ وَاللهُ أَكْبَرُ وَلَا حَوْلَ وَلَا قُوَّةَ إِلَّا بِاللهِ الْعَلِيِّ الْعَظِيمِ ﴿٢﴾

ثم يقرأ: ﴿اَللهُ لَآ إِلٰهَ إِلَّا هُوَ اَلْحَيُّ الْقَيُّومُ لَا تَأْخُذُهُ سِنَةٌ وَلَا نَوْمٌ لَهُ مَا فِي السَّمٰوَاتِ وَمَا فِي الْأَرْضِ مَنْ ذَا الَّذِي يَشْفَعُ عِنْدَهُ إِلَّا بِإِذْنِهِ يَعْلَمُ مَا بَيْنَ أَيْدِيهِمْ وَمَا خَلْفَهُمْ وَلَا يُحِيطُونَ بِشَيْءٍ مِنْ عِلْمِهِ إِلَّا بِمَا شَاءَ وَسِعَ كُرْسِيُّهُ السَّمٰوَاتِ وَالْأَرْضَ وَلَا يَؤُودُهُ حِفْظُهُمَا وَهُوَ الْعَلِيُّ الْعَظِيمُ﴾ ﴿٣﴾

٢٢

1. O Allah! I ask You for well-being in this life and in the hereafter.

   O Allah! I ask You for pardon and for preservation, in my religion, in my life in this world, in my family and in my wealth.

   O Allah! Conceal my imperfections and calm all my fears!

   O Allah! Protect me (against dangers) from in front, from behind, from my right, from my left, and from above, and I seek refuge in Your greatness from being swallowed by the earth beneath me.

2. Glory be to Allah and to Him be praise! Glory be to Allah the Almighty! (100)

3. Glory be to Allah, to Him be praise! There is no god but Allah, and Allah is the Greatest. (100)

4. O Allah! Verily I ask You for good health with faith, faith with good morality, success followed by salvation. I ask from You mercy and well-being, and for Your forgiveness and good pleasure.

5. O Allah! Make faith beloved to us, endearing it to our hearts, and make unbelief, impiety and disobedience hateful to us, and make us among the rightly guided.

6. O Allah! Verily I ask You for a soul that is at rest and contentment with You, believing in the meeting with You, content with Your decree, and satisfied with what You bestow.

اَللّٰهُمَّ إِنِّيٓ أَسْأَلُكَ الْعَافِيَةَ فِي الدُّنْيَا وَالْاٰخِرَةِ، اَللّٰهُمَّ إِنِّي أَسْأَلُكَ الْعَفْوَ وَالْعَافِيَةَ فِي دِينِي وَدُنْيَايَ وَأَهْلِي وَمَالِي، اَللّٰهُمَّ اسْتُرْ عَوْرَاتِي وَاٰمِنْ رَوْعَاتِي، اَللّٰهُمَّ احْفَظْنِي مِنْ بَيْنِ يَدَيَّ وَمِنْ خَلْفِي وَعَنْ يَمِينِي وَعَنْ شِمَالِي وَمِنْ فَوْقِي وَأَعُوذُ بِعَظَمَتِكَ أَنْ أُغْتَالَ مِنْ تَحْتِي ﴿١﴾

سُبْحَانَ اللّٰهِ وَبِحَمْدِهِ سُبْحَانَ اللّٰهِ الْعَظِيمِ (١٠٠) ﴿٢﴾

سُبْحَانَ اللّٰهِ، الْحَمْدُ لِلّٰهِ، لَآ إِلٰهَ إِلَّا اللّٰهُ، اللّٰهُ أَكْبَرُ (١٠٠) ﴿٣﴾

اَللّٰهُمَّ إِنِّيٓ أَسْأَلُكَ صِحَّةً فِيٓ إِيمَانٍ وَإِيمَانًا فِي حُسْنِ خُلُقٍ وَنَجَاحًا يَتْبَعُهُ فَلَاحٌ وَرَحْمَةً مِنْكَ وَعَافِيَةً وَمَغْفِرَةً مِنْكَ وَرِضْوَانًا ﴿٤﴾ اَللّٰهُمَّ حَبِّبْ إِلَيْنَا الْإِيمَانَ وَزَيِّنْهُ فِي قُلُوبِنَا وَكَرِّهْ إِلَيْنَا الْكُفْرَ وَالْفُسُوقَ وَالْعِصْيَانَ وَاجْعَلْنَا مِنَ الرَّاشِدِينَ ﴿٥﴾ اَللّٰهُمَّ إِنِّيٓ أَسْأَلُكَ نَفْسًا بِكَ مُطْمَئِنَّةً تُؤْمِنُ بِلِقَائِكَ وَتَرْضَى بِقَضَائِكَ وَتَقْنَعُ بِعَطَائِكَ ﴿٦﴾

1. We have risen with the pristine way of Islam, with the testimony of sincerity, as a member of the nation of our forefather Abraham the pure Muslim who was not among the polytheists, who turned toward the Lord, following the religion of Prophet Muhammad (peace and blessings be upon him).

2. O Allah! I take refuge in You from sloth, decrepitude, the troubles of old age, the temptation of this world and the punishment of the Hereafter. We and all the creation have reached the morning belonging to Allah, Lord of the worlds.

3. O Allah! I ask from You the goodness of this day, the triumph, support, light, grace and the guidance therein, and I seek refuge in You from the evil of this day and the evil of the days thereafter.

4. There is no god but Allah and Allah is the Greatest, there is no god but Allah Who is Alone, there is no god but Allah without associate, there is no god but Allah. His is the dominion and all praise is due to Him. There is no god but Allah and there is no strength or power except in Allah.

أَصْبَحْنَا عَلَى فِطْرَةِ الْإِسْلَامِ وَكَلِمَةِ الْإِخْلَاصِ وَعَلَى

دِينِ نَبِيِّنَا مُحَمَّدٍ ﷺ وَعَلَى مِلَّةِ أَبِينَا إِبْرٰهِيمَ حَنِيفًا

مُسْلِمًا وَمَا كَانَ مِنَ الْمُشْرِكِينَ ﴿١﴾

اَللّٰهُمَّ إِنِّي أَعُوذُ بِكَ مِنَ الْكَسَلِ وَالْهَرَمِ وَسُوءِ الْكِبَرِ

وَفِتْنَةِ الدُّنْيَا وَعَذَابِ الْآخِرَةِ، أَصْبَحْنَا وَأَصْبَحَ الْمُلْكُ للهِ

رَبِّ الْعَالَمِينَ ﴿٢﴾

اَللّٰهُمَّ إِنِّي أَسْأَلُكَ خَيْرَ هٰذَا الْيَوْمِ فَتْحَهُ وَنَصْرَهُ وَنُورَهُ

وَبَرَكَتَهُ وَهُدَاهُ وَأَعُوذُ بِكَ مِنْ شَرِّ مَا فِيهِ وَشَرِّ مَا بَعْدَهُ ﴿٣﴾

لَآ إِلٰهَ إِلَّا اللهُ وَاللهُ أَكْبَرُ لَآ إِلٰهَ إِلَّا اللهُ وَحْدَهُ لَآ إِلٰهَ

إِلَّا اللهُ لَا شَرِيكَ لَهُ لَآ إِلٰهَ إِلَّا اللهُ لَهُ الْمُلْكُ وَلَهُ الْحَمْدُ

لَآ إِلٰهَ إِلَّا اللهُ وَلَا حَوْلَ وَلَا قُوَّةَ إِلَّا بِاللهِ ﴿٤﴾

1. We and all the creation have reached the morning belonging to Allah. All praise is due to Allah, there is no god but Allah, alone without any associate, His is the kingdom, to Him belongs all praise and He has power over all things.

   O Lord! I ask You for the goodness of this day, and the goodness of the days thereafter and I seek refuge in You from the evil of this day and the evil thereafter.

   O Lord! I take refuge in You from sloth and troubles of old age.

   O Lord! I take refuge in You from torment in the hellfire, and torment of the grave.

2. O Allah! Grant me health in my body and health in my hearing. O Allah! Grant me health in my sight! There is no god but You.

3. O Allah! Truly I seek refuge in You from unbelief and from poverty. O Allah! I seek refuge in You from the punishment of the grave, there is no god but You. (3)

4. Glory be to Allah and to Him be praise! There is no strength except in Allah, Whatever He wills comes to be, and what He wills not does not come to pass. I know that Allah has power over all things and that Allah's knowledge encompasses everything.

أَصْبَحْنَا وَأَصْبَحَ الْمُلْكُ لِلّٰهِ وَالْحَمْدُ لِلّٰهِ وَلَا إِلٰهَ إِلَّا اللّٰهُ وَحْدَهُ لَا شَرِيكَ لَهُ، لَهُ الْمُلْكُ وَلَهُ الْحَمْدُ وَهُوَ عَلٰى كُلِّ شَيْءٍ قَدِيرٌ، رَبِّ إِنِّي أَسْأَلُكَ خَيْرَ مَا فِي هٰذَا الْيَوْمِ وَخَيْرَ مَا بَعْدَهُ وَأَعُوذُ بِكَ مِنْ شَرِّ مَا فِي هٰذَا الْيَوْمِ وَشَرِّ مَا بَعْدَهُ، رَبِّ أَعُوذُ بِكَ مِنَ الْكَسَلِ وَسُوءِ الْكِبَرِ، رَبِّ أَعُوذُ بِكَ مِنْ عَذَابٍ فِي النَّارِ وَعَذَابٍ فِي الْقَبْرِ ﴿١﴾

اَللّٰهُمَّ إِنِّي أَعُوذُ بِكَ مِنَ الْكُفْرِ وَالْفَقْرِ، اَللّٰهُمَّ إِنِّي أَعُوذُ بِكَ مِنْ عَذَابِ الْقَبْرِ لَآ إِلٰهَ إِلَّا أَنْتَ (٣) ﴿٢﴾

اَللّٰهُمَّ عَافِنِي فِي بَدَنِي، اَللّٰهُمَّ عَافِنِي فِي سَمْعِي، اَللّٰهُمَّ عَافِنِي فِي بَصَرِي لَآ إِلٰهَ إِلَّا أَنْتَ (٣) ﴿٣﴾

سُبْحَانَ اللّٰهِ وَبِحَمْدِهِ لَا قُوَّةَ إِلَّا بِاللّٰهِ مَا شَآءَ اللّٰهُ كَانَ وَمَا لَمْ يَشَأْ لَمْ يَكُنْ أَعْلَمُ أَنَّ اللّٰهَ عَلٰى كُلِّ شَيْءٍ قَدِيرٌ وَأَنَّ اللّٰهَ قَدْ أَحَاطَ بِكُلِّ شَيْءٍ عِلْمًا ﴿٤﴾

1. O Allah! I ask you for sudden [outpourings of] goodness and I seek refuge in You from sudden [assaults of] evil.

2. O Allah! I have risen this morning with grace, good health and concealment [of my sins], so complete Your blessing on me, Your protection of me and Your concealment [of my sins] in this world and the Hereafter.

3. My Lord is Allah, I have put my trust in Allah, there is no god but Him, on Him do I rely and He is the Lord of the Supreme Throne. There is no god but Allah, the All-High, the Almighty.

   Whatever He wills comes to be and what He wills not does not come to pass. I know that Allah has power over all things and that Allah's knowledge encompasses everything.

4. O Allah! You are my Lord, there is no god but You, in You I have put my trust, and You are the Lord of the Supreme Throne. Whatever He wills comes to be and what He wills not does not come to pass. There is no strength or power except in Allah, the All-High, the Almighty.

   O Allah! I seek refuge in You from the evil of my self and from the evil of every creature in Your grasp: "Verily my Lord is upon a Straight Path." (Hud 11:56)

اَللّٰهُمَّ إِنِّي أَسْأَلُكَ مِنْ فَجْأَةِ الْخَيْرِ وَأَعُوذُ بِكَ مِنْ فَجْأَةِ الشَّرِّ ۝١

اَللّٰهُمَّ إِنِّي أَصْبَحْتُ مِنْكَ فِي نِعْمَةٍ وَعَافِيَةٍ وَسَتْرٍ فَأَتِمَّ نِعْمَتَكَ عَلَيَّ وَعَافِيَتَكَ وَسَتْرَكَ فِي الدُّنْيَا وَالْاٰخِرَةِ ۝٢

رَبِّيَ اللّٰهُ تَوَكَّلْتُ عَلَى اللّٰهِ لَا إِلٰهَ إِلَّا هُوَ عَلَيْهِ تَوَكَّلْتُ وَهُوَ رَبُّ الْعَرْشِ الْعَظِيمِ لَا إِلٰهَ إِلَّا اللّٰهُ الْعَلِيُّ الْعَظِيمُ، مَا شَاءَ اللّٰهُ كَانَ وَمَا لَمْ يَشَأْ لَمْ يَكُنْ أَعْلَمُ أَنَّ اللّٰهَ عَلَى كُلِّ شَيْءٍ قَدِيرٌ وَأَنَّ اللّٰهَ قَدْ أَحَاطَ بِكُلِّ شَيْءٍ عِلْمًا ۝٣

اَللّٰهُمَّ أَنْتَ رَبِّي لَا إِلٰهَ إِلَّا أَنْتَ عَلَيْكَ تَوَكَّلْتُ وَأَنْتَ رَبُّ الْعَرْشِ الْعَظِيمِ، مَا شَاءَ اللّٰهُ كَانَ وَمَا لَمْ يَشَأْ لَمْ يَكُنْ، لَا حَوْلَ وَلَا قُوَّةَ إِلَّا بِاللّٰهِ الْعَلِيِّ الْعَظِيمِ، اَللّٰهُمَّ إِنِّي أَعُوذُ بِكَ مِنْ شَرِّ نَفْسِي وَمِنْ شَرِّ كُلِّ دَابَّةٍ أَنْتَ اٰخِذٌ بِنَاصِيَتِهَا ﴿إِنَّ رَبِّي عَلَى صِرَاطٍ مُسْتَقِيمٍ﴾ ۝٤

You have recorded their actions and set down their last moments. Hearts incline to You, and with You all that is secret is open to view. The lawful is only that which You have made lawful, and the forbidden is only that which You have forbidden. Religion is what You have prescribed and the command is what You have decreed. The creation is Your creation, and every servant is Your servant. You are Allah; the All-Pitying, the All-Compassionate.

I ask You by the light of Your Countenance by which the heavens and the earth became illuminated, by every right that is Yours and by the right of those who petition You, to forgive me in this morning and evening and to save me from the hellfire through Your Power.

1. Allah is my sufficiency, there is no god but Him. In Him have I put my trust and He is the Lord of the Supreme Throne. (Tawba 9:129) (7)

2. We are content with Allah as our Lord, with Islam as our religion and with Muhammad as our Messenger. I am content with Allah as my Lord, with Islam as my religion, and with Muhammad as my Prophet. (3)

3. O Allah! Whatever blessing is with me at the break of this day or with any other of your creatures, truly it is from You alone without associate, and all praise and thanks are due to You.

وَكَتَبْتَ الْآثَارَ وَنَسَخْتَ الْآجَالَ الْقُلُوبُ لَكَ مُفْضِيَةٌ

وَالسِّرُّ عِنْدَكَ عَلَانِيَةٌ، اَلْحَلَالُ مَا أَحْلَلْتَ وَالْحَرَامُ مَا

حَرَّمْتَ وَالدِّينُ مَا شَرَعْتَ وَالْأَمْرُ مَا قَضَيْتَ وَالْخَلْقُ

خَلْقُكَ وَالْعَبْدُ عَبْدُكَ وَأَنْتَ اللهُ الرَّؤُوفُ الرَّحِيمُ أَسْأَلُكَ

بِنُورِ وَجْهِكَ الَّذِي أَشْرَقَتْ لَهُ السَّمٰوَاتُ وَالْأَرْضُ وَبِكُلِّ

حَقٍّ هُوَ لَكَ وَبِحَقِّ السَّائِلِينَ عَلَيْكَ أَنْ تُقِيلَنِي فِي هٰذِهِ

الْغَدَاةِ وَفِي هٰذِهِ الْعَشِيَّةِ وَأَنْ تُجِيرَنِي مِنَ النَّارِ بِقُدْرَتِكَ ﴿٣﴾

﴿حَسْبِيَ اللهُ لَآ إِلٰهَ إِلَّا هُوَ عَلَيْهِ تَوَكَّلْتُ وَهُوَ رَبُّ

الْعَرْشِ الْعَظِيمِ﴾(٧) ﴿١﴾

رَضِينَا بِاللهِ رَبًّا وَبِالْإِسْلَامِ دِينًا وَبِمُحَمَّدٍ رَسُولًا،

رَضِيتُ بِاللهِ رَبًّا وَبِالْإِسْلَامِ دِينًا وَبِمُحَمَّدٍ نَبِيًّا (٣) ﴿٢﴾

اَللّٰهُمَّ مَآ أَصْبَحَ بِي مِنْ نِعْمَةٍ أَوْ بِأَحَدٍ مِنْ خَلْقِكَ فَمِنْكَ

وَحْدَكَ لَا شَرِيكَ لَكَ فَلَكَ الْحَمْدُ وَلَكَ الشُّكْرُ ﴿٣﴾

١٧

1. O Allah, Creator of the heavens and earth in a certain system, Knower of the unseen and the manifest, and Lord and Owner of everything! I bear witness that there is no god but You. I seek refuge in You from the evil of my self, the evil of Satan and his traps, and from committing wrong to myself or another Muslim. (4)

2. (O All-Living, Self-Subsistent [Lord]!) *Ya Hayyu Ya Qayyum!* For the sake of Your Mercy I beg for help. Rectify for all my states and leave me not to myself even for the blinking of an eye!

3. O Allah! You are the most worthy of remembrance and the most worthy of worship. You are the best helper of all those who are sought [for help], the most compassionate of owners, the most generous of those who are petitioned, and the most liberal of those who give. You are the Sovereign without associate, You are the only being without any equal or associate. Everything perishes except You. You are not obeyed except by Your leave and You are not disobeyed except in Your knowledge. When You are obeyed You reward in return, and when You are disobeyed You are forgiving. You are the closest Witness and the nearest Protector. You block [desires of] selves, and You grasp them by the neck.

اَللّٰهُمَّ فَاطِرَ السَّمٰوَاتِ وَالْأَرْضِ عَالِمَ الْغَيْبِ وَالشَّهَادَةِ

رَبَّ كُلِّ شَيْءٍ وَمَلِيكَهُ أَشْهَدُ أَنْ لَّا إِلٰهَ إِلَّا أَنْتَ أَعُوذُ بِكَ

مِنْ شَرِّ نَفْسِي وَشَرِّ الشَّيْطَانِ وَشَرَكِهٖ وَأَنْ أَقْتَرِفَ عَلٰى

نَفْسِي سُوءًا أَوْ أَنْ أَجُرَّهُ عَلٰى مُسْلِمٍ (٤) ﴿١﴾

يَا حَيُّ يَا قَيُّومُ بِرَحْمَتِكَ أَسْتَغِيثُ أَصْلِحْ لِي شَأْنِي

كُلَّهُ وَلَا تَكِلْنِي إِلٰى نَفْسِي طَرْفَةَ عَيْنٍ ﴿٢﴾

اَللّٰهُمَّ أَنْتَ أَحَقُّ مَنْ ذُكِرَ وَأَحَقُّ مَنْ عُبِدَ وَأَنْصَرُ مَنِ

ابْتُغِيَ وَأَرْأَفُ مَنْ مَلَكَ وَأَجْوَدُ مَنْ سُئِلَ وَأَوْسَعُ مَنْ

أَعْطٰى، أَنْتَ الْمَلِكُ لَا شَرِيكَ لَكَ وَالْفَرْدُ لَا نِدَّ لَكَ كُلُّ

شَيْءٍ هَالِكٌ إِلَّا وَجْهَكَ لَنْ تُطَاعَ إِلَّا بِإِذْنِكَ وَلَنْ تُعْصٰى

إِلَّا بِعِلْمِكَ تُطَاعُ فَتَشْكُرُ وَتُعْصٰى فَتَغْفِرُ، أَقْرَبُ شَهِيدٍ

وَأَدْنٰى حَفِيظٍ، حُلْتَ دُونَ النُّفُوسِ وَأَخَذْتَ بِالنَّوَاصِي

1. Praise be to Allah, Who created sleep and wakefulness! Praise be to Allah, Who awoke me sound and healthy! I bear witness that Allah brings the dead to life and has power over every thing.

2. The morning has broken upon us and upon the creation, and all belongs to Allah, All-Mighty and Majestic. All praise is due to Allah, and all pride and greatness is His. The creation, the command, the night, the day, and all that rests in them belong to Him alone.

   O Allah! Bless us with peace and righteousness at the beginning of this day, prosperity at its middle, and success at its end!

   I ask of You the goodness of this life and the Hereafter, O most Merciful of the merciful!

3. O Allah! I seek refuge in You from worry and grief, and I seek refuge in You from incapacity and sloth. I seek refuge in You from cowardice and miserliness and I seek refuge in You from overpowering debt and subjugation by men. (3)

4. The morning has broken upon us and upon the creation, and all belongs to Allah. He is without associate, there is no god but Him, and unto Him is the resurrection.

اَلْحَمْدُ لِلهِ الَّذِي خَلَقَ النَّوْمَ وَالْيَقَظَةَ، اَلْحَمْدُ لِلهِ

الَّذِي بَعَثَنِي سَالِمًا سَوِيًّا أَشْهَدُ أَنَّ اللهَ يُحْيِي الْمَوْتَى وَهُوَ

عَلَى كُلِّ شَيْءٍ قَدِيرٌ ﴿١﴾

أَصْبَحْنَا وَأَصْبَحَ الْمُلْكُ لِلهِ عَزَّ وَجَلَّ وَالْحَمْدُ لِلهِ

وَالْكِبْرِيَاءُ وَالْعَظَمَةُ لِلهِ وَالْخَلْقُ وَالْأَمْرُ وَاللَّيْلُ وَالنَّهَارُ

وَمَا يَسْكُنُ فِيهِمَا لِلهِ وَحْدَهُ اَللّٰهُمَّ اجْعَلْ أَوَّلَ هٰذَا النَّهَارِ

صَلَاحًا وَأَوْسَطَهُ فَلَاحًا وَآخِرَهُ نَجَاحًا أَسْأَلُكَ خَيْرَ

الدُّنْيَا وَالْآخِرَةِ يَا أَرْحَمَ الرَّاحِمِينَ ﴿٢﴾

اَللّٰهُمَّ إِنِّي أَعُوذُ بِكَ مِنَ الْهَمِّ وَالْحَزَنِ وَأَعُوذُ بِكَ

مِنَ الْعَجْزِ وَالْكَسَلِ وَأَعُوذُ بِكَ مِنَ الْجُبْنِ وَالْبُخْلِ

وَأَعُوذُ بِكَ مِنْ غَلَبَةِ الدَّيْنِ وَقَهْرِ الرِّجَالِ ﴿٣﴾

أَصْبَحْنَا وَأَصْبَحَ الْمُلْكُ لِلهِ لَا شَرِيكَ لَهُ لَا إِلٰهَ إِلَّا هُوَ

وَإِلَيْهِ النُّشُورُ ﴿٤﴾

I seek refuge in You from wronging others and being wronged, from committing aggression and being the object of aggression, and from committing an error or committing a sin which is not forgiven.

O Allah, the Originator of the heavens and the earth, Knower of the unseen and the manifest, Lord of Majesty and Bounty! Truly I have pledged faith in You in this life, and I bear witness before You, for sufficient are You as witness.

Verily I bear witness that there is no god but You, alone without partners. Yours is the dominion, to You is all praise and You have power over all things.

I bear witness that Muhammad is Your servant and Your Messenger and that Your promise is true, the meeting with You is true, that without doubt the last hour is coming, and without doubt You resurrect those in the graves. Truly if you leave me to myself, You leave me to weakness, need, sin and error.

Truly I rely on nothing except Your mercy, so forgive me all my sins, for no one forgives sins except You. Accept my repentance! For verily You are the One Who accepts the sincere repentance of His servants, Ever-Relenting, the All-Compassionate.

غَيْرِ ضَرَّاءَ مُضِرَّةٍ وَلَا فِتْنَةٍ مُضِلَّةٍ وَأَعُوذُ بِكَ أَنْ أَظْلِمَ

أَوْ أُظْلَمَ أَوْ أَعْتَدِيَ أَوْ يُعْتَدَى عَلَيَّ أَوْ أَكْسِبَ خَطِيئَةً

أَوْ ذَنْبًا لَا يُغْفَرُ اَللّٰهُمَّ فَاطِرَ السَّمٰوَاتِ وَالْأَرْضِ عَالِمَ

الْغَيْبِ وَالشَّهَادَةِ ذَا الْجَلَالِ وَالْإِكْرَامِ فَإِنِّي أَعْهَدُ إِلَيْكَ

فِي هٰذِهِ الْحَيَاةِ الدُّنْيَا وَأُشْهِدُكَ وَكَفَى بِكَ شَهِيدًا إِنِّي

أَشْهَدُ أَنْ لَا إِلٰهَ إِلَّا أَنْتَ وَحْدَكَ لَا شَرِيكَ لَكَ، لَكَ

الْمُلْكُ وَلَكَ الْحَمْدُ وَأَنْتَ عَلٰى كُلِّ شَيْءٍ قَدِيرٌ وَأَشْهَدُ

أَنَّ مُحَمَّدًا عَبْدُكَ وَرَسُولُكَ وَأَشْهَدُ أَنَّ وَعْدَكَ حَقٌّ

وَلِقَاءَكَ حَقٌّ وَالسَّاعَةَ اٰتِيَةٌ لَا رَيْبَ فِيهَا وَأَنَّكَ تَبْعَثُ

مَنْ فِي الْقُبُورِ، وَأَنَّكَ إِنْ تَكِلْنِي إِلٰى نَفْسِي تَكِلْنِي

إِلٰى ضَعْفٍ وَعَوْرَةٍ وَذَنْبٍ وَخَطِيئَةٍ وَإِنِّي لَا أَثِقُ إِلَّا

بِرَحْمَتِكَ فَاغْفِرْ لِي ذُنُوبِي كُلَّهَا إِنَّهُ لَا يَغْفِرُ الذُّنُوبَ إِلَّا

أَنْتَ وَتُبْ عَلَيَّ إِنَّكَ أَنْتَ التَّوَّابُ الرَّحِيمُ ۝

١٤

1. O Allah! Upon the breaking of this day, I do bear witness before You, before the bearers of Your Throne, Your angels, and before all of Your creation that You are Allah besides whom there is no other god and that Muhammad is Your servant and Messenger. (3)

2. At Your beckon and call, O Allah! At Your service and pleasure! All goodness is in Your hands, coming from You, and returning to You.

O Allah! Whatever words I have uttered, oaths I have sworn, vows I have made, or deeds I have done, all depends on Your will. Whatever You willed was and whatever You willed not was not. There is no strength or power except in You, and truly You have power over all things.

O Allah! Let whomsoever I have invoked blessings on, be those whom You have blessed, and whomsoever I invoked curses on, be those whom You have cursed. Verily You are my protector in this life and in the Hereafter, so take my soul as a Muslim and join me with the righteous.

O Allah! I ask You for contentment with what You decree, a life of bliss after death, the joy of beholding Your Countenance, and longing for the meeting with You, safe from injury by what is harmful and from any trial that might cause me to go astray.

اَللّٰهُمَّ إِنِّي أَصْبَحْتُ أُشْهِدُكَ وَأُشْهِدُ حَمَلَةَ عَرْشِكَ وَمَلَائِكَتَكَ وَجَمِيعَ خَلْقِكَ بِأَنَّكَ أَنْتَ اللهُ الَّذِي لَا إِلٰهَ إِلَّا أَنْتَ وَأَنَّ مُحَمَّدًا عَبْدُكَ وَرَسُولُكَ (٣) ﴿١﴾

لَبَّيْكَ اللّٰهُمَّ لَبَّيْكَ، لَبَّيْكَ وَسَعْدَيْكَ وَالْخَيْرُ فِي يَدَيْكَ وَمِنْكَ وَإِلَيْكَ اللّٰهُمَّ مَا قُلْتُ مِنْ قَوْلٍ أَوْ حَلَفْتُ مِنْ حَلِفٍ أَوْ نَذَرْتُ مِنْ نَذْرٍ أَوْ عَمِلْتُ مِنْ عَمَلٍ فَمَشِيئَتُكَ بَيْنَ يَدَيْ ذٰلِكَ كُلِّهِ، مَا شِئْتَ كَانَ وَمَا لَمْ تَشَأْ لَمْ يَكُنْ وَلَا حَوْلَ وَلَا قُوَّةَ إِلَّا بِكَ إِنَّكَ عَلَى كُلِّ شَيْءٍ قَدِيرٌ اَللّٰهُمَّ مَا صَلَّيْتُ مِنْ صَلَاةٍ فَعَلَى مَنْ صَلَّيْتَ وَمَا لَعَنْتُ مِنْ لَعْنٍ فَعَلَى مَنْ لَعَنْتَ إِنَّكَ وَلِيِّي فِي الدُّنْيَا وَالْآخِرَةِ تَوَفَّنِي مُسْلِمًا وَأَلْحِقْنِي بِالصَّالِحِينَ اَللّٰهُمَّ إِنِّي أَسْأَلُكَ الرِّضَا بَعْدَ الْقَضَى وَبَرْدَ الْعَيْشِ بَعْدَ الْمَوْتِ وَلَذَّةَ النَّظَرِ إِلَى وَجْهِكَ وَشَوْقًا إِلَى لِقَائِكَ مِنْ

1. O Allah! By Your grace we entered the day, by Your grace we reached the evening, by Your grace we live, by Your leave we die and unto You is the resurrection.

2. All praise be to Allah Who revived us after death and unto Him is the resurrection.

3. There is no god but You, and You have no partner. Glory be to You O Allah! I seek Your forgiveness for my sin and ask You for Your Mercy. O Allah! Increase me in knowledge, and let not my heart go astray after You guided me! Grant me mercy from Yourself for verily You are the One Who bestows.

4. O Allah! Send Your blessings upon our master Muhammad and the family of our master Muhammad as You sent blessings upon our master Abraham and the family of our master Abraham. Truly You are the Owner of Praise, the Glorious. (10)

5. O Allah! Send Your grace upon our master Muhammad and the family of our master Muhammad as You sent Your grace upon our master Abraham and the family of our master Abraham. Truly You are the Owner of Praise, the Glorious. (10)

اَللّٰهُمَّ بِكَ أَصْبَحْنَا وَبِكَ أَمْسَيْنَا وَبِكَ نَحْيَا وَبِكَ نَمُوتُ وَإِلَيْكَ النُّشُورُ ﴿١﴾

اَلْحَمْدُ لِلّٰهِ الَّذِي أَحْيَانَا بَعْدَ مَا أَمَاتَنَا وَإِلَيْهِ النُّشُورُ ﴿٢﴾ لَا إِلٰهَ إِلَّا أَنْتَ لَا شَرِيكَ لَكَ، سُبْحَانَكَ اللّٰهُمَّ أَسْتَغْفِرُكَ لِذَنْبِي وَأَسْأَلُكَ رَحْمَتَكَ، اَللّٰهُمَّ زِدْنِي عِلْمًا وَلَا تُزِغْ قَلْبِي بَعْدَ إِذْ هَدَيْتَنِي وَهَبْ لِي مِنْ لَدُنْكَ رَحْمَةً إِنَّكَ أَنْتَ الْوَهَّابُ ﴿٣﴾

اَللّٰهُمَّ صَلِّ عَلَى سَيِّدِنَا مُحَمَّدٍ وَعَلَى اٰلِ سَيِّدِنَا مُحَمَّدٍ كَمَا صَلَّيْتَ عَلَى سَيِّدِنَا إِبْرٰهِيمَ وَعَلَى اٰلِ سَيِّدِنَا إِبْرٰهِيمَ إِنَّكَ حَمِيدٌ مَجِيدٌ (١٠) ﴿٤﴾

اَللّٰهُمَّ بَارِكْ عَلَى سَيِّدِنَا مُحَمَّدٍ وَعَلَى اٰلِ سَيِّدِنَا مُحَمَّدٍ كَمَا بَارَكْتَ عَلَى سَيِّدِنَا إِبْرٰهِيمَ وَعَلَى اٰلِ سَيِّدِنَا إِبْرٰهِيمَ إِنَّكَ حَمِيدٌ مَجِيدٌ (١٠) ﴿٥﴾

1. "Say: He is Allah, the One and Only; ❂ Allah, the Absolute, Eternal; ❂ He begets not, nor is He begotten. ❂ And there is none like unto Him." (Ikhlas 112) (3)

2. "Say: I take refuge in the Lord of the Daybreak, ❂ From the evil of what He created, ❂ From the evil of the night as its darkness overspreads, ❂ From the evil of those who blow on knots, ❂ And from the evil of an envier when he envies." (Falaq 113) (3)

3. "Say: I take refuge in the Lord of humankind, ❂ The King of humankind, ❂ The God of humankind, ❂ From the evil of the sneaking whisperer ❂ Who whispers in the breasts of humankind, ❂ From jinn and humankind." (Nas 114) (3)

4. "So glorify Allah when you enter the night and when you rise in the morning. ❂ To Him belongs all praise in the heavens and the earth, in the late afternoon and when you enter midday. ❂ He brings forth the living from the dead, and He brings forth the dead from the living; even so shall you be brought forth." (Rum 30:17-19)

11

﴿قُلْ هُوَ اللهُ أَحَدٌ ۝ اَللهُ الصَّمَدُ ۝ لَمْ يَلِدْ وَلَمْ يُولَدْ ۝ وَلَمْ يَكُنْ لَهُ كُفُواً أَحَدٌ﴾ (٣) ۝١

﴿قُلْ أَعُوذُ بِرَبِّ الْفَلَقِ ۝ مِنْ شَرِّ مَا خَلَقَ ۝ وَمِنْ شَرِّ غَاسِقٍ إِذَا وَقَبَ ۝ وَمِنْ شَرِّ النَّفَّاثَاتِ فِي الْعُقَدِ ۝ وَمِنْ شَرِّ حَاسِدٍ إِذَا حَسَدَ﴾ (٣) ۝٢

﴿قُلْ أَعُوذُ بِرَبِّ النَّاسِ ۝ مَلِكِ النَّاسِ ۝ إِلهِ النَّاسِ ۝ مِنْ شَرِّ الْوَسْوَاسِ الْخَنَّاسِ ۝ اَلَّذِي يُوَسْوِسُ فِي صُدُورِ النَّاسِ ۝ مِنَ الْجِنَّةِ وَالنَّاسِ﴾ (٣) ۝٣

﴿فَسُبْحَانَ اللهِ حِينَ تُمْسُونَ وَحِينَ تُصْبِحُونَ ۝ وَلَهُ الْحَمْدُ فِي السَّمٰوَاتِ وَالْأَرْضِ وَعَشِيًّا وَحِينَ تُظْهِرُونَ ۝ يُخْرِجُ الْحَيَّ مِنَ الْمَيِّتِ وَيُخْرِجُ الْمَيِّتَ مِنَ الْحَيِّ وَيُحْيِي الْأَرْضَ بَعْدَ مَوْتِهَا وَكَذٰلِكَ تُخْرَجُونَ﴾ ۝٤

1. O Allah! You are my Lord, there is no god but You. You have created me, and I am Your servant. I try my best to keep my covenant with You. I seek refuge in You from the evil of what I have done. I acknowledge Your favors upon me and I acknowledge my sins. So, forgive me, for truly no one forgives sins except You. (3)

2. In the Name of God, by Whose Name nothing in Earth or in the heaven can do any harm, and He is the All-Hearing, the All-Knowing. (3)

3. I take refuge in the perfect words of Allah from the evil of what He created.

4. I seek refuge in Allah, the All-Hearing, the All-Knowing from Satan the accursed. (3)

5. In the name of Allah the Merciful, the Compassionate. "He is Allah besides Whom there is no other god; Knower of the Unseen and the visible. He is the All-Merciful, the All-Compassionate. ✿ He is Allah, there is no god but He; the Sovereign, the All-Holy, the Source of Peace, the Source of Security; the Guardian, the All-Mighty; the Compeller, the Majestic. Transcendent is He above all that they ascribe as partner (to Him)! ✿ He is Allah; the Creator, the Producer, the Fashioner (Who has brought His creatures to existence and fashioned them in the best form and perfect harmony, making them undergo different phases). His are the most beautiful names. All that is in the heavens and the earth glorifies Him. He is the All-Mighty, the All-Wise." (Hashr 59:22-4)

اَللّٰهُمَّ أَنْتَ رَبِّي لَا إِلٰهَ إِلَّا أَنْتَ خَلَقْتَنِي وَأَنَا عَبْدُكَ
وَأَنَا عَلٰى عَهْدِكَ وَوَعْدِكَ مَا اسْتَطَعْتُ أَعُوذُ بِكَ مِنْ
شَرِّ مَا صَنَعْتُ أَبُوءُ لَكَ بِنِعْمَتِكَ عَلَيَّ وَأَبُوءُ لَكَ بِذَنْبِي
فَاغْفِرْ لِي فَإِنَّهُ لَا يَغْفِرُ الذُّنُوبَ إِلَّا أَنْتَ (٣) ﴿١﴾

بِسْمِ اللهِ الَّذِي لَا يَضُرُّ مَعَ اسْمِهِ شَيْءٌ فِي الْأَرْضِ
وَلَا فِي السَّمَاءِ وَهُوَ السَّمِيعُ الْعَلِيمُ (٣) ﴿٢﴾

أَعُوذُ بِكَلِمَاتِ اللهِ التَّامَّاتِ مِنْ شَرِّ مَا خَلَقَ (١) ﴿٣﴾

اَعُوذُ بِاللهِ السَّمِيعِ الْعَلِيمِ مِنَ الشَّيْطَانِ الرَّجِيمِ (٣) ﴿٤﴾

بِسْمِ اللهِ الرَّحْمٰنِ الرَّحِيمِ ﴿هُوَ اللهُ الَّذِي لَا إِلٰهَ إِلَّا هُوَ
عَالِمُ الْغَيْبِ وَالشَّهَادَةِ هُوَ الرَّحْمٰنُ الرَّحِيمُ ۞ هُوَ اللهُ الَّذِي
لَا إِلٰهَ إِلَّا هُوَ اَلْمَلِكُ الْقُدُّوسُ السَّلَامُ الْمُؤْمِنُ الْمُهَيْمِنُ
الْعَزِيزُ الْجَبَّارُ الْمُتَكَبِّرُ سُبْحَانَ اللهِ عَمَّا يُشْرِكُونَ ۞ هُوَ اللهُ
الْخَالِقُ الْبَارِئُ الْمُصَوِّرُ لَهُ الْأَسْمَاءُ الْحُسْنٰى يُسَبِّحُ لَهُ مَا
فِي السَّمٰوَاتِ وَالْأَرْضِ وَهُوَ الْعَزِيزُ الْحَكِيمُ﴾ ﴿٥﴾

1. Then one recites the Verse of the Throne (Ayat al-Kursi):

   "Allah! There is no god but He, the All-Living, the Self-Subsistent. Neither does slumber overtake Him nor sleep, and to Him belongs whatever is in the heavens and the earth. Who can intercede with Him except by His leave? He knows what is before them and what is behind them, and they comprehend of His knowledge only that which He wills. His Throne encompasses the heavens and the earth, and maintaining them both tires Him not. He is the Exalted, the Sublime." (Baqara 2:255)

2. Then one says: Glory be to Allah! (*Subhan Allah*) (33) Praise be to Allah! (*Al-hamdu lillah*) (33), Allah is the Greatest! (*Allahu Akbar*) (33).

3. Then one supplicates with what comes to the heart from Allah, after which one invokes a hundred times: "There is no god but Allah." (*La ilaha illallah*)

4. Then the following is said: I seek refuge in Allah from Satan the accursed. In the name of Allah the Merciful, the Compassionate.

ثُمَّ يَقْرَأُ: ﴿اَللّٰهُ لَاۤ إِلٰهَ إِلَّا هُوَ اَلْحَيُّ اَلْقَيُّومُ لَا تَأْخُذُهُ سِنَةٌ وَلَا نَوْمٌ لَهُ مَا فِي السَّمٰوَاتِ وَمَا فِي الْأَرْضِ مَنْ ذَا الَّذِي يَشْفَعُ عِنْدَهُ إِلَّا بِإِذْنِهِ يَعْلَمُ مَا بَيْنَ أَيْدِيهِمْ وَمَا خَلْفَهُمْ وَلَا يُحِيطُونَ بِشَيْءٍ مِنْ عِلْمِهِ إِلَّا بِمَا شَاۤءَ وَسِعَ كُرْسِيُّهُ السَّمٰوَاتِ وَالْأَرْضَ وَلَا يَؤُدُهُ حِفْظُهُمَا وَهُوَ الْعَلِيُّ الْعَظِيمُ﴾ ﴿١﴾

ثُمَّ يَقُولُ: سُبْحَانَ اللهِ (٣٣)، اَلْحَمْدُ لِلهِ (٣٣)، اَللّٰهُ أَكْبَرُ (٣٣) ﴿٢﴾

ثُمَّ يَدْعُو مَا شَاءَ اللهُ... ثُمَّ يَقُولُ مِائَةَ مَرَّةٍ ''لَاۤ إِلٰهَ إِلَّا اللهُ'' ﴿٣﴾

ثُمَّ يَقُولُ: أَعُوذُ بِاللهِ مِنَ الشَّيْطَانِ الرَّجِيمِ، بِسْمِ اللهِ الرَّحْمٰنِ الرَّحِيمِ ﴿٤﴾

٩

Morning Prayers

After the morning (fajr) ritual prayer:

1. O Allah! You are the Source of Peace, and all peace comes from You. Blessed are You and Exalted, Possessor of Majesty and Bounty!

    And then:

2. Glory be to Allah! (*Subhan Allah*) Praise be to Allah! (*Al-hamdu lillah*) There is no god but Allah (*La ilaha illallah*), Allah is the Greatest (*Allahu Akbar*), and there is no strength or power except in Allah, the All-High, the All-Mighty. (*La hawla wa la quwwata illa billah, Al 'Aliyyu, Al 'Azim*).

أَذْكَارُ الصَّبَاحِ

بَعْدَ صَلَاةِ الصُّبْحِ يَقُولُ:

اَللّٰهُمَّ أَنْتَ السَّلَامُ وَمِنْكَ السَّلَامُ تَبَارَكْتَ وَتَعَالَيْتَ يَا ذَا الْجَلَالِ وَالْإِكْرَامِ ﴿١﴾

ويقول بعد ذلك: سُبْحَانَ اللهِ وَالْحَمْدُ لله وَلَا إِلٰهَ إِلَّا اللهُ وَاللهُ أَكْبَرُ وَلَا حَوْلَ وَلَا قُوَّةَ إِلَّا بِاللهِ الْعَلِيِّ الْعَظِيمِ ﴿٢﴾

أَذْكَارُ الصَّبَاحِ وَالْمَسَاءِ

MORNING AND EVENING
INVOCATIONS

وقال عليه الصلاة والسلام: «اَلدُّعَاءُ هُوَ الْعِبَادَةُ». وقال: «اَلدُّعَاءُ مُخُّ الْعِبَادَةِ». وقال: «اُدْعُوا فَإِنَّ الدُّعَاءَ يَرُدُّ الْقَضَاءَ». وقال: «لَنْ يَنْفَعَ حَذَرٌ مِنْ قَدَرٍ وَلَكِنَّ الدُّعَاءَ يَنْفَعُ مِمَّا نَزَلَ وَمِمَّا لَمْ يَنْزِلْ فَعَلَيْكُمْ بِالدُّعَاءِ عِبَادَ اللهِ!»

فاعلم بهذا أن أفضل حال الإنسان حال يدعو ربه ويناجيه ويشتغل بالأذكار الواردة من سيد المرسلين عليه أكمل التحايا...

وقد صنف علماؤنا من قديم الزمان في عمل اليوم والليلة من الدعوات والأذكار كتبا كثيرة -جزاهم الله خير الجزاء ونفع بها المسلمين أجمعين- فقصدت تسهيل ذلك على الراغبين واختصرت منها ما يمكن دوامه عليه للداعين والذاكرين والله الرؤف الرحيم والودود المجيب أسأل التوفيق والهداية والتقوى والدوام على أنواع العطايا والبهايا والجمع مع محمدﷺ وأصحابه.

حسبي الله لا إله إلا هو عليه توكلت وهو رب العرش العظيم وسبحان الله لا قوة إلا بالله ما شاء الله كان وما لم يشأ لم يكن أعلم أن الله على كل شيء قدير وأن الله قد أحاط بكل شيء علما وأستودع الله ديني ودنياي ووالدي وأستاذي وإخواني فإنه نعم الحفيظ!...

٦

بِسْمِ اللهِ الرَّحْمٰنِ الرَّحِيمِ

مقدمة

الحمد لله الواحد الأحد الحق المبين الذي لا شريك له
وكفرت بما سواه. وأشهد أن محمدا عبده ورسوله وصفيه وحبيبه
خير خلقه أكرم الأولين والأخرين صلوات الله وسلامه عليه وعلى
إخوانه من النبيين والمرسلين وعلى الملئكة المقربين وعلى عبادك
الصالحين من أهل السموات وأهل الأرضين.

أما بعد: فإن الدعاء هو العبادة إذ به يقبل العبد على الله
ويعرض عما سواه وهو سلاح المؤمن ويرد به القضاء. كيف لا
وقد قال الله تعالى: ﴿وَقَالَ رَبُّكُمُ ادْعُونِي أَسْتَجِبْ لَكُمْ﴾ وقال:
﴿وَإِذَا سَأَلَكَ عِبَادِي عَنِّي فَإِنِّي قَرِيبٌ أُجِيبُ دَعْوَةَ الدَّاعِ إِذَا دَعَانِ﴾
وقال: ﴿أَمَّنْ يُجِيبُ الْمُضْطَرَّ إِذَا دَعَاهُ وَيَكْشِفُ السُّوءَ﴾.

مجموعة الأدعية المأثورة

جَمَعَهَا

مُحَمَّد فَتْح الله كُولَن

مجموعة الأدعية المأثورة